OECD/G20 Base Erosion and Profit Shifting Project

Prevention of Treaty Abuse – Second Peer Review Report on Treaty Shopping

INCLUSIVE FRAMEWORK ON BEPS: ACTION 6

OECD
BETTER POLICIES FOR BETTER LIVES

Please cite this publication as:
OECD (2020), *Prevention of Treaty Abuse – Second Peer Review Report on Treaty Shopping: Inclusive Framework on BEPS: Action 6*, OECD/G20 Base Erosion and Profit Shifting Project, OECD Publishing, Paris, *https://doi.org/10.1787/d656738d-en*.

ISBN 978-92-64-40899-9 (print)
ISBN 978-92-64-75017-3 (pdf)

OECD/G20 Base Erosion and Profit Shifting Project
ISSN 2313-2604 (print)
ISSN 2313-2612 (online)

Photo credits: Cover © ninog-Fotolia.com.

Corrigenda to publications may be found on line at: *www.oecd.org/about/publishing/corrigenda.htm*.

Foreword

The integration of national economies and markets has increased substantially in recent years, putting a strain on the international tax rules, which were designed more than a century ago. Weaknesses in the current rules create opportunities for base erosion and profit shifting (BEPS), requiring bold moves by policy makers to restore confidence in the system and ensure that profits are taxed where economic activities take place and value is created.

Following the release of the report *Addressing Base Erosion and Profit Shifting* in February 2013, OECD and G20 countries adopted a 15-point Action Plan to address BEPS in September 2013. The Action Plan identified 15 actions along three key pillars: introducing coherence in the domestic rules that affect cross-border activities, reinforcing substance requirements in the existing international standards, and improving transparency as well as certainty.

After two years of work, measures in response to the 15 actions were delivered to G20 Leaders in Antalya in November 2015. All the different outputs, including those delivered in an interim form in 2014, were consolidated into a comprehensive package. The BEPS package of measures represents the first substantial renovation of the international tax rules in almost a century. Once the new measures become applicable, it is expected that profits will be reported where the economic activities that generate them are carried out and where value is created. BEPS planning strategies that rely on outdated rules or on poorly co-ordinated domestic measures will be rendered ineffective.

Implementation is now the focus of this work. The BEPS package is designed to be implemented via changes in domestic law and practices, and in tax treaties. With the negotiation of a multilateral instrument (MLI) having been finalised in 2016 to facilitate the implementation of the treaty related BEPS measures, over 90 jurisdictions are covered by the MLI. The entry into force of the MLI on 1 July 2018 paves the way for swift implementation of the treaty related measures. OECD and G20 countries also agreed to continue to work together to ensure a consistent and co-ordinated implementation of the BEPS recommendations and to make the project more inclusive. Globalisation requires that global solutions and a global dialogue be established which go beyond OECD and G20 countries.

A better understanding of how the BEPS recommendations are implemented in practice could reduce misunderstandings and disputes between governments. Greater focus on implementation and tax administration should therefore be mutually beneficial to governments and business. Proposed improvements to data and analysis will help support ongoing evaluation of the quantitative impact of BEPS, as well as evaluating the impact of the countermeasures developed under the BEPS Project.

As a result, the OECD established the OECD/G20 Inclusive Framework on BEPS (Inclusive Framework), bringing all interested and committed countries and jurisdictions on an equal footing in the Committee on Fiscal Affairs and all its subsidiary bodies. The Inclusive Framework, which already has more than 135 members, is monitoring and peer reviewing the implementation of the minimum standards as well as completing the work on standard setting to address BEPS issues. In addition to BEPS members, other international organisations and regional tax bodies are involved in the work of the Inclusive Framework, which also consults business and the civil society on its different work streams.

This report was approved by the Inclusive Framework on 30 January 2020 and prepared for publication by the OECD Secretariat.

Table of contents

TABLES

Executive summary

Action 6 of the BEPS Project identified treaty abuse, and in particular treaty shopping, as one of the principal sources of BEPS concerns. Owing to the seriousness of treaty shopping, jurisdictions have agreed to adopt, as a minimum standard, measures to address it, and to subject their efforts to an annual peer review. In 2018, the first peer review concluded that although few of the reported agreements met the minimum standard, many jurisdictions had begun in earnest to tackle the problem, principally by signing the multilateral instrument[1] (MLI).

This second peer review reveals that, by 30 June 2019, 91 Inclusive Framework members had begun to update their bilateral treaty network and were implementing the minimum standard. The data compiled for this peer review demonstrate that the MLI has been the tool used by the vast majority of jurisdictions that have begun to implement the minimum standard. By 30 June 2019, the MLI had already modified around 60 bilateral agreements.[2] The MLI's impact was expected to increase quickly as jurisdictions ratified it and that number has, as of 1 January 2020, increased to 180 bilateral agreements. Further, the MLI's coverage is also expected to increase as other jurisdictions with a large network of tax treaties are considering joining it.[3]

The success of the MLI as a tool to implement Action 6 minimum standard is clear: by 1 January 2020, 93 jurisdictions had signed the MLI, 38 had ratified it, and it had modified 180 bilateral tax treaties. Once all signatories have ratified the MLI, around 65% of all agreements between Inclusive Framework members will be modified by the MLI to include the minimum standard (and other BEPS treaty related provisions). Other jurisdictions have expressed interest in signing the MLI and, if all waiting agreements[4] become covered tax agreements, this figure could be as high as 85%.

In light of the experience in conducting the peer reviews, the peer review methodology will be reviewed in 2020.

Notes

[1] Formally, the Multilateral Convention to Implement Tax Treaty Related Measures to Prevent BEPS.

[2] As the MLI was not in force at the time of the first peer review, it had not updated any treaties at that time.

[3] For instance, Bahrain, Jordan, Lebanon, North Macedonia, Thailand and Viet Nam, jurisdictions with large tax treaty networks, have expressed their intention to join the MLI in the future.

[4] A "waiting agreement" is an agreement that has been listed under the MLI by only one of the treaty partners and is therefore waiting for the other partner to sign the MLI to create a match.

1 Background

Action 6 minimum standard and the terms of reference

1. The minimum standard requires jurisdictions to do two things in their tax treaties: include an express statement on non-taxation (generally in the preamble); and adopt one of three methods of addressing treaty shopping. It does not specify how these two things should be achieved (e.g. through the MLI or bilaterally). The Action 6 Final Report further states that (i) a jurisdiction is required to implement the minimum standard in a treaty only if asked to do so by another member of the Inclusive Framework[1]; (ii) the decision on which of the three methods to adopt has to be agreed (a solution cannot be imposed); and (iii) reflecting treaties' bilateral nature, there is no time limit within which a jurisdiction has to attain the minimum standard.

2. In May 2017, the Inclusive Framework agreed the Terms of Reference for the peer review and its methodology and decided that the methodology would be reviewed in 2020.

3. The MLI has proven to be an effective way of implementing the minimum standard. However, a jurisdiction that prefers to implement the minimum standard through a detailed limitation on benefits provision cannot use the MLI to do so.

4. The current peer review process measures jurisdictions' progress in updating their tax treaties to include a new preamble and an approved method of tackling treaty-shopping. The peer review will be reviewed in 2020 in light of the experience in conducting the peer reviews.

Notes

[1] Para. 23, OECD (2015), *Preventing the Granting of Treaty Benefits in Inappropriate Circumstances, Action 6 – 2015 Final Report,* OECD/G20 Base Erosion and Profit Shifting Project, OECD Publishing, Paris. http://dx.doi.org/10.1787/9789264241695-en (the "BEPS Action 6 Report"): "Countries commit to adopt in their bilateral treaties measures that implement the minimum standard described in the preceding paragraph if requested to do so by other countries that have made the same commitment and that will request the inclusion of these measures." The Inclusive Framework of committed jurisdictions had not yet been established.

2 The 2019 Peer Review

Implementation of the minimum standard

5. The data collected with respect to the implementation of the Action 6 minimum standard show that, by 30 June 2019, 91 Inclusive Framework members had begun to update their bilateral treaty network and were implementing the minimum standard. The MLI had, by that same date, already modified around 60 bilateral agreements.[1] The MLI's impact is expected to increase quickly as jurisdictions ratify it and additional jurisdictions with large tax treaty networks join the MLI.[2]

6. The 2019 peer review collected data on how the 129 jurisdictions that were members of the Inclusive Framework on 30 June 2019 are updating their tax treaties, as foreseen by the current Peer Review Document.[3] Aggregate data on updates to bilateral treaties are presented below and a jurisdictional section for every member of the Inclusive Framework can be found in Chapter 5.

7. The 129 jurisdictions in the Inclusive Framework reported a total of 2 145 agreements between Inclusive Framework members themselves, and about 1 020 agreements between Inclusive Framework members and non-members.[4]

8. The agreements between Inclusive Framework members and non-members are not subject to the peer review and the aggregate results in this chapter focus on the 2 145 agreements entered into between Inclusive Framework members. The jurisdictional sections in Chapter 5 show cases where agreements outside the peer review comply with the minimum standard or are subject to a complying instrument.[5]

9. On 30 June 2019, 91 jurisdictions of the Inclusive Framework had some agreements that already complied with the minimum standard or were subject to a complying instrument and will therefore become compliant shortly.[6] An additional seven jurisdictions had no comprehensive tax agreements in force subject to the peer review.[7] Thirty-one jurisdictions had not signed any complying instruments to implement the minimum standard.

Compliant agreements

10. As of 30 June 2019, 86 bilateral agreements between members of the Inclusive Framework complied with the minimum standard. An additional 14 agreements not subject to this review (i.e. agreements between Inclusive Framework members and non-members) also complied with the minimum standard.

11. In each of the 86 agreements that already comply with the minimum standard, the minimum standard is implemented through the inclusion of the preamble statement and the principal purposes test (PPT). Of these 86 agreements, 17 agreements supplement the PPT with a limitation on benefits (LOB) provision.

Non-compliant agreements subject to a complying instrument

12. Many jurisdictions in the Inclusive Framework have agreements currently subject to a signed complying instrument that is not yet in force, but that would implement the minimum standard.

13. On 30 June 2019, about 1 330 of the 2 145 bilateral agreements between Inclusive Framework members were set to become covered tax agreements under the MLI (i.e. both Contracting Jurisdictions had listed the agreement under the MLI and, as a result, the MLI will modify the agreement once in effect) and were thereby set to become compliant with the minimum standard.[8] These agreements, to be modified by the MLI, would comply with the minimum standard once its provisions take effect, following ratification by both Contracting Jurisdictions.[9]

14. Around another 430 of these 2 145 bilateral agreements could be modified by the MLI in the future. This is because these agreements have been listed under the MLI by only one of the treaty partners and are waiting for a match.[10] These include “waiting” agreements between Inclusive Framework members that have signed the MLI and those that have not yet signed it.[11]

15. As things stand, the MLI will modify around 65% of all agreements between Inclusive Framework members. Some additional jurisdictions have expressed interest in signing the MLI.[12] If all waiting agreements become covered tax agreements, this figure could be as high as 85%.

16. A further 22 agreements are subject to a bilateral amending instrument that is not yet in force.[13] For example, the Nordic Convention is currently subject to a complying instrument, which was signed in August 2018. The Convention will comply with the minimum standard once that instrument enters into effect.

17. The number of agreements subject to a bilateral amending instrument,, when compared with those that are subject to the MLI, shows the efficiency of the MLI in implementing the minimum standard.

18. For the agreements listed under the MLI, all 85 members of the Inclusive Framework that are parties and signatories to the MLI are implementing the preamble statement and the PPT. Twelve jurisdictions have also opted to apply the simplified LOB through the MLI to supplement the PPT when possible. Six additional jurisdictions agreed to accept a simplified LOB in agreements with partners that opted for it under the MLI.

19. In total, the PPT will be implemented in all agreements to be covered under the MLI. Around 60 of these agreements will also include a simplified LOB provision.

Notes

[1] The MLI was not in force at the time of the first peer review.

[2] As set out above, Bahrain, Jordan, Lebanon, North Macedonia, Thailand and Viet Nam, jurisdictions with large tax treaty networks, have expressed their intention to join the MLI in the future.

[3] The BEPS Action 6 Report.

[4] In 2018, the Inclusive Framework reported 1 940 agreements entered into between Inclusive Framework members. The additional 205 agreements reviewed in 2019 includes new agreements entered into between Inclusive Framework members between 30 June 2018 and 30 June 2019 and, importantly, the

relevant existing agreements of the 13 new Inclusive Framework members, which were not subject to the 2018 Peer Review.

[5] A "complying instrument" could be the MLI or a suitable new amending protocol yet to enter into force. It could also be a completely new agreement that has not yet entered into force.

[6] Eighty-nine jurisdictions were signatories or parties to the MLI as of 30 June 2019, but four of them are not members of the Inclusive Framework. As of 30 June 2019, 85 Inclusive Framework members were signatories or parties to the MLI. Three additional members (Brazil, North Macedonia and Zambia), although not signatories or parties to the MLI, have concluded one or two amending protocols to implement the minimum standard.

[7] Angola, the Bahamas, the Cayman Islands, the Cook Islands, Djibouti, Haiti and Turks and Caicos Islands have no agreements in force.

[8] On 30 June 2019, most signatories' MLI positions, including the list of notified tax agreements, were provisional and could be subject to future changes.

[9] Article 35 of the MLI governs its entry into effect. The provisions of the MLI take effect for covered tax agreements on different dates.

[10] Under Article 2 of the MLI, a Covered Tax Agreement means an agreement with respect to which each Party [to the agreement] has made a notification to the Depositary of the MLI listing the agreement as one which it wishes to be covered by the MLI.

[11] In addition, around 175 agreements concluded amongst Inclusive Framework members that have signed the MLI were only listed under the MLI by one of the treaty partners.

[12] As set out above, Bahrain, Jordan, Lebanon, North Macedonia, Thailand and Viet Nam, jurisdictions with large tax treaty networks, have expressed their intention to join the MLI in the future.

[13] Some agreements subject to a bilateral complying instrument were also listed under the MLI as the MLI allows jurisdictions to implement other (non-minimum standard) treaty-related BEPS measures.

3 Difficulties in implementing the minimum standard

20. The peer review also provided a way for a jurisdiction that encountered difficulties in reaching agreement with another jurisdiction to implement the Action 6 minimum standard an opportunity to raise its concerns in writing to the Secretariat.

21. In the course of this year's peer review, a jurisdiction raised a concern with respect to the CARICOM Agreement, a multilateral agreement concluded by eleven jurisdictions, ten of which are members of the Inclusive Framework. The CARICOM Agreement was concluded in 1994 to encourage regional trade and investment within the Community and contains several unusual features[1] not found in the OECD Model Tax Convention or the UN Model Double Taxation Convention, which could lead to certain income flows escaping tax altogether. These departures from standard tax treaty provisions may have encouraged greater economic integration within the CARICOM Community at the time. But they may also have made the CARICOM Agreement more vulnerable to treaty shopping and other forms of abuse.

22. Previous renegotiation attempts of the CARICOM Agreement have proven to be difficult. However, with the impetus of the Inclusive Framework, and the commitment of its jurisdiction members to implement the BEPS minimum standards, now could provide an opportune time to modernise the CARICOM Agreement.

Notes

[1] The CARICOM Agreement provides for an almost exclusive source-based taxation of all income, gains and profits. Some income – for instance dividends – are also entirely exempted from tax under the CARICOM Agreement.

4 Conclusion and next steps

23. The implementation of the minimum standard will continue to be monitored and, as set out in the Peer Review Document, the next peer review exercise will be launched in the first half of 2020.

24. As noted at paragraph 14 of the Peer Review document, the methodology for the review of the implementation of the Action 6 minimum standard will be reviewed in 2020, in light of the experience in conducting the peer review.

25. The Inclusive Framework on BEPS, together with Working Party No. 1 will carry out the 2020 review mindful of available resources, and recognising that many treaties that would implement the minimum standard have not yet entered into force.

Background

Context of the peer review

26. Over the last decades, bilateral tax agreements, concluded by nearly every jurisdiction in the world, have served to prevent harmful double taxation and remove obstacles to cross-border trade in goods and services, and movements of capital, technology and persons. This extensive network of tax agreements has, however, also given rise to so-called "treaty-shopping" arrangements.

27. As set out in the Action 6 Final Report, treaty shopping typically involves the attempt by a person to indirectly access the benefits of a tax agreement between two jurisdictions without being a resident of one of those jurisdictions.[1]

28. Treaty shopping is undesirable for several reasons, including:

- Treaty benefits negotiated between the parties to an agreement are economically extended to residents of a third jurisdiction in a way the parties did not intend. The principle of reciprocity is therefore breached and the balance of concessions that the parties make is altered;
- Income may escape taxation altogether or be subject to inadequate taxation in a way the parties did not intend; and
- The jurisdiction of residence of the ultimate income beneficiary has less incentive to enter into a tax agreement with the jurisdiction of source, because residents of the jurisdiction of residence can indirectly receive treaty benefits from the jurisdiction of source without the need for the jurisdiction of residence to provide reciprocal benefits.

Some previous attempts to tackle treaty shopping

29. Concerns about treaty shopping are not new. For example, in 1977, the concept of "beneficial owner" was introduced into the dividends, interest, and royalties articles of the OECD Model Tax Convention to clarify the meaning of the words "paid to", and deal with simple treaty-shopping situations where income is paid to an intermediary resident of a treaty country who is not treated as the owner of that income for tax purposes (such as an agent or nominee).[2]

30. In 1977, the Commentary on Article 1 of the OECD Model Tax Convention was also updated to include a section on the improper use of tax agreements.[3] In 1986, the Committee on Fiscal Affairs (CFA) published two reports: *Double Taxation and the Use of Base Companies* and *Double Taxation and the Use of Conduit Companies*. In 2002, the Committee published the report, *Restricting the Entitlement to Treaty Benefits*. The Commentary on Article 1 of the OECD Model Tax Convention was expanded on several occasions, notably in 2003, with the inclusion of sample provisions that countries could use to counter treaty shopping.

31. A review of jurisdictions' practices shows that they have tried to address treaty shopping in the past and have used different approaches to do so. Some have relied on specific anti-abuse rules based on the legal nature, ownership, and general activities of residents of a jurisdiction party to a tax agreement.[4] Others have favoured a general anti-abuse rule based on the purpose of transactions or arrangements.

BEPS and treaty shopping

32. The BEPS Action Plan[5], developed by the CFA and endorsed by the G20 Leaders in September 2013[6], identified 15 actions to address base erosion and profit shifting (BEPS). It identified treaty abuse, and in particular treaty shopping, as one of the most important sources of BEPS concerns.

33. Action 6 (Prevent Treaty Abuse) of the BEPS Action Plan called for the development of treaty provisions to prevent the granting of treaty benefits in inappropriate circumstances. In parallel, Action 15 of the BEPS Action Plan called for an analysis of the possible development of a multilateral instrument "to enable jurisdictions that wish to do so to implement measures developed in the course of the work on BEPS and amend bilateral tax treaties".

34. After two years of work, the CFA, in which OECD and G20 countries work on an equal footing, produced the final BEPS Package,[7] which was endorsed by the OECD Council and the G20 Leaders in November 2015.

35. Jurisdictions agreed that four of the BEPS measures would be minimum standards that participating jurisdictions would commit to implement. The Action 6 Report sets out one of these minimum standards. The Action 6 minimum standard requires jurisdictions to commit to include in their tax treaties provisions dealing with treaty shopping to ensure a minimum level of protection against treaty abuse.

The Action 6 minimum standard

36. The minimum standard on treaty shopping requires jurisdictions to include two components in their tax agreements: an express statement on non-taxation (generally in the preamble) and one of three methods of addressing treaty shopping.

37. The minimum standard does not provide how these two components should be implemented (i.e. through the MLI or amending instruments). It recognises, however, that these provisions need to be agreed bilaterally and that a jurisdiction will be required to implement the minimum standard when requested to do so by another member of the Inclusive Framework.

The express statement

38. As set out in paragraphs 22 and 23 of the Final Report on Action 6, jurisdictions have agreed to include in their tax agreements an express statement that their common intention is to eliminate double taxation without creating opportunities for non-taxation or reduced taxation through tax evasion or avoidance, including through treaty-shopping arrangements. The following provision now appears in the 2017 OECD Model Tax Convention:

39. Intending to conclude a Convention for the elimination of double taxation with respect to taxes on income and on capital without creating opportunities for non-taxation or reduced taxation through tax

evasion or avoidance (including through treaty-shopping arrangements aimed at obtaining reliefs provided in this Convention for the indirect benefit of residents of third States)

Three methods of addressing treaty shopping

40. Jurisdictions have also committed to implement that "common intention" through the inclusion of treaty provisions in one of the following three forms:

- a principal purpose test (PPT) equivalent to paragraph 9 of Article 29 of the 2017 OECD Model Tax Convention together with either a simplified or a detailed version of the limitation on benefits (LOB) rule that appears in paragraphs 1 to 7 of the 2017 OECD Model Tax Convention; or
- the PPT alone; or
- a detailed version of the LOB rule together with a mechanism (such as a treaty rule that might take the form of a PPT rule restricted to conduit arrangements, or domestic anti-abuse rules or judicial doctrines that would achieve a similar result) that would deal with conduit arrangements not already dealt with in tax treaties.

The obligation to implement the minimum standard

41. The Action 6 Report recognised that "some flexibility in the implementation of the Action 6 minimum standard [would be] required, as these provisions need to be adapted to each country's specificities and to the circumstances of the negotiation of bilateral conventions." In particular:

- a jurisdiction is required to implement the minimum standard in a treaty only if asked to do so by another member of the Inclusive Framework;
- its form (which of the three options used) has to be agreed (a solution cannot be imposed); and
- the commitment to adopt in bilateral treaties measures that implement the minimum standard should not be interpreted as a commitment to conclude new treaties or amend existing treaties within a specified period of time.

42. The Action 6 Report itself recognised that since participation in the multilateral instrument (see next section) was not mandatory and because jurisdictions could have different preferences about how the minimum standard should be met, monitoring its implementation would be necessary.

The 2018 peer review

43. The first peer review was conducted in 2018 and covered the 116 jurisdictions that were members of the Inclusive Framework on 30 June 2018. The Peer Review Report, which was adopted by the Inclusive Framework in January 2019, was published on 14 February 2019.

44. The 2018 peer review revealed that, as the provisions of the MLI had not taken effect at the time of the first peer review, nearly all of the agreements reviewed for the 2018 report did not at that time comply with the minimum standard. Substantial progress had, however, been made in 2017 and 2018 towards its implementation and a large majority of Inclusive Framework members had begun to translate their commitment on treaty shopping into actions and were in the process of modifying their treaty networks.

45. In total, on 30 June 2018, the peer review showed that 82 jurisdictions had some agreements that were already compliant with the minimum standard or were subject to a complying instrument that would bring their agreements into compliance.[8] The first Peer Review highlighted the effectiveness of the MLI in implementing the treaty-related BEPS measures. It was by far the preferred tool of Inclusive Framework members for implementing the minimum standard.

46. In the course of the first peer review, all concerns raised by jurisdictions on the implementation of the minimum standard in their agreements had been resolved when the Report was approved by the Inclusive Framework and therefore no recommendation was made under the first peer review.

Conduct of the 2019 peer review

47. The review started with a questionnaire sent to members of the Inclusive Framework in March 2019. The questionnaire was based on the 2018 Action 6 peer review[9] questionnaire with a few modifications. In 2018, each jurisdiction was asked to list all of its comprehensive income tax agreements in force. Those lists indicated whether each agreement included the provisions of the minimum standard, i.e. a complying preamble and the necessary anti-abuse provision(s), whether it was subject to a "complying instrument" that would soon bring it into compliance, what that instrument was, and which of the three methods of meeting the minimum standard had been used.

In 2019, each jurisdiction was invited to update its 2018 questionnaire, taking into consideration any new agreements that had entered into force by adding them to their list of agreements. Jurisdictions that joined the Inclusive Framework after 30 June 2018 were asked to complete the original questionnaire.

Notes

1 See paragraph 17 of the BEPS Action 6 Final Report (2015). As the Report also notes, cases where a resident of the Contracting State in which income originates seeks to obtain treaty benefits (e.g. through a transfer of residence to the other Contracting State or through the use of an entity established in that other State) could also be considered a form of treaty shopping.

2 See paragraph 2 of Articles 10 and 11, and paragraph 1 of Article 12 of the OECD Model Tax Convention

3 See paragraphs 7-10 of the Commentary on Article 1 of the 1977 Model Tax Convention.

4 "Limitation on benefits" provisions commonly found in treaties concluded by the United States are the best-known example.

5 OECD (2013), Action Plan on Base Erosion and Profit Shifting, OECD Publishing. http://dx.doi.org/10.1787/9789264202719-en

6 G20 Research Group (2013), G20 Leaders' Declaration, http://www.g20.utoronto.ca/2013/2013-0906-declaration.html

7 In October 2015, the CFA, including OECD and G20 countries working on an equal footing, produced the Final BEPS Package, in the form of reports on each of the 15 actions accompanied by an Explanatory Statement. The Final BEPS Package gives countries and economies the tools they need to ensure that profits are taxed where economic activities generating the profits are performed and where value is created, while at the same time giving businesses greater certainty by reducing disputes over the application of international tax rules and standardising compliance requirements.

8 A further seven jurisdictions had no comprehensive tax agreements and were outside the scope of this exercise.

9 OECD (2017), BEPS Action 6 on Preventing the Granting of Treaty Benefits in Inappropriate Circumstances – Peer Review Documents, OECD/G20 Base Erosion and Profit Shifting Project, OECD,

Paris. www.oecd.org/tax/beps/beps-action-6-preventing-the-granting-of-treaty-benefits-in-inappropriate-circumstance-peer-review-documents.pdf

5 Data for each jurisdiction of the Inclusive Framework

Jurisdictional data

Explanation of the jurisdictional data

The jurisdictional sections in this chapter provide specific information for each of the 129 jurisdictions in the Inclusive Framework subject to the Peer Review. The information is based on the lists of tax agreements provided by those jurisdictions.

Each jurisdictional section contains information on the progress made in the implementation of the minimum standard and on implementation issues reported. It also includes a summary of the jurisdiction's response to the Peer Review questionnaire (i.e. the list of tax agreements provided). The summary of the jurisdiction's response is presented in the form of a table in which all its tax agreements in force are listed.

Although the tax agreements between Inclusive Framework members and non-members are not subject to the Peer Review, to recognise the progress made by some jurisdictions, and for the sake of completeness, information on these agreements is also reported.

This section of Chapter 5 includes a list of the 129 jurisdictions subject to the Peer Review.

It should be recalled that a jurisdiction is required to implement the minimum standard in a treaty if asked to do so by another member of the Inclusive Framework.

Explanations of the data shown in the jurisdictional sections

The number of tax agreements:

- The jurisdictional sections indicate the number of tax agreements for each jurisdiction and include tax agreements with jurisdictions that are not members of the Inclusive Framework. Such agreements are indicated with an asterisk.
- For the purpose of the Peer Review, a tax agreement is a comprehensive agreement for the avoidance of double taxation with respect to taxes on income (whether or not other taxes are also covered) that is presently in force. It does not include other types of agreements such as inheritance tax treaties, tax information exchange agreements (TIEAs) or other administrative agreements, shipping and air transport agreements, nor does it include non-comprehensive agreements covering only individuals.
- The term "agreement" should also be interpreted to mean a treaty relationship. For example, if a state has split into two and each successor state is honouring an agreement concluded by the predecessor state, each successor state is treated as having a separate agreement. In this example, the number of bilateral treaty relationships therefore exceeds the number of signed agreements.

The tax agreements compliant with the minimum standard:

- The jurisdictional sections indicate the number of tax agreements that fully comply with the minimum standard for each jurisdiction. Partially compliant agreements, i.e. agreements that contain only one element of the minimum standard, are shown as non-compliant.
- Where jurisdictions have concluded a new tax agreement or an amending protocol, it is shown as meeting the minimum standard only when its provisions are in force.
- Where the minimum standard has been implemented through the MLI, *the relevant provisions of the MLI (Article 6 and Article 7) must have started to take effect as of 30 June 2019 for this agreement to meet the minimum standard (Article 35 of the MLI).*

The tax agreements subject to a complying instrument:

- The jurisdictional sections indicate the number of tax agreements that do not comply with the minimum standard but that are subject to a complying instrument.
- A "complying instrument" can be the MLI or an amending protocol that has not entered into force and that could bring the tax agreement into compliance with the minimum standard. It can also be a completely new agreement that complies with the minimum standard that has not yet entered into force.
- The complying instrument can only be the MLI if the agreement is notified as an agreement the jurisdiction wishes to cover under the MLI *irrespective of whether or not its treaty partner has notified the tax agreement.*
- MLI information shown for each jurisdiction is generally based on its latest publicly available positions, which will be the definitive position for those jurisdictions that have already deposited their instrument of ratification and provisional for those that have not yet done so.

Table 5.1. List of jurisdictions in the Inclusive Framework subject to the Peer Review

On 30 June 2019, the following jurisdictions were members of the Inclusive Framework:

1.	Andorra	51.	Greenland	101.	Saint Kitts and Nevis
2.	Angola	52.	Grenada	102.	Saint Lucia
3.	Anguilla	53.	Guernsey	103.	Saint Vincent and the Grenadines
4.	Antigua and Barbuda	54.	Haiti	104.	San Marino
5.	Argentina	55.	Hong Kong (China)	105.	Saudi Arabia
6.	Armenia	56.	Hungary	106.	Senegal
7.	Aruba	57.	Iceland	107.	Serbia
8.	Australia	58.	India	108.	Seychelles
9.	Austria	59.	Indonesia	109.	Sierra Leone
10.	The Bahamas	60.	Ireland	110.	Singapore
11.	Bahrain	61.	Isle of Man	111.	Slovak Republic
12.	Barbados	62.	Israel	112.	Slovenia
13.	Belgium	63.	Italy	113.	South Africa
14.	Belize	64.	Jamaica	114.	Spain
15.	Benin	65.	Japan	115.	Sri Lanka
16.	Bermuda	66.	Jersey	116.	Sweden
17.	Botswana	67.	Kazakhstan	117.	Switzerland
18.	Brazil	68.	Kenya	118.	Thailand
19.	British Virgin Islands	69.	Korea	119.	Trinidad and Tobago
20.	Brunei Darussalam	70.	Latvia	120.	Tunisia
21.	Bulgaria	71.	Liberia	121.	Turks and Caicos Islands
22.	Burkina Faso	72.	Liechtenstein	122.	Turkey
23.	Cabo Verde	73.	Lithuania	123.	Ukraine
24.	Cameroon	74.	Luxembourg	124.	United Arab Emirates
25.	Canada	75.	Macau (China)	125.	United Kingdom
26.	Cayman Islands	76.	Malaysia	126.	United States
27.	Chile	77.	Maldives	127.	Uruguay
28.	China (People's Republic of)	78.	Malta	128.	Viet Nam
29.	Colombia	79.	Mauritius	129.	Zambia
30.	Congo	80.	Mexico		
31.	Costa Rica	81.	Monaco		
32.	Cook Islands	82.	Mongolia		
33.	Côte d'Ivoire	83.	Montserrat		
34.	Croatia	84.	Morocco		
35.	Curacao	85.	Netherlands		
36.	Czech Republic	86.	New Zealand		
37.	Democratic Republic of the Congo	87.	Nigeria		
38.	Denmark	88.	North Macedonia		
39.	Djibouti	89.	Norway		
40.	Dominica	90.	Oman		
41.	Dominican Republic	91.	Pakistan		
42.	Egypt	92.	Panama		
43.	Estonia	93.	Papua New Guinea		
44.	Faroe Islands	94.	Paraguay		
45.	Finland	95.	Peru		
46.	France	96.	Poland		
47.	Gabon	97.	Portugal		
48.	Georgia	98.	Qatar		

49.	Germany	99.	Romania		
50.	Greece	100.	Russian Federation		

Andorra

A. Progress in the implementation of the minimum standard

Andorra has eight tax agreements in force, as reported in its response to the Peer Review questionnaire. Its agreement with Cyprus complies with the minimum standard.

Andorra signed the MLI in 2017, listing seven tax agreements.

Andorra is implementing the minimum standard in its tax agreements through the inclusion of the preamble statement and the PPT.[1]

The agreements that will be modified by the MLI will come into compliance with the minimum standard once the provisions of the MLI take effect.

B. Implementation issues

No jurisdiction has raised any concerns about their agreements with Andorra.

Summary of the jurisdiction response – Andorra

	Treaty partners	Compliance with the standard	If compliant, the alternative implemented	Signature of a complying instrument		The alternative implemented through the complying instrument (if not the MLI)	Comments
1	Cyprus*	Yes	PPT alone	N/A	N/A		
2	France	No	N/A	Yes		N/A	
3	Liechtenstein	No	N/A	Yes		N/A	
4	Luxembourg	No	N/A	Yes	N/A		
5	Malta	No	N/A	Yes	N/A		
6	Portugal	No	N/A	Yes	N/A		
7	Spain	No	N/A	Yes	N/A		
8	United Arab Emirates	No	N/A	Yes	N/A		

Angola

A. Progress in the implementation of the minimum standard

Angola has no tax agreements, as reported in its response to the Peer Review questionnaire.

B. Implementation issues

No jurisdiction has raised any concerns about Angola.

Anguilla

A. Progress in the implementation of the minimum standard

Anguilla has one tax agreement in force with Switzerland, as reported in its response to the Peer Review questionnaire.

Anguilla's agreement does not comply with the minimum standard and is not subject to a complying instrument.

B. Implementation issues

No jurisdiction has raised any concerns about the agreement with Anguilla.

Anguilla is encouraged to implement the minimum standard in its agreement.

Summary of the jurisdiction response – Anguilla

	Treaty partners	Compliance with the standard	If compliant, the alternative implemented	Signature of a complying instrument	The alternative implemented through the complying instrument (if not the MLI)		Comments
1	Switzerland	No	N/A	No	N/A		

Antigua and Barbuda

A. Progress in the implementation of the minimum standard

Antigua and Barbuda has three tax agreements in force, as reported in its response to the Peer Review questionnaire, including the multilateral agreement among the members of the CARICOM concluded with ten treaty partners (the CARICOM Agreement).[2]

None of Antigua and Barbuda's agreements comply with the minimum standard or are subject to a complying instrument.

B. Implementation issues

Antigua and Barbuda is encouraged to implement the minimum standard in its agreements.

Antigua and Barbuda is encouraged to bring the CARICOM Agreement up to date by commencing talks among all the treaty partners.[3]

Summary of the jurisdiction response – Antigua and Barbuda

	Treaty partners	Compliance with the standard	If compliant, the alternative implemented	Signature of a complying instrument	The alternative implemented through the complying instrument (if not the MLI)	Comments
1	Barbados	No	N/A	No	N/A	*CARICOM*
2	Belize	No	N/A	No	N/A	*CARICOM*
3	Dominica	No	N/A	No	N/A	*CARICOM*
4	Grenada	No	N/A	No	N/A	*CARICOM*
5	Guyana*	No	N/A	No	N/A	*CARICOM*
6	Jamaica	No	N/A	No	N/A	*CARICOM*
7	Saint Kitts and Nevis	No	N/A	No	N/A	*CARICOM*
8	Saint Lucia	No	N/A	No	N/A	*CARICOM*
9	Saint Vincent and the Grenadines	No	N/A	No	N/A	*CARICOM*
10	Switzerland	No	N/A	No	N/A	
11	Trinidad and Tobago	No	N/A	No	N/A	*CARICOM*
12	United Kingdom	No	N/A	No	N/A	

Argentina

A. Progress in the implementation of the minimum standard

Argentina has 20 tax agreements in force, as reported in its response to the Peer Review questionnaire. Three of those agreements, the agreements with Brazil, Chile and Mexico, comply with the minimum standard.

Argentina signed the MLI in 2017, listing 17 tax agreements.

Argentina is implementing the minimum standard through the inclusion of the preamble statement and the PPT combined with the LOB.[4]

The agreements that will be modified by the MLI will come into compliance with the minimum standard once the provisions of the MLI take effect.

Argentina indicated in its response to the Peer Review questionnaire that bilateral negotiations would be used with respect to its agreement with Germany.

B. Implementation issues

No jurisdiction has raised any concerns about their agreements with Argentina.

Summary of the jurisdiction response – Argentina

	Treaty partners	Compliance with the standard	If compliant, the alternative implemented	Signature of a complying instrument	The alternative implemented through the complying instrument (if not the MLI)	Comments
1	Australia	No	N/A	Yes	N/A	
2	Belgium	No	N/A	Yes	N/A	
3	Bolivia*	No	N/A	No	N/A	
4	Brazil	Yes	PPT and LOB	N/A	N/A	
5	Canada	No	N/A	Yes	N/A	
6	Chile	Yes	PPT and LOB	N/A	N/A	
7	Denmark	No	N/A	Yes	N/A	
8	Finland	No	N/A	Yes	N/A	
9	France	No	N/A	Yes	N/A	
10	Germany	No	N/A	No	N/A	
11	Italy	No	N/A	Yes	N/A	
12	Mexico	Yes	PPT and LOB	N/A	N/A	
13	Netherlands	No	N/A	Yes	N/A	
14	Norway	No	N/A	Yes	N/A	
15	Russia	No	N/A	Yes	N/A	
16	Spain	No	N/A	Yes	N/A	
17	Sweden	No	N/A	Yes	N/A	
18	Switzerland	No	N/A	Yes	N/A	
19	United Arab Emirates	No	N/A	Yes	N/A	
20	United Kingdom	No	N/A	Yes	N/A	

Armenia

A. Progress in the implementation of the minimum standard

Armenia has 46 tax agreements in force, as reported in its response to the Peer Review questionnaire.

Armenia signed the MLI in 2017, listing 46 tax agreements.

Armenia is implementing the minimum standard through the inclusion of the preamble statement and the PPT combined with the LOB.[5]

The agreements that will be modified by the MLI will come into compliance with the minimum standard once the provisions of the MLI take effect.

B. Implementation issues

No jurisdiction has raised any concerns about their agreements with Armenia.

Summary of the jurisdiction response – Armenia

	Treaty partners	Compliance with the standard	If compliant, the alternative implemented	Signature of a complying instrument	The alternative implemented through the complying instrument (if not the MLI)	Comments
1	Austria	No	N/A	Yes	N/A	
2	Belarus*	No	N/A	Yes	N/A	
3	Belgium	No	N/A	Yes	N/A	
4	Bulgaria	No	N/A	Yes	N/A	
5	Canada	No	N/A	Yes	N/A	
6	China (People's Republic of)	No	N/A	Yes	N/A	
7	Croatia	No	N/A	Yes	N/A	
8	Cyprus*	No	N/A	Yes	N/A	
9	Czech Republic	No	N/A	Yes	N/A	
10	Estonia	No	N/A	Yes	N/A	
11	Finland	No	N/A	Yes	N/A	
12	France	No	N/A	Yes	N/A	
13	Georgia	No	N/A	Yes	N/A	
14	Germany	No	N/A	Yes	N/A	
15	Greece	No	N/A	Yes	N/A	
16	Hungary	No	N/A	Yes	N/A	
17	India	No	N/A	Yes	N/A	
18	Indonesia	No	N/A	Yes	N/A	
19	Iran*	No	N/A	Yes	N/A	
20	Ireland	No	N/A	Yes	N/A	
21	Italy	No	N/A	Yes	N/A	
22	Japan	No	N/A	No	N/A	

23	Kazakhstan	No	N/A	Yes	N/A	
24	Kuwait*	No	N/A	Yes	N/A	
25	Latvia	No	N/A	Yes	N/A	
26	Lebanon*	No	N/A	Yes	N/A	
27	Lithuania	No	N/A	Yes	N/A	
28	Luxembourg	No	N/A	Yes	N/A	
29	Moldova*	No	N/A	Yes	N/A	
30	Netherlands	No	N/A	Yes	N/A	
31	Poland	No	N/A	Yes	N/A	
32	Qatar	No	N/A	Yes	N/A	
33	Romania	No	N/A	Yes	N/A	
34	Russian Federation	No	N/A	Yes	N/A	
35	Serbia	No	N/A	Yes	N/A	
36	Slovak Republic	No	N/A	Yes	N/A	
37	Slovenia	No	N/A	Yes	N/A	
38	Spain	No	N/A	Yes	N/A	
39	Sweden	No	N/A	Yes	N/A	
40	Switzerland	No	N/A	Yes	N/A	
41	Syrian Arab Republic*	No	N/A	Yes	N/A	
42	Tajikistan*	No	N/A	Yes	N/A	
43	Thailand	No	N/A	Yes	N/A	
44	Turkmenistan*	No	N/A	Yes	N/A	
45	Ukraine	No	N/A	Yes	N/A	
46	United Arab Emirates	No	N/A	Yes	N/A	
47	United Kingdom	No	N/A	Yes	N/A	

Aruba

A. Progress in the implementation of the minimum standard

Aruba has one tax agreement in force, as reported in its response to the Peer Review questionnaire.

Aruba's agreement does not comply with the minimum standard and is not subject to a complying instrument.

Aruba's agreement with the Netherlands is an arrangements governed by the domestic law of the Kingdom of the Netherlands.

B. Implementation issues

No jurisdiction has raised any concerns about the agreement with Aruba.

Aruba is encouraged to implement the minimum standard in its agreement.

Summary of the jurisdiction response – Aruba

	Treaty partners	Compliance with the standard	If compliant, the alternative implemented	Signature of a complying instrument	The alternative implemented through the complying instrument (if not the MLI)	Comments
1	Netherlands	No	N/A	No	N/A	A new treaty is under negotiation or multilateral

Australia

A. Progress in the implementation of the minimum standard

Australia has 44 tax agreements in force, as reported in its response to the Peer Review questionnaire.[6] Seven of those agreements, the agreements with France, Germany, Japan, New Zealand, Poland, the Slovak Republic and the United Kingdom, comply with the minimum standard.

Australia signed the MLI in 2017 and deposited its instrument of ratification on 26 September 2018, listing 42 tax agreements.[7] The MLI entered into force for Australia on 1 January 2019.

Australia is implementing the minimum standard through the inclusion of the preamble statement and the PPT.[8]

The agreements modified by the MLI come into compliance with the minimum standard once the provisions of the MLI take effect. Other agreements listed under the MLI are expected to become compliant with the minimum standard in early 2020 and throughout future years as the MLI continues to take effect for other jurisdictions.

B. Implementation issues

No jurisdiction has raised any concerns about their agreements with Australia.

Summary of the jurisdiction response – Australia

	Treaty partners	Compliance with the standard	If compliant, the alternative implemented	Signature of a complying instrument	The alternative implemented through the complying instrument (if not the MLI)	Comments
1	Argentina	No	N/A	Yes	N/A	
2	Austria	No	N/A	Yes	N/A	Austria has not listed this agreement as a CTA
3	Belgium	No	N/A	Yes	N/A	MLI entered into force on 1/10/2019
4	Canada	No	N/A	Yes	N/A	MLI entered into force on 1/12/2019
5	Chile	No	N/A	Yes	N/A	
6	China (People's Republic of)	No	N/A	Yes	N/A	
7	Chinese Taipei*	No	N/A	No	N/A	
8	Czech Republic	No	N/A	Yes	N/A	
9	Denmark	No	N/A	Yes	N/A	MLI entered

						into force on 1/1/2020
10	Fiji*	No	N/A	Yes	N/A	
11	Finland	No	N/A	Yes	N/A	MLI entered into force on 1/6/2019
12	France	Yes	PPT alone	N/A	N/A	MLI entered into force on 1/1/2019
13	Germany	Yes	PPT alone	N/A	N/A	
14	Hungary	No	N/A	Yes	N/A	
15	India	No	N/A	Yes	N/A	MLI entered into force on 1/10/2019
16	Indonesia	No	N/A	Yes	N/A	
17	Ireland	No	N/A	Yes	N/A	MLI entered into force on 1/5/2019
18	Italy	No	N/A	Yes	N/A	
19	Japan	Yes	PPT and LOB	N/A	N/A	MLI entered into force on 1/1/2019
20	Kiribati*	No	N/A	Yes	N/A	
21	Korea	No	N/A	Yes	N/A	
22	Malaysia	No	N/A	Yes	N/A	
23	Malta	No	N/A	Yes	N/A	MLI entered into force on 1/4/2019
24	Mexico	No	N/A	Yes	N/A	
25	Netherlands	No	N/A	Yes	N/A	MLI will enter into force on 1 July 2019
26	New Zealand	Yes	PPT alone	N/A	N/A	MLI entered into force on 1/1/2019
27	Norway	No	N/A	Yes	N/A	MLI entered into force on 1/11/2019
28	Papua New Guinea	No	N/A	Yes	N/A	
29	Philippines*	No	N/A	Yes	N/A	
30	Poland	Yes	PPT alone	N/A	N/A	MLI entered

						into force on 1/1/2019
31	Romania	No	N/A	Yes	N/A	
32	Russia	No	N/A	Yes	N/A	MLI entered into force on 1/10/2019
33	Singapore	No	N/A	Yes	N/A	MLI entered into force on 1/4/2019
34	Slovak Republic	Yes	PPT alone	N/A	N/A	MLI entered into force on 1/1/2019
35	South Africa	No	N/A	Yes	N/A	
36	Spain	No	N/A	Yes	N/A	
37	Sri Lanka	No	N/A	Yes	N/A	
38	Sweden	No	N/A	Yes	N/A	Sweden has not listed this agreement as a CTA
39	Switzerland	No	N/A	Yes	N/A	Switzerland has not listed this agreement as a CTA
40	Thailand	No	N/A	Yes	N/A	
41	Turkey	No	N/A	Yes	N/A	
42	United Kingdom	Yes	PPT alone	N/A	N/A	MLI entered into force on 1/1/2019
43	United States	No	N/A	Yes	N/A	
44	Viet Nam	No	N/A	Yes	N/A	

Austria

A. Progress in the implementation of the minimum standard

Austria has 91 tax agreements in force, as reported in its response to the Peer Review questionnaire. Eleven of those agreements, the agreements with France, Israel, Japan, Kosovo*, Liechtenstein, Lithuania, Poland, Serbia, the Slovak Republic, Slovenia, and the United Kingdom, comply with the minimum standard.

Austria signed the MLI in 2017 and deposited its instrument of ratification on 22 September 2017, listing 38 tax agreements. The MLI entered into force for Austria on 1 July 2018.

Austria is implementing the minimum standard through the inclusion of the preamble statement and the PPT.[9]

The agreements modified by the MLI come into compliance with the minimum standard once the provisions of the MLI take effect.[10] Other agreements listed under the MLI are expected to become compliant with the minimum standard by the end of 2019.

Austria indicated in its response to the Peer Review questionnaire that bilateral negotiations would be used with respect to its agreement with Korea.

B. Implementation issues

No jurisdiction has raised any concerns about their agreements with Austria.

Summary of the jurisdiction response – Austria

	Treaty partners	Compliance with the standard	If compliant, the alternative implemented	Signature of a complying instrument	The alternative implemented through the complying instrument (if not the MLI)	Comments
1	Albania*	No	N/A	No	N/A	
2	Algeria*	No	N/A	No	N/A	
3	Armenia	No	N/A	No	N/A	
4	Australia	No	N/A	No	N/A	
5	Azerbaijan*	No	N/A	No	N/A	
6	Bahrain	No	N/A	No	N/A	
7	Barbados	No	N/A	No	N/A	
8	Belarus*	No	N/A	No	N/A	
9	Belgium	No	N/A	Yes	N/A	
10	Belize	No	N/A	No	N/A	
11	Bosnia and Herzegovina*	No	N/A	No	N/A	
12	Brazil	No	N/A	No	N/A	
13	Bulgaria	No	N/A	Yes	N/A	
14	Canada	No	N/A	Yes	N/A	
15	Chile	No	N/A	Yes	N/A	

16	China (People's Republic of)	No	N/A	Yes	N/A	
17	Chinese Taipei*	No	N/A	No	N/A	
18	Croatia	No	N/A	Yes	N/A	
19	Cuba*	No	N/A	No	N/A	
20	Cyprus*	No	N/A	Yes	N/A	
21	Czech Republic	No	N/A	Yes	N/A	
22	Denmark	No	N/A	No	N/A	
23	Egypt	No	N/A	No	N/A	
24	Estonia	No	N/A	Yes	N/A	
25	Finland	No	N/A	Yes	N/A	
26	France	Yes	PPT alone	No	N/A	
27	Georgia	No	N/A	No	N/A	
28	Germany	No	N/A	Yes	N/A	
29	Greece	No	N/A	Yes	N/A	
30	Hong Kong (China)	No	N/A	Yes	N/A	
31	Hungary	No	N/A	Yes	N/A	
32	Iceland	No	N/A	No	N/A	
33	India	No	N/A	Yes	N/A	
34	Indonesia	No	N/A	No	N/A	
35	Iran*	No	N/A	No	N/A	
36	Ireland	No	N/A	Yes	N/A	
37	Israel	Yes	PPT alone	No	N/A	
38	Italy	No	N/A	Yes	N/A	
39	Japan	Yes	PPT and LOB	N/A	N/A	
40	Kazakhstan	No	N/A	No	N/A	
41	Korea	No	N/A	No	N/A	
42	Kosovo*	Yes	PPT alone	No	N/A	
43	Kuwait*	No	N/A	No	N/A	
44	Kyrgyzstan*	No	N/A	No	N/A	
45	Latvia	No	N/A	Yes	N/A	
46	Libya*	No	N/A	No	N/A	
47	Liechtenstein	Yes	PPT alone	N/A	N/A	
48	Lithuania	Yes	PPT alone	No	N/A	
49	Luxembourg	No	N/A	Yes	N/A	
50	North Macedonia	No	N/A	No	N/A	
51	Malaysia	No	N/A	No	N/A	
52	Malta	No	N/A	Yes	N/A	
53	Mexico	No	N/A	Yes	N/A	
54	Moldova*	No	N/A	No	N/A	
55	Mongolia	No	N/A	No	N/A	
56	Montenegro*	No	N/A	No	N/A	
57	Morocco	No	N/A	No	N/A	
58	Nepal*	No	N/A	No	N/A	
59	Netherlands	No	N/A	Yes	N/A	
60	New Zealand	No	N/A	No	N/A	
61	Norway	No	N/A	No	N/A	
62	Pakistan	No	N/A	Yes	N/A	
63	Philippines*	No	N/A	No	N/A	
64	Poland	Yes	PPT alone	No	N/A	
65	Portugal	No	N/A	Yes	N/A	
66	Qatar	No	N/A	No	N/A	
67	Romania	No	N/A	Yes	N/A	
68	Russia	No	N/A	Yes	N/A	

69	San Marino	No	N/A	No	N/A	
70	Saudi Arabia	No	N/A	No	N/A	
71	Serbia	Yes	PPT alone	No	N/A	
72	Singapore	No	N/A	Yes	N/A	
73	Slovak Republic	Yes	PPT alone	No	N/A	
74	Slovenia	Yes	PPT alone	No	N/A	
75	South Africa	No	N/A	Yes	N/A	
76	Spain	No	N/A	Yes	N/A	
77	Sweden	No	N/A	No	N/A	
78	Switzerland	No	N/A	Yes	N/A	
79	Syrian Arab Republic*	No	N/A	No	N/A	
80	Tajikistan*	No	N/A	No	N/A	
81	Thailand	No	N/A	No	N/A	
82	Tunisia	No	N/A	No	N/A	
83	Turkey	No	N/A	Yes	N/A	
84	Turkmenistan*	No	N/A	No	N/A	
85	Ukraine	No	N/A	No	N/A	
86	United Arab Emirates	No	N/A	No	N/A	
87	United Kingdom	Yes	PPT alone	No	N/A	
88	United States	No	N/A	No	N/A	
89	Uzbekistan*	No	N/A	No	N/A	
90	Venezuela*	No	N/A	No	N/A	
91	Viet Nam	No	N/A	No	N/A	

The Bahamas

A. Progress in the implementation of the minimum standard

The Bahamas has no tax agreements, as reported in its response to the Peer Review questionnaire.

B. Implementation issues

No jurisdiction has raised any concerns about the Bahamas.

Bahrain

A. Progress in the implementation of the minimum standard

Bahrain has 44 tax agreements in force, as reported in its response to the Peer Review questionnaire.

None of Bahrain's agreements comply with the minimum standard or are subject to a complying instrument.

Bahrain indicated in its response to the Peer Review questionnaire that it is currently working towards signing the MLI in 2020.

Bahrain further indicated that bilateral negotiations would be used with respect to several agreements.

B. Implementation issues

No jurisdiction has raised any concerns about their agreements with Bahrain.

Bahrain is encouraged to implement the minimum standard in its agreements.

Summary of the jurisdiction response – Bahrain

	Treaty partners	Compliance with the standard	If compliant, the alternative implemented	Signature of a complying instrument	The alternative implemented through the complying instrument (if not the MLI)	Comments
1	Algeria*	No	N/A	No	N/A	
2	Austria	No	N/A	No	N/A	
3	Barbados	No	N/A	No	N/A	
4	Bangladesh*	No	N/A	No	N/A	
5	Belarus*	No	N/A	No	N/A	
6	Belgium	No	N/A	No	N/A	
7	Bermuda	No	N/A	No	N/A	
8	Brunei Darussalam	No	N/A	No	N/A	
9	Bulgaria	No	N/A	No	N/A	
10	China (People's Republic of)	No	N/A	No	N/A	
11	Cyprus*	No	N/A	No	N/A	
12	Czech Republic	No	N/A	No	N/A	
13	Egypt	No	N/A	No	N/A	
14	Estonia	No	N/A	No	N/A	
15	France	No	N/A	No	N/A	
16	Georgia	No	N/A	No	N/A	
17	Hungary	No	N/A	No	N/A	
18	Iran*	No	N/A	No	N/A	
19	Ireland	No	N/A	No	N/A	
20	Isle of Man	No	N/A	No	N/A	
21	Jordan*	No	N/A	No	N/A	
22	Korea	No	N/A	No	N/A	
23	Lebanon*	No	N/A	No	N/A	

24	Luxembourg	No	N/A	No	N/A	
25	Malaysia	No	N/A	No	N/A	
26	Malta	No	N/A	No	N/A	
27	Mexico	No	N/A	No	N/A	
28	Morocco	No	N/A	No	N/A	
29	Netherlands	No	N/A	No	N/A	
30	Pakistan	No	N/A	No	N/A	
31	Philippines*	No	N/A	No	N/A	
32	Portugal	No	N/A	No	N/A	
33	Seychelles	No	N/A	No	N/A	
34	Singapore	No	N/A	No	N/A	
35	Sri Lanka	No	N/A	No	N/A	
36	Sudan*	No	N/A	No	N/A	
37	Syrian Arab Republic*	No	N/A	No	N/A	
38	Tajikistan*	No	N/A	No	N/A	
39	Thailand	No	N/A	No	N/A	
40	Turkey	No	N/A	No	N/A	
41	Turkmenistan*	No	N/A	No	N/A	
42	United Kingdom	No	N/A	No	N/A	
43	Uzbekistan*	No	N/A	No	N/A	
44	Yemen*	No	N/A	No	N/A	

Barbados

A. Progress in the implementation of the minimum standard

Barbados has 31 tax agreements in force, including the multilateral agreement among the members of the CARICOM concluded with ten treaty partners (the CARICOM Agreement).[11]

Barbados signed the MLI in 2018, listing 30 tax agreements.[12]

Barbados is implementing the minimum standard through the inclusion of the preamble statement and the PPT.[13]

The agreements that will be modified by the MLI will come into compliance with the minimum standard once the provisions of the MLI take effect.

B. Implementation issues

Barbados is encouraged to bring the CARICOM Agreement up to date by commencing talks among all the treaty partners.[14]

Summary of the jurisdiction response – Barbados

	Treaty partners	Compliance with the standard	If compliant, the alternative implemented	Signature of a complying instrument	The alternative implemented through the complying instrument (if not the MLI)	Comments
1	Antigua and Barbuda	No	N/A	Yes	N/A	CARICOM
2	Austria	No	N/A	Yes	N/A	
3	Bahrain	No	N/A	Yes	N/A	
4	Belize	No	N/A	Yes	N/A	CARICOM
5	Botswana	No	N/A	Yes	N/A	
6	Canada	No	N/A	Yes	N/A	
7	China (People's Republic of)	No	N/A	Yes	N/A	
8	Cuba*	No	N/A	No	N/A	
9	Cyprus*	No	N/A	Yes	N/A	
10	Czech Republic	No	N/A	Yes	N/A	
11	Dominica	No	N/A	Yes	N/A	CARICOM
12	Finland	No	N/A	Yes	N/A	
13	Grenada	No	N/A	Yes	N/A	CARICOM
14	Guyana*	No	N/A	Yes	N/A	CARICOM
15	Iceland	No	N/A	Yes	N/A	
16	Italy	No	N/A	Yes	N/A	
17	Jamaica	No	N/A	Yes	N/A	CARICOM
18	Luxembourg	No	N/A	Yes	N/A	
19	Malta	No	N/A	Yes	N/A	
20	Mauritius	No	N/A	Yes	N/A	
21	Mexico	No	N/A	Yes	N/A	

22	Netherlands	No	N/A	Yes	N/A	
23	Norway	No	N/A	Yes	N/A	
24	Panama	No	N/A	Yes	N/A	
25	Portugal	No	N/A	Yes	N/A	
26	Qatar	No	N/A	Yes	N/A	
27	Saint Kitts and Nevis	No	N/A	Yes	N/A	CARICOM
28	Saint Lucia	No	N/A	Yes	N/A	CARICOM
29	Saint Vincent and the Grenadines	No	N/A	Yes	N/A	CARICOM
30	San Marino	No	N/A	Yes	N/A	
31	Seychelles	No	N/A	Yes	N/A	
32	Singapore	No	N/A	Yes	N/A	
33	Spain	No	N/A	Yes	N/A	
34	Sweden	No	N/A	Yes	N/A	
35	Switzerland	No	N/A	Yes	N/A	
36	Trinidad and Tobago	No	N/A	Yes	N/A	CARICOM
37	United Arab Emirates	No	N/A	Yes	N/A	
38	United Kingdom	No	N/A	Yes	N/A	
39	United States	No	N/A	Yes	N/A	
40	Venezuela*	No	N/A	Yes	N/A	

Belgium

A. Progress in the implementation of the minimum standard

Belgium has 95 tax agreements in force, as reported in its response to the Peer Review questionnaire. Its agreement with Japan complies with the minimum standard.

Belgium signed the MLI in 2017 and deposited its instrument of ratification on 26 June 2019, listing 90 tax agreements.[15] The MLI entered into force for Belgium on 1 October 2019.

Belgium is generally implementing the minimum standard through the inclusion of the preamble statement and the PPT.[16]

The agreements that will be modified by the MLI will come into compliance with the minimum standard once the provisions of the MLI take effect.

Belgium indicated in its response of the Peer Review questionnaire that bilateral negotiations would be used with Chinese Taipei, Germany, Norway and Switzerland.

B. Implementation issues

No jurisdiction has raised any concerns about their agreements with Belgium.

Summary of the jurisdiction response – Belgium

	Treaty partners	Compliance with the standard	If compliant, the alternative implemented	Signature of a complying instrument	The alternative implemented through the complying instrument (if not the MLI)	Comments
1	Albania*	No	N/A	Yes	N/A	
2	Algeria*	No	N/A	Yes	N/A	
3	Argentina	No	N/A	Yes	N/A	
4	Armenia	No	N/A	Yes	N/A	
5	Australia	No	N/A	Yes	N/A	
6	Austria	No	N/A	Yes	N/A	
7	Azerbaijan*	No	N/A	Yes	N/A	
8	Bahrain	No	N/A	Yes	N/A	
9	Bangladesh*	No	N/A	Yes	N/A	
10	Belarus*	No	N/A	Yes	N/A	
11	Bosnia and Herzegovina*	No	N/A	Yes	N/A	
12	Brazil	No	N/A	Yes	N/A	
13	Bulgaria	No	N/A	Yes	N/A	
14	Canada	No	N/A	Yes	N/A	
15	Chile	No	N/A	Yes	N/A	
16	China (People's Republic of)	No	N/A	Yes	N/A	
17	Chinese Taipei*	No	N/A	No	N/A	
18	Congo	No	N/A	Yes	N/A	

19	Cote d'Ivoire	No	N/A	Yes	N/A	
20	Croatia	No	N/A	Yes	N/A	
21	Cyprus*	No	N/A	Yes	N/A	
22	Czech Republic	No	N/A	Yes	N/A	
23	Denmark	No	N/A	Yes	N/A	
24	Ecuador*	No	N/A	Yes	N/A	
25	Egypt	No	N/A	Yes	N/A	
26	Estonia	No	N/A	Yes	N/A	
27	Finland	No	N/A	Yes	N/A	
28	France	No	N/A	Yes	N/A	
29	Gabon	No	N/A	Yes	N/A	
30	Georgia	No	N/A	Yes	N/A	
31	Germany	No	N/A	No	N/A	
32	Ghana*	No	N/A	Yes	N/A	
33	Greece	No	N/A	Yes	N/A	
34	Hong Kong (China)	No	N/A	Yes	N/A	
35	Hungary	No	N/A	Yes	N/A	
36	Iceland	No	N/A	Yes	N/A	
37	India	No	N/A	Yes	N/A	
38	Indonesia	No	N/A	Yes	N/A	
39	Ireland	No	N/A	Yes	N/A	
40	Israel	No	N/A	Yes	N/A	
41	Italy	No	N/A	Yes	N/A	
42	Japan	Yes	PPT and LOB	N/A	N/A	
43	Kazakhstan	No	N/A	Yes	N/A	
44	Korea	No	N/A	Yes	N/A	
45	Kosovo*	No	N/A	Yes	N/A	
46	Kuwait*	No	N/A	Yes	N/A	
47	Kyrgyzstan*	No	N/A	Yes	N/A	
48	Latvia	No	N/A	Yes	N/A	
49	Lithuania	No	N/A	Yes	N/A	
50	Luxembourg	No	N/A	Yes	N/A	
51	North Macedonia	No	N/A	Yes	N/A	
52	Malaysia	No	N/A	Yes	N/A	
53	Malta	No	N/A	Yes	N/A	
54	Mauritius	No	N/A	Yes	N/A	
55	Mexico	No	N/A	Yes	N/A	
56	Moldova*	No	N/A	Yes	N/A	
57	Mongolia	No	N/A	Yes	N/A	
58	Montenegro*	No	N/A	Yes	N/A	
59	Morocco	No	N/A	Yes	N/A	
60	Netherlands	No	N/A	Yes	N/A	
61	New Zealand	No	N/A	Yes	N/A	
62	Nigeria	No	N/A	Yes	N/A	
63	Norway	No	N/A	No	N/A	
64	Pakistan	No	N/A	Yes	N/A	
65	Philippines*	No	N/A	Yes	N/A	
66	Poland	No	N/A	Yes	N/A	
67	Portugal	No	N/A	Yes	N/A	
68	Romania	No	N/A	Yes	N/A	
69	Russia	No	N/A	Yes	N/A	
70	Rwanda*	No	N/A	Yes	N/A	
71	San Marino	No	N/A	Yes	N/A	

72	Senegal	No	N/A	Yes	N/A	
73	Serbia	No	N/A	Yes	N/A	
74	Seychelles	No	N/A	Yes	N/A	
75	Singapore	No	N/A	Yes	N/A	
76	Slovak Republic	No	N/A	Yes	N/A	
77	Slovenia	No	N/A	Yes	N/A	
78	South Africa	No	N/A	Yes	N/A	
79	Spain	No	N/A	Yes	N/A	
80	Sri Lanka	No	N/A	Yes	N/A	
81	Sweden	No	N/A	Yes	N/A	
82	Switzerland	No	N/A	No	N/A	
83	Tajikistan*	No	N/A	Yes	N/A	
84	Thailand	No	N/A	Yes	N/A	
85	Tunisia	No	N/A	Yes	N/A	
86	Turkey	No	N/A	Yes	N/A	
87	Turkmenistan*	No	N/A	Yes	N/A	
88	Ukraine	No	N/A	Yes	N/A	
89	United Arab Emirates	No	N/A	Yes	N/A	
90	United Kingdom	No	N/A	Yes	N/A	
91	United States	No	N/A	Yes	N/A	
92	Uruguay	No	N/A	Yes	N/A	
93	Uzbekistan*	No	N/A	Yes	N/A	
94	Venezuela*	No	N/A	Yes	N/A	
95	Viet Nam	No	N/A	Yes	N/A	

Belize

A. Progress in the implementation of the minimum standard

Belize has four tax agreements in force, as reported in its response to the Peer Review questionnaire, including the multilateral agreement among the members of the CARICOM concluded with ten of its treaty partners (the CARICOM Agreement).[17]

Belize signed the MLI in 2019, listing four tax agreements.

Belize is implementing the minimum standard through the inclusion of the preamble statement and the PPT.

The agreements that will be modified by the MLI will come into compliance with the minimum standard once the provisions of the MLI take effect.

B. Implementation issues

Belize is encouraged to bring the CARICOM Agreement up to date by commencing talks among all the treaty partners.[18]

Summary of the jurisdiction response – Belize

	Treaty partners	Compliance with the standard	If compliant, the alternative implemented	Signature of a complying instrument	The alternative implemented through the complying instrument (if not the MLI)	Comments
1	Antigua and Barbuda	No	N/A	Yes	N/A	CARICOM
2	Austria	No	N/A	Yes	N/A	
3	Barbados	No	N/A	Yes	N/A	CARICOM
4	Dominica	No	N/A	Yes	N/A	CARICOM
5	Grenada	No	N/A	Yes	N/A	CARICOM
6	Guyana*	No	N/A	Yes	N/A	CARICOM
7	Jamaica	No	N/A	Yes	N/A	CARICOM
8	Saint Kitts and Nevis	No	N/A	Yes	N/A	CARICOM
9	Saint Lucia	No	N/A	Yes	N/A	CARICOM
10	Saint Vincent and the Grenadines	No	N/A	Yes	N/A	CARICOM
11	Switzerland	No	N/A	Yes	N/A	
12	Trinidad and Tobago	No	N/A	Yes	N/A	CARICOM
13	United Kingdom	No	N/A	Yes	N/A	

Benin

A. Progress in the implementation of the minimum standard

Benin has three tax agreements in force, as reported in its response to the Peer Review questionnaire, including the multilateral Regulation 08/2008/COM adopting the rules for the avoidance of double taxation within the West African Economic and Monetary Union and the rule for assistance in tax matters (the UEMOA) concluded with seven partners.[19]

None of Benin's agreements comply with the minimum standard or are subject to a complying instrument.

B. Implementation issues

No jurisdiction has raised any concerns about their agreements with Benin.

Benin is encouraged to implement the minimum standard in its agreements.

Summary of the jurisdiction response – Benin

	Treaty partners	Compliance with the standard	If compliant, the alternative implemented	Signature of a complying instrument	The alternative implemented through the complying instrument (if not the MLI)	Comments
1	France	No	N/A	No	N/A	
2	Norway	No	N/A	No	N/A	
3	Burkina Faso	No	N/A	No	N/A	UEMOA
4	Côte d'Ivoire	No	N/A	No	N/A	UEMOA
5	Guinea-Bissau*	No	N/A	No	N/A	UEMOA
6	Togo*	No	N/A	No	N/A	UEMOA
7	Mali*	No	N/A	No	N/A	UEMOA
8	Niger*	No	N/A	No	N/A	UEMOA
9	Senegal	No	N/A	No	N/A	UEMOA

Bermuda

A. Progress in the implementation of the minimum standard

Bermuda has two tax agreements in force as reported in its response to the Peer Review questionnaire.

Neither of Bermuda's agreements comply with the minimum standard or are subject to a complying instrument.

B. Implementation issues

No jurisdiction has raised any concerns about their agreements with Bermuda.

Bermuda is encouraged to implement the minimum standard in its agreements.

Summary of the jurisdiction response – Bermuda

	Treaty partners	Compliance with the standard	If compliant, the alternative implemented	Signature of a complying instrument	The alternative implemented through the complying instrument (if not the MLI)	Comments
1	Bahrain	No	N/A	No	N/A	
2	Seychelles	No	N/A	No	N/A	

Botswana

A. Progress in the implementation of the minimum standard

Botswana has 16 tax agreements in force, as reported in its response to the Peer Review questionnaire.

None of Botswana's agreements comply with the minimum standard or are subject to a complying instrument.

B. Implementation issues

No jurisdiction has raised any concerns about their agreements with Botswana.

Botswana is encouraged to implement the minimum standard in its agreements.

Summary of the jurisdiction response – Botswana

	Treaty partners	Compliance with the standard	If compliant, the alternative implemented	Signature of a complying instrument	The alternative implemented through the complying instrument (if not the MLI)	Comments
1	Barbados	No	N/A	No	N/A	
2	France	No	N/A	No	N/A	
3	India	No	N/A	No	N/A	
4	Ireland	No	N/A	No	N/A	
5	Malta	No	N/A	No	N/A	
6	Mauritius	No	N/A	No	N/A	
7	Mozambique*	No	N/A	No	N/A	
8	Namibia*	No	N/A	No	N/A	
9	Russia	No	N/A	No	N/A	
10	Seychelles	No	N/A	No	N/A	
11	South Africa	No	N/A	No	N/A	
12	Eswatini*	No	N/A	No	N/A	
13	Sweden	No	N/A	No	N/A	
14	United Kingdom	No	N/A	No	N/A	
15	Zambia	No	N/A	No	N/A	
16	Zimbabwe*	No	N/A	No	N/A	

Brazil

A. Progress in the implementation of the minimum standard

Brazil has 33 tax agreements in force, as reported in its response to the Peer Review questionnaire. Its agreement with Argentina complies with the minimum standard. Brazil has not signed the MLI.

Brazil is implementing the minimum standard through the inclusion of the preamble statement and the PPT combined with the LOB.

Brazil also signed one bilateral complying instrument with respect to its agreement with Sweden.

Brazil indicated in its response to the Peer Review questionnaire that bilateral negotiations would be used with respect to its agreements and that it already contacted its treaty partners for negotiations.

B. Implementation issues

No jurisdiction has raised any concerns about their agreements with Brazil.

Summary of the jurisdiction response – Brazil

	Treaty partners	Compliance with the standard	If compliant, the alternative implemented	Signature of a complying instrument	The alternative implemented through the complying instrument (if not the MLI)	Comments
1	Argentina	Yes	PPT and LOB	N/A	N/A	
2	Austria	No	N/A	No	N/A	
3	Belgium	No	N/A	No	N/A	
4	Canada	No	N/A	No	N/A	
5	Chile	No	N/A	No	N/A	
6	China (People's Republic of)	No	N/A	No	N/A	
7	Czech Republic	No	N/A	No	N/A	
8	Denmark	No	N/A	No	N/A	
9	Ecuador*	No	N/A	No	N/A	
10	Finland	No	N/A	No	N/A	
11	France	No	N/A	No	N/A	
12	Hungary	No	N/A	No	N/A	
13	India	No	N/A	No	N/A	
14	Israel	No	N/A	No	N/A	
15	Italy	No	N/A	No	N/A	
16	Japan	No	N/A	No	N/A	
17	Korea	No	N/A	No	N/A	
18	Luxembourg	No	N/A	No	N/A	
19	Mexico	No	N/A	No	N/A	
20	Netherlands	No	N/A	No	N/A	
21	Norway	No	N/A	No	N/A	
22	Peru	No	N/A	No	N/A	

23	Philippines*	No	N/A	No	N/A	
24	Portugal	No	N/A	No	N/A	
25	Russia	No	N/A	No	N/A	
26	Slovak Republic	No	N/A	No	N/A	
27	South Africa	No	N/A	No	N/A	
28	Spain	No	N/A	No	N/A	
29	Sweden	No	N/A	Yes	PPT and LOB	
30	Trinidad and Tobago	No	N/A	No	N/A	
31	Turkey	No	N/A	No	N/A	
32	Ukraine	No	N/A	No	N/A	
33	Venezuela*	No	N/A	No	N/A	

British Virgin Islands

A. Progress in the implementation of the minimum standard

The British Virgin Islands has one tax agreement in force, as reported in its response to the Peer Review questionnaire.

The British Virgin Islands' agreement does not comply with the minimum standard and is not subject to any complying instruments.

B. Implementation issues

No jurisdiction has raised any concerns about the agreement with the British Virgin Islands.

The British Virgin Islands is encouraged to implement the minimum standard in its agreement.

Summary of the jurisdiction response – British Virgin Islands

	Treaty partners	Compliance with the standard	If compliant, the alternative implemented	Signature of a complying instrument	The alternative implemented through the complying instrument (if not the MLI)	Comments
1	Switzerland	No	N/A	No	N/A	

Brunei Darussalam

A. Progress in the implementation of the minimum standard

Brunei Darussalam has 18 tax agreements in force, as reported in its response to the Peer Review questionnaire.

None of Brunei Darussalam's agreements comply with the minimum standard or are subject to a complying instrument.

Brunei Darussalam indicated in its response to the Peer Review questionnaire that it is updating its Model Tax Convention with the treaty-related BEPS minimum standards and it considers signing the MLI.

B. Implementation issues

No jurisdiction has raised any concerns about their agreements with Brunei Darussalam.

Brunei Darussalam is encouraged to implement the minimum standard in its agreements.

Summary of the jurisdiction response – Brunei Darussalam

	Treaty partners	Compliance with the standard	If compliant, the alternative implemented	Signature of a complying instrument	The alternative implemented through the complying instrument (if not the MLI)	Comments
1	Bahrain	No	N/A	No	N/A	
2	Cambodia*	No	N/A	No	N/A	
3	China (People's Republic of)	No	N/A	No	N/A	
4	Hong Kong (China)	No	N/A	No	N/A	
5	Indonesia	No	N/A	No	N/A	
6	Japan	No	N/A	No	N/A	
7	Korea	No	N/A	No	N/A	
8	Kuwait*	No	N/A	No	N/A	
9	Lao People's Democratic Republic*	No	N/A	No	N/A	
10	Luxembourg	No	N/A	No	N/A	
11	Malaysia	No	N/A	No	N/A	
12	Oman	No	N/A	No	N/A	
13	Pakistan	No	N/A	No	N/A	
14	Qatar	No	N/A	No	N/A	
15	Singapore	No	N/A	No	N/A	
16	United Arab Emirates	No	N/A	No	N/A	
17	United Kingdom	No	N/A	No	N/A	
18	Viet Nam	No	N/A	No	N/A	

Bulgaria

A. Progress in the implementation of the minimum standard

Bulgaria has 70 tax agreements in force, as reported in its response to the Peer Review questionnaire. Its agreement with Saudi Arabia complies with the minimum standard.

Bulgaria signed the MLI in 2017, listing 66 tax agreements.

Bulgaria is implementing the minimum standard through the inclusion of the preamble statement and the PPT combined with the LOB.[20]

The agreements that will be modified by the MLI will come into compliance with the minimum standard once the provisions of the MLI take effect.

Bulgaria indicated in its response to the Peer Review questionnaire that bilateral negotiations would be used for agreements with Finland, Germany, Malta, the Netherlands and Switzerland.

B. Implementation issues

No jurisdiction has raised any concerns about their agreements with Bulgaria.

Summary of the jurisdiction response – Bulgaria

	Treaty partners	Compliance with the standard	If compliant, the alternative implemented	Signature of a complying instrument	The alternative implemented through the complying instrument (if not the MLI)	Comments
1	Albania*	No	N/A	Yes	N/A	
2	Algeria*	No	N/A	Yes	N/A	
3	Armenia	No	N/A	Yes	N/A	
4	Austria	No	N/A	Yes	N/A	
5	Azerbaijan*	No	N/A	Yes	N/A	
6	Bahrain	No	N/A	Yes	N/A	
7	Belarus*	No	N/A	Yes	N/A	
8	Belgium	No	N/A	Yes	N/A	
9	Canada	No	N/A	Yes	N/A	
10	China (People's Republic of)	No	N/A	Yes	N/A	
11	Croatia	No	N/A	Yes	N/A	
12	Cyprus*	No	N/A	Yes	N/A	
13	Czech Republic	No	N/A	Yes	N/A	
14	Democratic People's Republic of Korea*	No	N/A	Yes	N/A	
15	Denmark	No	N/A	Yes	N/A	
16	Egypt	No	N/A	Yes	N/A	
17	Estonia	No	N/A	Yes	N/A	
18	Finland	No	N/A	No	N/A	
19	France	No	N/A	Yes	N/A	

20	Georgia	No	N/A	Yes	N/A	
21	Germany	No	N/A	Yes	N/A	
22	Greece	No	N/A	Yes	N/A	
23	Hungary	No	N/A	Yes	N/A	
24	India	No	N/A	Yes	N/A	
25	Indonesia	No	N/A	Yes	N/A	
26	Iran*	No	N/A	Yes	N/A	
27	Ireland	No	N/A	Yes	N/A	
28	Israel	No	N/A	Yes	N/A	
29	Italy	No	N/A	Yes	N/A	
30	Japan	No	N/A	Yes	N/A	
31	Jordan*	No	N/A	Yes	N/A	
32	Kazakhstan	No	N/A	Yes	N/A	
33	Korea	No	N/A	Yes	N/A	
34	Kuwait*	No	N/A	Yes	N/A	
35	Latvia	No	N/A	Yes	N/A	
36	Lebanon*	No	N/A	Yes	N/A	
37	Lithuania	No	N/A	Yes	N/A	
38	Luxembourg	No	N/A	Yes	N/A	
39	North Macedonia	No	N/A	Yes	N/A	
40	Malta	No	N/A	No	N/A	
41	Moldova*	No	N/A	Yes	N/A	
42	Mongolia	No	N/A	Yes	N/A	
43	Montenegro*	No	N/A	Yes	N/A	
44	Morocco	No	N/A	Yes	N/A	
45	Netherlands	No	N/A	No	N/A	
46	Norway	No	N/A	Yes	N/A	
47	Poland	No	N/A	Yes	N/A	
48	Portugal	No	N/A	Yes	N/A	
49	Qatar	No	N/A	Yes	N/A	
50	Romania	No	N/A	Yes	N/A	
51	Russia	No	N/A	Yes	N/A	
52	Saudi Arabia	Yes	PPT alone	N/A	N/A	
53	Serbia	No	N/A	Yes	N/A	
54	Singapore	No	N/A	Yes	N/A	
55	Slovak Republic	No	N/A	Yes	N/A	
56	Slovenia	No	N/A	Yes	N/A	
57	South Africa	No	N/A	Yes	N/A	
58	Spain	No	N/A	Yes	N/A	
59	Sweden	No	N/A	Yes	N/A	
60	Switzerland	No	N/A	Yes	N/A	
61	Syrian Arab Republic*	No	N/A	Yes	N/A	
62	Thailand	No	N/A	Yes	N/A	
63	Turkey	No	N/A	Yes	N/A	
64	Ukraine	No	N/A	Yes	N/A	
65	United Arab Emirates	No	N/A	Yes	N/A	
66	United Kingdom	No	N/A	Yes	N/A	
67	United States	No	N/A	Yes	N/A	
68	Uzbekistan*	No	N/A	Yes	N/A	
69	Viet Nam	No	N/A	Yes	N/A	
70	Zimbabwe*	No	N/A	Yes	N/A	

Burkina Faso

A. Progress in the implementation of the minimum standard

Burkina Faso has three tax agreements in force, as reported in its response to the Peer Review questionnaire, including the multilateral Regulation 08/2008/COM adopting the rules for the avoidance of double taxation within the West African Economic and Monetary Union and the rule for assistance in tax matters (the UEMOA) concluded with seven partners.[21]

Burkina Faso signed the MLI in 2017, listing two tax agreements.[22]

Burkina Faso is implementing the minimum standard through the inclusion of the preamble statement and the PPT.[23]

The agreements that will be modified by the MLI will come into compliance with the minimum standard once the provisions of the MLI take effect.

Burkina Faso indicated in its response to the Peer Review questionnaire that the agreement the UEMOA has not been listed under the MLI as it is a regulation of the West African Economic and Monetary Union.

B. Implementation issues

No jurisdiction has raised any concerns about their agreements with Burkina Faso.

Summary of the jurisdiction response – Burkina Faso

	Treaty partners	Compliance with the standard	If compliant, the alternative implemented	Signature of a complying instrument	The alternative implemented through the complying instrument (if not the MLI)	Comments
1	Benin	No	N/A	No	N/A	UEMOA
2	Cote d'Ivoire	No	N/A	No	N/A	UEMOA
3	France	No	N/A	Yes	N/A	
4	Guinea-Bissau*	No	N/A	No	N/A	UEMOA
5	Mali*	No	N/A	No	N/A	UEMOA
6	Niger*	No	N/A	No	N/A	UEMOA
7	Senegal	No	N/A	No	N/A	UEMOA
8	Togo*	No	N/A	No	N/A	UEMOA
9	Tunisia	No	N/A	Yes	N/A	

Cabo Verde

A. Progress in the implementation of the minimum standard

Cabo Verde has three tax agreements in force, as reported in its response to the Peer Review questionnaire.

None of Cabo Verde's agreements comply with the minimum standard or are subject to a complying instrument.

B. Implementation issues

No jurisdiction has raised any concerns about their agreements with Cabo Verde.

Cabo Verde is encouraged to implement the minimum standard in its agreements.

Summary of the jurisdiction response – Cabo Verde

	Treaty partners	Compliance with the standard	If compliant, the alternative implemented	Signature of a complying instrument	The alternative implemented through the complying instrument (if not the MLI)	Comments
1	Macau (China)	No	N/A	No	N/A	
2	Mauritius	No	N/A	No	N/A	
3	Portugal	No	N/A	No	N/A	

Cameroon

A. Progress in the implementation of the minimum standard

Cameroon has four tax agreements in force, as reported in its response to the Peer Review questionnaire.

Cameroon signed the MLI in 2017, listing four tax agreements.[24]

Cameroon is implementing the minimum standard through the inclusion of the preamble statement and the PPT.[25]

The agreements that will be modified by the MLI will come into compliance with the minimum standard once the provisions of the MLI take effect.

B. Implementation issues

No jurisdiction has raised any concerns about their agreements with Cameroon.

Summary of the jurisdiction response – Cameroon

	Treaty partners	Compliance with the standard	If compliant, the alternative implemented	Signature of a complying instrument	The alternative implemented through the complying instrument (if not the MLI)	Comments
1	Canada	No	N/A	Yes	N/A	
2	France	No	N/A	Yes	N/A	
3	South Africa	No	N/A	Yes	N/A	
4	Tunisie	No	N/A	Yes	N/A	

Canada

A. Progress in the implementation of the minimum standard

Canada has 93 tax agreements in force, as reported in its response to the Peer Review questionnaire.

Canada signed the MLI in 2017, with a provisional listing of 75 tax agreements.

Canada is implementing the minimum standard through the inclusion of the preamble statement and the PPT.[26]

The agreements that will be modified by the MLI will come into compliance with the minimum standard once the provisions of the MLI take effect.

Canada indicated in its response to the Peer Review questionnaire that bilateral negotiations would be used with respect to its agreements with Germany and Switzerland.

B. Implementation issues

No jurisdiction has raised any concerns about their agreements with Canada.

Summary of the jurisdiction response – Canada

	Treaty partners	Compliance with the standard	If compliant, the alternative implemented	Signature of a complying instrument	The alternative implemented through the complying instrument (if not the MLI)	Comments
1	Algeria*	No	N/A	No	N/A	
2	Argentina	No	N/A	Yes	N/A	
3	Armenia	No	N/A	No	N/A	
4	Australia	No	N/A	Yes	N/A	
5	Austria	No	N/A	Yes	N/A	
6	Azerbaijan*	No	N/A	Yes	N/A	
7	Bangladesh*	No	N/A	Yes	N/A	
8	Barbados	No	N/A	Yes	N/A	
9	Belgium	No	N/A	Yes	N/A	
10	Brazil	No	N/A	Yes	N/A	
11	Bulgaria	No	N/A	Yes	N/A	
12	Cameroon	No	N/A	Yes	N/A	
13	Chile	No	N/A	Yes	N/A	
14	China (People's Republic of)	No	N/A	Yes	N/A	
15	Chinese Taipei*[27]	No	N/A	No	N/A	
16	Colombia	No	N/A	Yes	N/A	
17	Cote d'Ivoire	No	N/A	No	N/A	
18	Croatia	No	N/A	Yes	N/A	
19	Cyprus*	No	N/A	Yes	N/A	
20	Czech Republic	No	N/A	Yes	N/A	
21	Denmark	No	N/A	Yes	N/A	

22	Dominican Republic	No	N/A	Yes	N/A	
23	Ecuador*	No	N/A	No	N/A	
24	Egypt	No	N/A	Yes	N/A	
25	Estonia	No	N/A	Yes	N/A	
26	Finland	No	N/A	Yes	N/A	
27	France	No	N/A	Yes	N/A	
28	Gabon	No	N/A	Yes	N/A	
29	Germany	No	N/A	No	N/A	
30	Greece	No	N/A	Yes	N/A	
31	Guyana*	No	N/A	No	N/A	
32	Hong Kong (China)	No	N/A	Yes	N/A	
33	Hungary	No	N/A	Yes	N/A	
34	Iceland	No	N/A	Yes	N/A	
35	India	No	N/A	Yes	N/A	
36	Indonesia	No	N/A	Yes	N/A	
37	Ireland	No	N/A	Yes	N/A	
38	Israel	No	N/A	Yes	N/A	
39	Italy	No	N/A	Yes	N/A	
40	Jamaica	No	N/A	Yes	N/A	
41	Japan	No	N/A	Yes	N/A	
42	Jordan*	No	N/A	Yes	N/A	
43	Kazakhstan	No	N/A	Yes	N/A	
44	Kenya	No	N/A	Yes	N/A	
45	Korea	No	N/A	Yes	N/A	
46	Kuwait*	No	N/A	No	N/A	
47	Kyrgyzstan*	No	N/A	No	N/A	
48	Latvia	No	N/A	Yes	N/A	
49	Lithuania	No	N/A	Yes	N/A	
50	Luxembourg	No	N/A	Yes	N/A	
51	Malaysia	No	N/A	Yes	N/A	
52	Malta	No	N/A	Yes	N/A	
53	Mexico	No	N/A	Yes	N/A	
54	Moldova*	No	N/A	Yes	N/A	
55	Mongolia	No	N/A	Yes	N/A	
56	Morocco	No	N/A	Yes	N/A	
57	Netherlands	No	N/A	Yes	N/A	
58	New Zealand	No	N/A	Yes	N/A	
59	Nigeria	No	N/A	Yes	N/A	
60	Norway	No	N/A	Yes	N/A	
61	Oman	No	N/A	No	N/A	
62	Pakistan	No	N/A	Yes	N/A	
63	Papua New Guinea	No	N/A	No	N/A	
64	Peru	No	N/A	No	N/A	
65	Philippines*	No	N/A	Yes	N/A	
66	Poland	No	N/A	Yes	N/A	
67	Portugal	No	N/A	Yes	N/A	
68	Romania	No	N/A	Yes	N/A	
69	Russia	No	N/A	Yes	N/A	
70	Senegal	No	N/A	Yes	N/A	
71	Serbia	No	N/A	Yes	N/A	
72	Singapore	No	N/A	Yes	N/A	

73	Slovak Republic	No	N/A	Yes	N/A	
74	Slovenia	No	N/A	Yes	N/A	
75	South Africa	No	N/A	Yes	N/A	
76	Spain	No	N/A	Yes	N/A	
77	Sri Lanka	No	N/A	Yes	N/A	
78	Sweden	No	N/A	Yes	N/A	
79	Switzerland	No	N/A	No	N/A	
80	Tanzania*	No	N/A	Yes	N/A	
81	Thailand	No	N/A	Yes	N/A	
82	Trinidad and Tobago	No	N/A	No	N/A	
83	Tunisia	No	N/A	Yes	N/A	
84	Turkey	No	N/A	Yes	N/A	
85	Ukraine	No	N/A	Yes	N/A	
86	United Arab Emirates	No	N/A	No	N/A	
87	United Kingdom	No	N/A	Yes	N/A	
88	United States	No	N/A	No	N/A	
89	Uzbekistan*	No	N/A	No	N/A	
90	Venezuela*	No	N/A	No	N/A	
91	Viet Nam	No	N/A	Yes	N/A	
92	Zambia	No	N/A	Yes	N/A	
93	Zimbabwe*	No	N/A	Yes	N/A	

Cayman Islands

A. Progress in the implementation of the minimum standard

The Cayman Islands has no tax agreements, as reported in its response to the Peer Review questionnaire.

B. Implementation issues

No jurisdiction has raised any concerns about the Cayman Islands.

Chile

A. Progress in the implementation of the minimum standard

Chile has 33 tax agreements in force, as reported in its response to the Peer Review questionnaire. Five of those agreements, the agreements with Argentina, China, Italy, Japan and Uruguay, comply with the minimum standard.

Chile signed the MLI in 2017, listing 33 tax agreements.[28]

Chile is implementing the minimum standard through the inclusion of the preamble statement and the PPT combined with the LOB. For its compliant agreements with Italy and Japan, the minimum standard is implemented through the inclusion of the preamble statement and the PPT.[29] Chile notes that all of its agreements that do not contain a PPT provision include a main purpose test in the dividends, interest and royalties articles.

The agreements that will be modified by the MLI will come into compliance with the minimum standard once the provisions of the MLI take effect.

B. Implementation issues

No jurisdiction has raised any concerns about their agreements with Chile.

Summary of the jurisdiction response – Chile

	Treaty partners	Compliance with the standard	If compliant, the alternative implemented	Signature of a complying instrument	The alternative implemented through the complying instrument (if not the MLI)	Comments
1	Argentina	Yes	PPT and LOB	N/A	N/A	
2	Australia	No	N/A	Yes	N/A	
3	Austria	No	N/A	Yes	N/A	
4	Belgium	No	N/A	Yes	N/A	
5	Brazil	No	N/A	Yes	N/A	
6	Canada	No	N/A	Yes	N/A	
7	China (People's Republic of)	Yes	PPT and LOB	N/A	N/A	
8	Colombia	No	N/A	Yes	N/A	
9	Croatia	No	N/A	Yes	N/A	
10	Czech Republic	No	N/A	Yes	N/A	
11	Denmark	No	N/A	Yes	N/A	
12	Ecuador*	No	N/A	Yes	N/A	
13	France	No	N/A	Yes	N/A	
14	Ireland	No	N/A	Yes	N/A	
15	Italy	Yes	PPT alone	N/A	N/A	
16	Japan	Yes	PPT alone	N/A	N/A	
17	Korea	No	N/A	Yes	N/A	
18	Malaysia	No	N/A	Yes	N/A	

19	Mexico	No	N/A	Yes	N/A	
20	New Zealand	No	N/A	Yes	N/A	
21	Norway	No	N/A	Yes	N/A	
22	Paraguay	No	N/A	Yes	N/A	
23	Peru	No	N/A	Yes	N/A	
24	Poland	No	N/A	Yes	N/A	
25	Portugal	No	N/A	Yes	N/A	
26	Russia	No	N/A	Yes	N/A	
27	South Africa	No	N/A	Yes	N/A	
28	Spain	No	N/A	Yes	N/A	
29	Sweden	No	N/A	Yes	N/A	
30	Switzerland	No	N/A	Yes	N/A	
31	Thailand	No	N/A	Yes	N/A	
32	United Kingdom	No	N/A	Yes	N/A	
33	Uruguay	Yes	PPT and LOB	N/A	N/A	

China (People's Republic of)

A. Progress in the implementation of the minimum standard

China has 102 tax agreements in force, as reported in its response to the Peer Review questionnaire. Two of those agreements, the agreements with Chile and India, comply with the minimum standard.

China signed the MLI in 2017, listing 100 tax agreements.[30]

China is generally implementing the minimum standard through the inclusion of the preamble statement and the PPT.[31]

The agreements that will be modified by the MLI will come into compliance with the minimum standard once the provisions of the MLI take effect.

B. Implementation issues

No jurisdiction has raised any concerns about their agreements with China.

Summary of the jurisdiction response – China (People's Republic of)

	Treaty partners	Compliance with the standard	If compliant, the alternative implemented	Signature of a complying instrument	The alternative implemented through the complying instrument (if not the MLI)	Comments
1	Albania*	No	N/A	Yes	N/A	
2	Algeria*	No	N/A	Yes	N/A	
3	Armenia	No	N/A	Yes	N/A	
4	Australia	No	N/A	Yes	N/A	
5	Austria	No	N/A	Yes	N/A	
6	Azerbaijan*	No	N/A	Yes	N/A	
7	Bahrain	No	N/A	Yes	N/A	
8	Bangladesh*	No	N/A	Yes	N/A	
9	Barbados	No	N/A	Yes	N/A	
10	Belarus*	No	N/A	Yes	N/A	
11	Belgium	No	N/A	Yes	N/A	
12	Bosnia and Herzegovina*	No	N/A	Yes	N/A	
13	Brazil	No	N/A	Yes	N/A	
14	Brunei Darussalam	No	N/A	Yes	N/A	
15	Bulgaria	No	N/A	Yes	N/A	
16	Cambodia*	No	N/A	Yes	N/A	
17	Canada	No	N/A	Yes	N/A	
18	Chile	Yes	PPT and LOB	N/A	N/A	
19	Croatia	No	N/A	Yes	N/A	
20	Cuba*	No	N/A	Yes	N/A	
21	Cyprus*	No	N/A	Yes	N/A	
22	Czech Republic	No	N/A	Yes	N/A	

23	Denmark	No	N/A	Yes	N/A	
24	Ecuador*	No	N/A	Yes	N/A	
25	Egypt	No	N/A	Yes	N/A	
26	Estonia	No	N/A	Yes	N/A	
27	Ethiopia*	No	N/A	Yes	N/A	
28	Finland	No	N/A	Yes	N/A	
29	France	No	N/A	Yes	N/A	
30	Georgia	No	N/A	Yes	N/A	
31	Germany	No	N/A	Yes	N/A	
32	Greece	No	N/A	Yes	N/A	
33	Hungary	No	N/A	Yes	N/A	
34	Iceland	No	N/A	Yes	N/A	
35	India	Yes	PPT alone	N/A	N/A	
36	Indonesia	No	N/A	Yes	N/A	
37	Iran*	No	N/A	Yes	N/A	
38	Ireland	No	N/A	Yes	N/A	
39	Israel	No	N/A	Yes	N/A	
40	Italy	No	N/A	Yes	PPT alone	
41	Jamaica	No	N/A	Yes	N/A	
42	Japan	No	N/A	Yes	N/A	
43	Kazakhstan	No	N/A	Yes	N/A	
44	Korea	No	N/A	Yes	N/A	
45	Kuwait*	No	N/A	Yes	N/A	
46	Kyrgyzstan*	No	N/A	Yes	N/A	
47	Lao People's Democratic Republic*	No	N/A	Yes	N/A	
48	Latvia	No	N/A	Yes	N/A	
49	Lithuania	No	N/A	Yes	N/A	
50	Luxembourg	No	N/A	Yes	N/A	
51	North Macedonia	No	N/A	Yes	N/A	
52	Malaysia	No	N/A	Yes	N/A	
53	Malta	No	N/A	Yes	N/A	
54	Mauritius	No	N/A	Yes	N/A	
55	Mexico	No	N/A	Yes	N/A	
56	Moldova*	No	N/A	Yes	N/A	
57	Mongolia	No	N/A	Yes	N/A	
58	Montenegro*	No	N/A	Yes	N/A	
59	Morocco	No	N/A	Yes	N/A	
60	Nepal*	No	N/A	Yes	N/A	
61	Netherlands	No	N/A	Yes	N/A	
62	New Zealand	No	N/A	Yes	PPT alone	
63	Nigeria	No	N/A	Yes	N/A	
64	Norway	No	N/A	Yes	N/A	
65	Oman	No	N/A	Yes	N/A	
66	Pakistan	No	N/A	Yes	N/A	
67	Papua New Guinea	No	N/A	Yes	N/A	
68	Philippines*	No	N/A	Yes	N/A	
69	Poland	No	N/A	Yes	N/A	
70	Portugal	No	N/A	Yes	N/A	
71	Qatar	No	N/A	Yes	N/A	
72	Romania	No	N/A	Yes	N/A	
73	Russia	No	N/A	Yes	N/A	
74	Saudi Arabia	No	N/A	Yes	N/A	

75	Serbia	No	N/A	Yes	N/A	
76	Seychelles	No	N/A	Yes	N/A	
77	Singapore	No	N/A	Yes	N/A	
78	Slovak Republic	No	N/A	Yes	N/A	
79	Slovenia	No	N/A	Yes	N/A	
80	South Africa	No	N/A	Yes	N/A	
81	Spain	No	N/A	Yes	PPT alone	
82	Sri Lanka	No	N/A	Yes	N/A	
83	Sudan*	No	N/A	Yes	N/A	
84	Sweden	No	N/A	Yes	N/A	
85	Switzerland	No	N/A	Yes	N/A	
86	Syrian Arab Republic*	No	N/A	Yes	N/A	
87	Tajikistan*	No	N/A	Yes	N/A	
88	Thailand	No	N/A	Yes	N/A	
89	Trinidad and Tobago	No	N/A	Yes	N/A	
90	Tunisia	No	N/A	Yes	N/A	
91	Turkey	No	N/A	Yes	N/A	
92	Turkmenistan*	No	N/A	Yes	N/A	
93	Ukraine	No	N/A	Yes	N/A	
94	United Arab Emirates	No	N/A	Yes	N/A	
95	United Kingdom	No	N/A	Yes	N/A	
96	United States	No	N/A	Yes	N/A	
97	Uzbekistan*	No	N/A	Yes	N/A	
98	Venezuela*	No	N/A	Yes	N/A	
99	Viet Nam	No	N/A	Yes	N/A	
100	Zambia	No	N/A	Yes	N/A	
101	Zimbabwe*	No	N/A	Yes	N/A	
102	Botswana	No	N/A	Yes	N/A	

Colombia

A. Progress in the implementation of the minimum standard

Colombia has ten tax agreements in force, as reported in its response to the Peer Review questionnaire, including the Decision 578 of the Andean Community Commission for the members of the Andean Community (the Andean Community Agreement).[32]

Colombia signed the MLI in 2017, listing nine tax agreements.[33]

Colombia is implementing the minimum standard through the inclusion of the preamble statement and the PPT combined with the LOB.[34]

The agreements that will be modified by the MLI will come into compliance with the minimum standard once the provisions of the MLI take effect.

Colombia indicated in its response to the Peer Review questionnaire that the Andean Community Agreement has not been listed under the MLI as it is a decision of the Andean Community Commission.

Colombia further indicated that bilateral negotiations would be used with respect to its agreement with Switzerland.

B. Implementation issues

No jurisdiction has raised any concerns about their agreements with Colombia.

Colombia indicated that it encountered difficulties in the renegotiation of the Andean Community Agreement.[35]

Summary of the jurisdiction response – Colombia

	Treaty partners	Compliance with the standard	If compliant, the alternative implemented	Signature of a complying instrument	The alternative implemented through the complying instrument (if not the MLI)	Comments
1	Bolivia*	No	N/A	No	N/A	Currently renegotiating Decision 578
2	Canada	No	N/A	Yes	N/A	
3	Chile	No	N/A	Yes	N/A	
4	Czech Republic	No	N/A	Yes	N/A	
5	Ecuador*	No	N/A	No	N/A	Currently renegotiating Decision 578
6	India	No	N/A	Yes	N/A	
7	Korea	No	N/A	Yes	N/A	
8	Mexico	No	N/A	Yes	N/A	
9	Peru	No	N/A	No	N/A	Currently renegotiating Decision 578

10	Portugal	No	N/A	Yes	N/A	
11	Spain	No	N/A	Yes	N/A	
12	Switzerland[36]	No	N/A	No	N/A	

Congo

A. Progress in the implementation of the minimum standard

Congo has three tax agreements in force, as reported in its response to the Peer Review questionnaire.

None of Congo's agreements comply with the minimum standard or are subject to a complying instrument.

B. Implementation issues

No jurisdiction has raised any concerns about their agreements with Congo.

Congo is encouraged to implement the minimum standard in its agreements.

Summary of the jurisdiction response – Congo

	Treaty partners	Compliance with the standard	If compliant, the alternative implemented	Signature of a complying instrument	The alternative implemented through the complying instrument (if not the MLI)	Comments
1	France	No	N/A	No	N/A	
2	Italy	No	N/A	No	N/A	
3	Mauritius	No	N/A	No	N/A	

Costa Rica

A. Progress in the implementation of the minimum standard

Costa Rica has three tax agreements in force, as reported in its response to the Peer Review questionnaire.

Costa Rica signed the MLI in 2017, listing three tax agreements.

Costa Rica is implementing the minimum standard through the inclusion of the preamble statement and the PPT.[37]

The agreements that will be modified by the MLI will come into compliance with the minimum standard once the provisions of the MLI take effect.

Costa Rica indicated in its response to the Peer Review questionnaire that bilateral negotiations would be used with respect to its agreement with Germany.

B. Implementation issues

No jurisdiction has raised any concerns about their agreements with Costa Rica.

Summary of the jurisdiction response – Costa Rica

	Treaty partners	Compliance with the standard	If compliant, the alternative implemented	Signature of a complying instrument	The alternative implemented through the complying instrument (if not the MLI)	Comments
1	Germany	No	N/A	Yes	N/A	
2	Mexico	No	N/A	Yes	N/A	
3	Spain	No	N/A	Yes	N/A	

Cook Islands

A. Progress in the implementation of the minimum standard

The Cook Islands has no tax agreements, as reported in its response to the Peer Review questionnaire.

B. Implementation issues

No jurisdiction has raised any concerns about the Cook Islands.

Côte d'Ivoire

A. Progress in the implementation of the minimum standard

Côte d'Ivoire has 12 tax agreements in force, as reported in its response to the Peer Review questionnaire, including the multilateral Regulation 08/2008/COM adopting the rules for the avoidance of double taxation within the West African Economic and Monetary Union and the rule for assistance in tax matters (the UEMOA) concluded with seven partners.[38]

Côte d'Ivoire signed the MLI in 2018, listing ten tax agreements.[39]

Côte d'Ivoire is implementing the minimum standard through the inclusion of the preamble statement and the PPT.[40]

The agreements that will be modified by the MLI will come into compliance with the minimum standard once the provisions of the MLI take effect.

B. Implementation issues

No jurisdiction has raised any concerns about their agreements with Côte d'Ivoire.

Summary of the jurisdiction response – Côte d'Ivoire

	Treaty partners	Compliance with the standard	If compliant, the alternative implemented	Signature of a complying instrument	The alternative implemented through the complying instrument (if not the MLI)	Comments
1	Belgium	No	N/A	Yes	N/A	
2	Benin	No	N/A	No	N/A	UEMOA
3	Burkina Faso	No	N/A	No	N/A	UEMOA
4	Canada	No	N/A	Yes	N/A	
5	France	No	N/A	Yes	N/A	
6	Germany	No	N/A	Yes	N/A	
7	Guinea-Bissau*	No	N/A	No	N/A	UEMOA
8	Italy	No	N/A	Yes	N/A	
9	Mali*	No	N/A	No	N/A	UEMOA
10	Morocco	No	N/A	Yes	N/A	
11	Niger*	No	N/A	No	N/A	UEMOA
12	Norway	No	N/A	Yes	N/A	
13	Portugal	No	N/A	Yes	N/A	
14	Senegal	No	N/A	No	N/A	UEMOA
15	Switzerland	No	N/A	No	N/A	
16	Togo*	No	N/A	No	N/A	UEMOA
17	Tunisia	No	N/A	Yes	N/A	
18	United Kingdom	No	N/A	Yes	N/A	

Croatia

A. Progress in the implementation of the minimum standard

Croatia has 65 tax agreements in force, as reported in its response to the Peer Review questionnaire.

Croatia signed the MLI in 2017, listing 65 tax agreements.[41]

Croatia is implementing the minimum standard through the inclusion of the preamble statement and the PPT.

The agreements that will be modified by the MLI will come into compliance with the minimum standard once the provisions of the MLI take effect.

B. Implementation issues

No jurisdiction has raised any concerns about their agreements with Croatia.

Summary of the jurisdiction response – Croatia

	Treaty partners	Compliance with the standard	If compliant, the alternative implemented	Signature of a complying instrument	The alternative implemented through the complying instrument (if not the MLI)	Comments
1	Albania*	No	N/A	Yes	N/A	
2	Armenia	No	N/A	Yes	N/A	
3	Austria	No	N/A	Yes	N/A	
4	Azerbaijan*	No	N/A	Yes	N/A	
5	Belarus*	No	N/A	Yes	N/A	
6	Belgium	No	N/A	Yes	N/A	
7	Bosnia and Herzegovina*	No	N/A	Yes	N/A	
8	Bulgaria	No	N/A	Yes	N/A	
9	Canada	No	N/A	Yes	N/A	
10	Chile	No	N/A	Yes	N/A	
11	China (People's Republic of)	No	N/A	Yes	N/A	
12	Czech Republic	No	N/A	Yes	N/A	
13	Denmark	No	N/A	Yes	N/A	
14	Estonia	No	N/A	Yes	N/A	
15	Finland	No	N/A	Yes	N/A	
16	France	No	N/A	Yes	N/A	
17	Georgia	No	N/A	Yes	N/A	
18	Germany	No	N/A	Yes	N/A	
19	Greece	No	N/A	Yes	N/A	
20	Hungary	No	N/A	Yes	N/A	
21	Iceland	No	N/A	Yes	N/A	
22	India	No	N/A	Yes	N/A	
23	Indonesia	No	N/A	Yes	N/A	

24	Iran*	No	N/A	Yes	N/A	
25	Ireland	No	N/A	Yes	N/A	
26	Israel	No	N/A	Yes	N/A	
27	Italy	No	N/A	Yes	N/A	
28	Jordan*	No	N/A	Yes	N/A	
29	Kazakhstan	No	N/A	Yes	N/A	
30	Korea	No	N/A	Yes	N/A	
31	Kosovo*	No	N/A	Yes	N/A	
32	Kuwait*	No	N/A	Yes	N/A	
33	Latvia	No	N/A	Yes	N/A	
34	Lithuania	No	N/A	Yes	N/A	
35	Luxembourg	No	N/A	Yes	N/A	
36	North Macedonia	No	N/A	Yes	N/A	
37	Malaysia	No	N/A	Yes	N/A	
38	Malta	No	N/A	Yes	N/A	
39	Mauritius	No	N/A	Yes	N/A	
40	Moldova*	No	N/A	Yes	N/A	
41	Montenegro*	No	N/A	Yes	N/A	
42	Morocco	No	N/A	Yes	N/A	
43	Netherlands	No	N/A	Yes	N/A	
44	Norway	No	N/A	Yes	N/A	
45	Oman	No	N/A	Yes	N/A	
46	Poland	No	N/A	Yes	N/A	
47	Portugal	No	N/A	Yes	N/A	
48	Qatar	No	N/A	Yes	N/A	
49	Romania	No	N/A	Yes	N/A	
50	Russia	No	N/A	Yes	N/A	
51	San Marino	No	N/A	Yes	N/A	
52	Serbia	No	N/A	Yes	N/A	
53	Slovak Republic	No	N/A	Yes	N/A	
54	Slovenia	No	N/A	Yes	N/A	
55	South Africa	No	N/A	Yes	N/A	
56	Spain	No	N/A	Yes	N/A	
57	Sweden	No	N/A	Yes	N/A	
58	Switzerland	No	N/A	Yes	N/A	
59	Syrian Arab Republic*	No	N/A	Yes	N/A	
60	Turkey	No	N/A	Yes	N/A	
61	Turkmenistan*	No	N/A	Yes	N/A	
62	Ukraine	No	N/A	Yes	N/A	
63	United Arab Emirates	No	N/A	Yes	N/A	
64	United Kingdom	No	N/A	Yes	N/A	
65	Viet Nam	No	N/A	Yes	N/A	

Curacao

A. Progress in the implementation of the minimum standard

Curacao has three tax agreements in force, as reported in its response to the Peer Review questionnaire.

Curacao signed the MLI in 2017 and the Kingdom of the Netherlands deposited its instrument of acceptance on 29 March 2019, listing two tax agreements. The MLI entered into force for Curacao on 1 July 2019.

Curacao is implementing the minimum standard through the inclusion of the preamble statement and the PPT.[42]

The agreements that will be modified by the MLI will come into compliance with the minimum standard once the provisions of the MLI take effect.

Curacao indicated in its response to the Peer Review questionnaire that its agreement with the Netherlands has not been listed under the MLI as it is an arrangement governed by the domestic law of the Kingdom of the Netherlands.

B. Implementation issues

No jurisdiction has raised any concerns about their agreements with Curacao.

Summary of the jurisdiction response – Curacao

	Treaty partners	Compliance with the standard	If compliant, the alternative implemented	Signature of a complying instrument	The alternative implemented through the complying instrument (if not the MLI)	Comments
1	Norway	No	N/A	Yes	N/A	
2	Netherlands	No	N/A	No	N/A	
3	Malta	No	N/A	Yes	N/A	

Czech Republic

A. Progress in the implementation of the minimum standard

The Czech Republic has 88 tax agreements in force, as reported in its response to the Peer Review questionnaire.[43]

The Czech Republic signed the MLI in 2017, provisionally listing 86 tax agreements.

The Czech Republic is implementing the minimum standard through the inclusion of the preamble statement and the PPT.[44]

The agreements that will be modified by the MLI will come into compliance with the minimum standard once the provisions of the MLI take effect.

The Czech Republic signed a bilateral complying instrument with Korea.

B. Implementation issues

No jurisdiction has raised any concerns about their agreements with the Czech Republic.

Summary of the jurisdiction response – Czech Republic

	Treaty partners	Compliance with the standard	If compliant, the alternative implemented	Signature of a complying instrument	The alternative implemented through the complying instrument (if not the MLI)	Comments
1	Albania*	No	N/A	Yes	N/A	
2	Armenia	No	N/A	Yes	N/A	
3	Australia	No	N/A	Yes	N/A	
4	Austria	No	N/A	Yes	N/A	
5	Azerbaijan*	No	N/A	Yes	N/A	
6	Bahrain	No	N/A	Yes	N/A	
7	Barbados	No	N/A	Yes	N/A	
8	Belarus*	No	N/A	Yes	N/A	
9	Belgium	No	N/A	Yes	N/A	
10	Bosnia and Herzegovina*	No	N/A	Yes	N/A	
11	Brazil	No	N/A	Yes	N/A	
12	Bulgaria	No	N/A	Yes	N/A	
13	Canada	No	N/A	Yes	N/A	
14	Chile	No	N/A	Yes	N/A	
15	China (People's Republic of)	No	N/A	Yes	N/A	
16	Colombia	No	N/A	Yes	N/A	
17	Croatia	No	N/A	Yes	N/A	
18	Cyprus*	No	N/A	Yes	N/A	
19	Democratic People's Republic of Korea*	No	N/A	Yes	N/A	

20	Denmark	No	N/A	Yes	N/A	
21	Egypt	No	N/A	Yes	N/A	
22	Estonia	No	N/A	Yes	N/A	
23	Ethiopia*	No	N/A	Yes	N/A	
24	Finland	No	N/A	Yes	N/A	
25	France	No	N/A	Yes	N/A	
26	Georgia	No	N/A	Yes	N/A	
27	Germany	No	N/A	Yes	N/A	
28	Greece	No	N/A	Yes	N/A	
29	Hong Kong (China)	No	N/A	Yes	N/A	
30	Hungary	No	N/A	Yes	N/A	
31	Iceland	No	N/A	Yes	N/A	
32	India	No	N/A	Yes	N/A	
33	Indonesia	No	N/A	Yes	N/A	
34	Iran*	No	N/A	Yes	N/A	
35	Ireland	No	N/A	Yes	N/A	
36	Israel	No	N/A	Yes	N/A	
37	Italy	No	N/A	Yes	N/A	
38	Japan	No	N/A	Yes	N/A	
39	Jordan*	No	N/A	Yes	N/A	
40	Kazakhstan	No	N/A	Yes	N/A	
41	Korea	No	N/A	Yes	PPT alone	
42	Kuwait*	No	N/A	Yes	N/A	
43	Latvia	No	N/A	Yes	N/A	
44	Lebanon*	No	N/A	Yes	N/A	
45	Liechtenstein	No	N/A	Yes	N/A	
46	Lithuania	No	N/A	Yes	N/A	
47	Luxembourg	No	N/A	Yes	N/A	
48	North Macedonia	No	N/A	Yes	N/A	
49	Malaysia	No	N/A	Yes	N/A	
50	Malta	No	N/A	Yes	N/A	
51	Mexico	No	N/A	Yes	N/A	
52	Moldova*	No	N/A	Yes	N/A	
53	Mongolia	No	N/A	Yes	N/A	
54	Montenegro*	No	N/A	Yes	N/A	
55	Morocco	No	N/A	Yes	N/A	
56	Netherlands	No	N/A	Yes	N/A	
57	New Zealand	No	N/A	Yes	N/A	
58	Nigeria	No	N/A	Yes	N/A	
59	Norway	No	N/A	Yes	N/A	
60	Pakistan	No	N/A	Yes	N/A	
61	Panama	No	N/A	Yes	N/A	
62	Philippines*	No	N/A	Yes	N/A	
63	Poland	No	N/A	Yes	N/A	
64	Portugal	No	N/A	Yes	N/A	
65	Romania	No	N/A	Yes	N/A	
66	Russia	No	N/A	Yes	N/A	
67	Saudi Arabia	No	N/A	Yes	N/A	
68	Serbia	No	N/A	Yes	N/A	
69	Singapore	No	N/A	Yes	N/A	
70	Slovak Republic	No	N/A	Yes	N/A	
71	Slovenia	No	N/A	Yes	N/A	
72	South Africa	No	N/A	Yes	N/A	

73	Spain	No	N/A	Yes	N/A	
74	Sri Lanka	No	N/A	Yes	N/A	
75	Sweden	No	N/A	Yes	N/A	
76	Switzerland	No	N/A	Yes	N/A	
77	Syrian Arab Republic*	No	N/A	Yes	N/A	
78	Tajikistan*	No	N/A	Yes	N/A	
79	Thailand	No	N/A	Yes	N/A	
80	Tunisia	No	N/A	Yes	N/A	
81	Turkey	No	N/A	Yes	N/A	
82	Turkmenistan*	No	N/A	No	N/A	
83	Ukraine	No	N/A	Yes	N/A	
84	United Arab Emirates	No	N/A	Yes	N/A	
85	United Kingdom	No	N/A	Yes	N/A	
86	United States	No	N/A	Yes	N/A	
87	Uzbekistan*	No	N/A	Yes	N/A	
88	Venezuela*	No	N/A	Yes	N/A	
89	Viet Nam	No	N/A	Yes	N/A	

Democratic Republic of the Congo

A. Progress in the implementation of the minimum standard

The Democratic Republic of the Congo has two tax agreements in force, as reported in its response to the Peer Review questionnaire.

Neither of the Democratic Republic of the Congo's agreements comply with the minimum standard or are subject to a complying instrument.

B. Implementation issues

No jurisdiction has raised any concerns about their agreements with the Democratic Republic of the Congo.

The Democratic Republic of the Congo is encouraged to implement the minimum standard in its agreements.

Summary of the jurisdiction response – Democratic Republic of the Congo

	Treaty partners	Compliance with the standard	If compliant, the alternative implemented	Signature of a complying instrument	The alternative implemented through the complying instrument (if not the MLI)	Comments
1	Belgium	No	N/A	No	N/A	
2	South Africa	No	N/A	No	N/A	

Denmark

A. Progress in the implementation of the minimum standard

Denmark has 70 tax agreements in force, as reported in its response to the Peer Review questionnaire, including the multilateral Nordic Convention concluded with Finland, Iceland, Norway and Sweden (the "Nordic Convention").[45] Two of its agreements, the agreements with Japan and the Netherlands, comply with the minimum standard.

Denmark signed the MLI in 2017, listing 64 tax agreements.

Denmark is implementing the minimum standard through the inclusion of the preamble statement and the PPT.[46]

The agreements that will be modified by the MLI will come into compliance with the minimum standard once the provisions of the MLI take effect.

Denmark indicated in its response to the Peer Review questionnaire that it expects to ratify the MLI by the end of October 2019.

The Parties to the Nordic Convention signed a complying instrument in 2018.

B. Implementation issues

No jurisdiction has raised any concerns about their agreements with Denmark.

Summary of the jurisdiction response – Denmark

	Treaty partners	Compliance with the standard	If compliant, the alternative implemented	Signature of a complying instrument	The alternative implemented through the complying instrument (if not the MLI)	Comments
1	Argentina	No	N/A	Yes	N/A	
2	Australia	No	N/A	Yes	N/A	
3	Austria	No	N/A	Yes	N/A	
4	Azerbaijan*	No	N/A	Yes	N/A	
5	Bangladesh*	No	N/A	Yes	N/A	
6	Belarus*	No	N/A	No	N/A	
7	Belgium	No	N/A	Yes	N/A	
8	Brazil	No	N/A	Yes	N/A	
9	Bulgaria	No	N/A	Yes	N/A	
10	Canada	No	N/A	Yes	N/A	
11	Chile	No	N/A	Yes	N/A	
12	China (People's Republic of)	No	N/A	Yes	N/A	
13	Chinese Taipei*	No	N/A	Yes	N/A	
14	Croatia	No	N/A	Yes	N/A	
15	Cyprus*	No	N/A	Yes	N/A	
16	Czech Republic	No	N/A	Yes	N/A	

17	Egypt	No	N/A	Yes	N/A	
18	Estonia	No	N/A	Yes	N/A	
19	Finland	No	N/A	Yes	PPT alone	
20	Georgia	No	N/A	Yes	N/A	
21	Germany	No	N/A	No	N/A	
22	Ghana*	No	N/A	Yes	N/A	
23	Greece	No	N/A	Yes	N/A	
24	Hungary	No	N/A	Yes	N/A	
25	Iceland	No	N/A	Yes	PPT alone	
26	India	No	N/A	Yes	N/A	
27	Indonesia	No	N/A	Yes	N/A	
28	Ireland	No	N/A	Yes	N/A	
29	Israel	No	N/A	Yes	N/A	
30	Italy	No	N/A	Yes	N/A	
31	Jamaica	No	N/A	Yes	N/A	
32	Japan	Yes	PPT and LOB	N/A	N/A	
33	Kenya	No	N/A	Yes	N/A	
34	Korea	No	N/A	Yes	N/A	
35	Kuwait*	No	N/A	Yes	N/A	
36	Latvia	No	N/A	Yes	N/A	
37	Lithuania	No	N/A	Yes	N/A	
38	Luxembourg	No	N/A	Yes	N/A	
39	North Macedonia	No	N/A	Yes	N/A	
40	Malaysia	No	N/A	Yes	N/A	
41	Malta	No	N/A	Yes	N/A	
42	Mexico	No	N/A	Yes	N/A	
43	Montenegro*	No	N/A	Yes	N/A	
44	Morocco	No	N/A	Yes	N/A	
45	Netherlands	Yes	PPT alone	N/A	N/A	
46	New Zealand	No	N/A	Yes	N/A	
47	Norway	No	N/A	Yes	PPT alone	
48	Pakistan	No	N/A	Yes	N/A	
49	Philippines*	No	N/A	Yes	N/A	
50	Poland	No	N/A	Yes	N/A	
51	Portugal	No	N/A	Yes	N/A	
52	Romania	No	N/A	Yes	N/A	
53	Russia	No	N/A	Yes	N/A	
54	Serbia	No	N/A	Yes	N/A	
55	Singapore	No	N/A	Yes	N/A	
56	Slovak Republic	No	N/A	Yes	N/A	
57	Slovenia	No	N/A	Yes	N/A	
58	South Africa	No	N/A	Yes	N/A	
59	Sri Lanka	No	N/A	Yes	N/A	
60	Sweden	No	N/A	Yes	PPT alone	
61	Switzerland	No	N/A	No	N/A	
62	Tanzania*	No	N/A	Yes	N/A	
63	Thailand	No	N/A	Yes	N/A	
64	Trinidad and Tobago	No	N/A	Yes	N/A	
65	Tunisia	No	N/A	Yes	N/A	
66	Turkey	No	N/A	Yes	N/A	
67	Uganda*	No	N/A	Yes	N/A	
68	Ukraine	No	N/A	Yes	N/A	
69	United Kingdom	No	N/A	Yes	N/A	

70	United States	No	N/A	Yes	N/A	
71	Venezuela*	No	N/A	Yes	N/A	
72	Viet Nam	No	N/A	Yes	N/A	
73	Zambia	No	N/A	Yes	N/A	

Djibouti

A. Progress in the implementation of the minimum standard

Djibouti has no tax agreements, as reported in its response to the Peer Review questionnaire.

B. Implementation issues

No jurisdiction has raised any concerns about Djibouti.

Dominica

A. Progress in the implementation of the minimum standard

Dominica has three tax agreements in force, as reported in its response to the Peer Review questionnaire, including the multilateral agreement among the members of the CARICOM concluded with ten treaty partners (the CARICOM Agreement).[47]

None of Dominica's agreements comply with the minimum standard or are subject to a complying instrument.

B. Implementation issues

Dominica is encouraged to implement the minimum standard in its agreements.

Dominica is encouraged to bring the CARICOM Agreement up to date by commencing talks among all the treaty partners.[48]

Summary of the jurisdiction response – Dominica

	Treaty partners	Compliance with the standard	If compliant, the alternative implemented	Signature of a complying instrument	The alternative implemented through the complying instrument (if not the MLI)	Comments
1	Antigua and Barbuda	No	N/A	No	N/A	CARICOM
2	Barbados	No	N/A	No	N/A	CARICOM
3	Belize	No	N/A	No	N/A	CARICOM
4	Grenada	No	N/A	No	N/A	CARICOM
5	Guyana*	No	N/A	No	N/A	CARICOM
6	Jamaica	No	N/A	No	N/A	CARICOM
7	Saint Kitts and Nevis	No	N/A	No	N/A	CARICOM
8	Saint Lucia	No	N/A	No	N/A	CARICOM
9	Saint Vincent and the Grenadines	No	N/A	No	N/A	CARICOM
10	Switzerland	No	N/A	No	N/A	
11	Trinidad and Tobago	No	N/A	No	N/A	CARICOM
12	United Kingdom	No	N/A	No	N/A	

Dominican Republic

A. Progress in the implementation of the minimum standard

The Dominican Republic has two tax agreements in force, as reported in its response to the Peer Review questionnaire.

Neither of the Dominican Republic's agreements comply with the minimum standard or are subject to a complying instrument.

B. Implementation issues

No jurisdiction has raised any concerns about their agreements with the Dominican Republic.

Dominican Republic is encouraged to implement the minimum standard in its agreements.

Summary of the jurisdiction response – Dominican Republic

	Treaty partners	Compliance with the standard	If compliant, the alternative implemented	Signature of a complying instrument	The alternative implemented through the complying instrument (if not the MLI)	Other comments
1	Canada	No	N/A	No	N/A	
2	Spain	No	N/A	No	N/A	Partial compliance. Treaty has a PPT, but no new preamble

Egypt

A. Progress in the implementation of the minimum standard

Egypt has 57 tax agreements in force, as reported in its response to the Peer Review questionnaire.

Egypt signed the MLI in 2017, listing 55 tax agreements.

Egypt is implementing the minimum standard through the inclusion of the preamble statement and the PPT.[49]

The agreements that will be modified by the MLI will come into compliance with the minimum standard once the provisions of the MLI take effect.

B. Implementation issues

No jurisdiction has raised any concerns about their agreements with Egypt.

Summary of the jurisdiction response – Egypt

	Treaty partners	Compliance with the standard	If compliant, the alternative implemented	Signature of a complying instrument	The alternative implemented through the complying instrument (if not the MLI)	Comments
1	Albania*	No	N/A	Yes	N/A	
2	Algeria*	No	N/A	Yes	N/A	
3	Austria	No	N/A	Yes	N/A	
4	Bahrain	No	N/A	Yes	N/A	
5	Belarus*	No	N/A	Yes	N/A	
6	Belgium	No	N/A	Yes	N/A	
7	Bulgaria	No	N/A	Yes	N/A	
8	Canada	No	N/A	Yes	N/A	
9	China (People's Republic of)	No	N/A	Yes	N/A	
10	Cyprus*	No	N/A	Yes	N/A	
11	Czech Republic	No	N/A	Yes	N/A	
12	Denmark	No	N/A	Yes	N/A	
13	Ethiopia*	No	N/A	Yes	N/A	
14	Finland	No	N/A	Yes	N/A	
15	France	No	N/A	Yes	N/A	
16	Georgia	No	N/A	Yes	N/A	
17	Germany	No	N/A	Yes	N/A	
18	Greece	No	N/A	Yes	N/A	
19	Hungary	No	N/A	Yes	N/A	
20	India	No	N/A	Yes	N/A	
21	Indonesia	No	N/A	Yes	N/A	
22	Iraq*	No	N/A	Yes	N/A	
23	Ireland	No	N/A	Yes	N/A	

24	Italy	No	N/A	Yes	N/A	
25	Japan	No	N/A	Yes	N/A	
26	Jordan*	No	N/A	Yes	N/A	
27	Korea	No	N/A	Yes	N/A	
28	Kuwait*	No	N/A	Yes	N/A	
29	Lebanon*	No	N/A	Yes	N/A	
30	Libya*	No	N/A	Yes	N/A	
31	Malaysia	No	N/A	Yes	N/A	
32	Malta	No	N/A	Yes	N/A	
33	Mauritius	No	N/A	Yes	N/A	
34	Morocco	No	N/A	Yes	N/A	
35	Netherlands	No	N/A	Yes	N/A	
36	Norway	No	N/A	Yes	N/A	
37	Pakistan	No	N/A	Yes	N/A	
38	Palestinian Authority*	No	N/A	Yes	N/A	
39	Poland	No	N/A	Yes	N/A	
40	Romania	No	N/A	Yes	N/A	
41	Russia	No	N/A	Yes	N/A	
42	Saudi Arabia	No	N/A	No	N/A	
43	Serbia	No	N/A	Yes	N/A	
44	Singapore	No	N/A	Yes	N/A	
45	South Africa	No	N/A	Yes	N/A	
46	Spain	No	N/A	Yes	N/A	
47	Sudan*	No	N/A	Yes	N/A	
48	Sweden	No	N/A	Yes	N/A	
49	Switzerland	No	N/A	Yes	N/A	
50	Syrian Arab Republic*	No	N/A	Yes	N/A	
51	Tunisia	No	N/A	Yes	N/A	
52	Turkey	No	N/A	Yes	N/A	
53	Ukraine	No	N/A	Yes	N/A	
54	United Arab Emirates	No	N/A	Yes	N/A	
55	United Kingdom	No	N/A	Yes	N/A	
56	United States	No	N/A	No	N/A	
57	Yemen*	No	N/A	Yes	N/A	

Estonia

A. Progress in the implementation of the minimum standard

Estonia has 59 tax agreements in force, as reported in its response to the Peer Review questionnaire. Its agreement with Japan complies with the minimum standard.

Estonia signed the MLI in 2018, listing 56 tax agreements.[50]

Estonia is generally implementing the minimum standard through the inclusion of the preamble statement and the PPT.[51]

The agreements that will be modified by the MLI will come into compliance with the minimum standard once the provisions of the MLI take effect.

Estonia indicated in its response to the Peer Review questionnaire that bilateral negotiations would be used with respect to its agreements with Germany and Switzerland.

B. Implementation issues

No jurisdiction has raised any concerns about their agreements with Estonia.

Summary of the jurisdiction response – Estonia

	Treaty partners	Compliance with the standard	If compliant, the alternative implemented	Signature of a complying instrument	The alternative implemented through the complying instrument (if not the MLI)	Comments
1	Albania*	No	N/A	Yes	N/A	
2	Armenia	No	N/A	Yes	N/A	
3	Austria	No	N/A	Yes	N/A	
4	Azerbaijan*	No	N/A	Yes	N/A	
5	Bahrain	No	N/A	Yes	N/A	
6	Belarus*	No	N/A	Yes	N/A	
7	Belgium	No	N/A	Yes	N/A	
8	Bulgaria	No	N/A	Yes	N/A	
9	Canada	No	N/A	Yes	N/A	
10	China (People's Republic of)	No	N/A	Yes	N/A	
11	Croatia	No	N/A	Yes	N/A	
12	Cyprus*	No	N/A	Yes	N/A	
13	Czech Republic	No	N/A	Yes	N/A	
14	Denmark	No	N/A	Yes	N/A	
15	Finland	No	N/A	Yes	N/A	
16	France	No	N/A	Yes	N/A	
17	Georgia	No	N/A	Yes	N/A	
18	Germany	No	N/A	No	N/A	
19	Greece	No	N/A	Yes	N/A	
20	Hungary	No	N/A	Yes	N/A	

21	Iceland	No	N/A	Yes	N/A	
22	India	No	N/A	Yes	N/A	
23	Ireland	No	N/A	Yes	N/A	
24	Isle of Man	No	N/A	Yes	N/A	
25	Israel	No	N/A	Yes	N/A	
26	Italy	No	N/A	Yes	N/A	
27	Japan	Yes	PPT and LOB	N/A	N/A	
28	Jersey	No	N/A	Yes	N/A	
29	Kazakhstan	No	N/A	Yes	N/A	
30	Korea	No	N/A	Yes	N/A	
31	Kyrgyzstan*	No	N/A	Yes	N/A	
32	Latvia	No	N/A	Yes	N/A	
33	Lithuania	No	N/A	Yes	N/A	
34	Luxembourg	No	N/A	Yes	N/A	
35	North Macedonia	No	N/A	Yes	N/A	
36	Malta	No	N/A	Yes	N/A	
37	Mexico	No	N/A	Yes	N/A	
38	Moldova*	No	N/A	Yes	N/A	
39	Netherlands	No	N/A	Yes	N/A	
40	Norway	No	N/A	Yes	N/A	
41	Poland	No	N/A	Yes	N/A	
42	Portugal	No	N/A	Yes	N/A	
43	Romania	No	N/A	Yes	N/A	
44	Serbia	No	N/A	Yes	N/A	
45	Singapore	No	N/A	Yes	N/A	
46	Slovak Republic	No	N/A	Yes	N/A	
47	Slovenia	No	N/A	Yes	N/A	
48	Spain	No	N/A	Yes	N/A	
49	Sweden	No	N/A	Yes	N/A	
50	Switzerland	No	N/A	No	N/A	
51	Thailand	No	N/A	Yes	N/A	
52	Turkey	No	N/A	Yes	N/A	
53	Turkmenistan*	No	N/A	Yes	N/A	
54	Ukraine	No	N/A	Yes	N/A	
55	United Arab Emirates	No	N/A	Yes	N/A	
56	United Kingdom	No	N/A	Yes	N/A	
57	United States	No	N/A	Yes	N/A	
58	Uzbekistan*	No	N/A	Yes	N/A	
59	Viet Nam	No	N/A	Yes	N/A	

Faroe Islands

A. Progress in the implementation of the minimum standard

The Faroe Islands has five tax agreements in force, as reported in its response to the Peer Review questionnaire, including the multilateral Nordic Convention concluded with Denmark, Finland, Iceland, Norway and Sweden (the "Nordic Convention")[52]. The Faroe Islands has not signed the MLI.

The Faroe Islands is implementing the minimum standard through the inclusion of the preamble statement and the PPT.

The Faroe Islands signed a complying instrument with respect to its agreement with Greenland.

The Faroe Islands indicated in its response to the Peer Review questionnaire that the agreements with India and Switzerland are agreements concluded by Denmark that apply to its territory.

The Parties to the Nordic Convention signed a complying instrument in 2018.

B. Implementation issues

No jurisdiction has raised any concerns about their agreements with the Faroe Islands.

Summary of the jurisdiction response – Faroe Islands

	Treaty partners	Compliance with the standard	If compliant, the alternative implemented	Signature of a complying instrument	The alternative implemented through the complying instrument (if not the MLI)	Comments
1	Denmark	No	N/A	Yes	PPT alone	Nordic Convention
2	Finland	No	N/A	Yes	PPT alone	Nordic Convention
2	Greenland	No	N/A	Yes	N/A	
3	India	No	N/A	Yes	N/A	DK MLI
4	Iceland	No	N/A	Yes	PPT alone	Nordic Convention
5	Norway	No	N/A	Yes	PPT alone	Nordic Convention
6	Sweden	No	N/A	Yes	PPT alone	Nordic Convention
7	Switzerland	No	N/A	No	N/A	DK Protocol
8	United Kingdom	No	N/A	No	N/A	Awaiting UK

Finland

A. Progress in the implementation of the minimum standard

Finland has 73 tax agreements in force, as reported in its response to the Peer Review questionnaire, including the multilateral Nordic Convention concluded with Denmark, the Faroe Islands, Iceland, Norway and Sweden ("Nordic Convention").[53] Its agreement with Hong Kong (China) complies with the minimum standard.

Finland signed the MLI in 2017 and deposited its instrument of acceptance on 25 February 2019, listing 69 tax agreements.[54] The MLI entered into force for Finland on 1st June 2019.

Finland is implementing the minimum standard through the inclusion of the preamble statement and the PPT.[55]

The agreements that will be modified by the MLI will come into compliance with the minimum standard once the provisions of the MLI take effect. Some agreements listed under the MLI are expected to become compliant with the minimum standard by the end of 2019.Finland indicated in its response to the Peer Review questionnaire that bilateral negotiations would be used with respect to its agreements with Bulgaria and Germany.

The Parties to the Nordic Convention signed a complying instrument in 2018.

B. Implementation issues

No jurisdiction has raised any concerns about their agreements with Finland.

Summary of the jurisdiction response – Finland

	Treaty partners	Compliance with the standard	If compliant, the alternative implemented	Signature of a complying instrument	The alternative implemented through the complying instrument (if not the MLI)	Comments
1	Argentina	No	N/A	Yes	N/A	
2	Armenia	No	N/A	Yes	N/A	
3	Australia	No	N/A	Yes	N/A	MLI in force for both Treaty partners.
4	Austria	No	N/A	Yes	N/A	MLI in force for both Treaty partners.
5	Azerbaijan*	No	N/A	Yes	N/A	
6	Barbados	No	N/A	Yes	N/A	
7	Belarus*	No	N/A	Yes	N/A	
8	Belgium	No	N/A	Yes	N/A	
9	Bosnia and Herzegovina*	No	N/A	Yes	N/A	
10	Brazil	No	N/A	Yes	N/A	
11	Bulgaria	No	N/A	No	N/A	

12	Canada	No	N/A	Yes	N/A	
13	China (People's Republic of)	No	N/A	Yes	N/A	
14	Croatia	No	N/A	Yes	N/A	
15	Cyprus*	No	N/A	Yes	N/A	
16	Czech Republic	No	N/A	Yes	N/A	
17	Denmark	No	N/A	Yes	PPT alone	Nordic Convention
18	Egypt	No	N/A	Yes	N/A	
19	Estonia	No	N/A	Yes	N/A	
20	Faroe Islands	No	N/A	Yes	PPT alone	Nordic Convention
21	France	No	N/A	Yes	N/A	MLI in force for both Treaty partners.
22	Georgia	No	N/A	Yes	N/A	
23	Germany	No	N/A	No	N/A	
24	Greece	No	N/A	Yes	N/A	
25	Hong Kong (China)	Yes	PPT alone	N/A	N/A	
26	Hungary	No	N/A	Yes	N/A	
27	Iceland	No	N/A	Yes	PPT alone	Nordic Convention
28	India	No	N/A	Yes	N/A	
29	Indonesia	No	N/A	Yes	N/A	
30	Ireland	No	N/A	Yes	N/A	MLI in force for both Treaty partners.
31	Israel	No	N/A	Yes	N/A	MLI in force for both Treaty partners.
32	Italy	No	N/A	Yes	N/A	
33	Japan	No	N/A	Yes	N/A	MLI in force for both Treaty partners.
34	Kazakhstan	No	N/A	Yes	N/A	
35	Korea	No	N/A	Yes	N/A	
36	Kosovo*	No	N/A	Yes	N/A	
37	Kyrgyzstan*	No	N/A	Yes	N/A	
38	Latvia	No	N/A	Yes	N/A	
39	Lithuania	No	N/A	Yes	N/A	MLI in force for both Treaty partners.
40	Luxembourg	No	N/A	Yes	N/A	
41	North Macedonia	No	N/A	Yes	N/A	
42	Malaysia	No	N/A	Yes	N/A	
43	Malta	No	N/A	Yes	N/A	MLI in force for both Treaty partners.
44	Mexico	No	N/A	Yes	N/A	
45	Moldova*	No	N/A	Yes	N/A	
46	Montenegro*	No	N/A	Yes	N/A	

47	Morocco	No	N/A	Yes	N/A	
48	Netherlands	No	N/A	Yes	N/A	
49	New Zealand	No	N/A	Yes	N/A	MLI in force for both Treaty partners.
50	Norway	No	N/A	Yes	PPT alone	Nordic Convention
51	Pakistan	No	N/A	Yes	N/A	
52	Philippines*	No	N/A	Yes	N/A	
53	Poland	No	N/A	Yes	N/A	MLI in force for both Treaty partners.
54	Romania	No	N/A	Yes	N/A	
55	Russia	No	N/A	Yes	N/A	
56	Serbia	No	N/A	Yes	N/A	MLI in force for both Treaty partners.
57	Singapore	No	N/A	Yes	N/A	MLI in force for both Treaty partners.
58	Slovak Republic	No	N/A	Yes	N/A	MLI in force for both Treaty partners.
59	Slovenia	No	N/A	Yes	N/A	MLI in force for both Treaty partners.
60	South Africa	No	N/A	Yes	N/A	
61	Spain	No	N/A	Yes	N/A	
62	Sri Lanka	No	N/A	Yes	N/A	
63	Sweden	No	N/A	Yes	PPT alone	Nordic Convention
64	Switzerland	No	N/A	Yes	N/A	
65	Tajikistan*	No	N/A	Yes	N/A	
66	Tanzania*	No	N/A	Yes	N/A	
67	Thailand	No	N/A	Yes	N/A	
68	Turkey	No	N/A	Yes	N/A	
69	Turkmenistan*	No	N/A	Yes	N/A	
70	Ukraine	No	N/A	Yes	N/A	
71	United Arab Emirates	No	N/A	Yes	N/A	
72	United Kingdom	No	N/A	Yes	N/A	MLI in force for both Treaty partners.
73	United States	No	N/A	Yes	N/A	
74	Uruguay	No	N/A	Yes	N/A	
75	Uzbekistan*	No	N/A	Yes	N/A	
76	Viet Nam	No	N/A	Yes	N/A	
77	Zambia	No	N/A	Yes	N/A	

France

A. Progress in the implementation of the minimum standard

France has 118 tax agreements in force, as reported in its response to the Peer Review questionnaire. Eleven of those agreements, the agreements with Australia, Austria, Israel, Japan, Lithuania, New Zealand, Poland, Serbia, Slovak Republic, Slovenia and United Kingdom, comply with the minimum standard.

France signed the MLI in 2017 and deposited its instrument of ratification on 26 September 2018, listing 90 tax agreements.[56] The MLI entered into force for France on 1 January 2019.

France is implementing the minimum standard through the inclusion of the preamble statement and the PPT.[57]

The agreements modified by the MLI come into compliance with the minimum standard once the provisions of the MLI take effect. Other agreements listed under the MLI are expected to become compliant with the minimum standard by the end of 2019. France indicated in its response to the Peer Review questionnaire that the agreements not listed under the MLI were concluded with treaty partners that were not members of the ad hoc Group at the time of France's signature of the MLI.

B. Implementation issues

No jurisdiction has raised any concerns about their agreements with France.

Summary of the jurisdiction response – France

	Treaty partners	Compliance with the standard	If compliant, the alternative implemented	Signature of a complying instrument	The alternative implemented through the complying instrument (if not the MLI)	Comments
1	Albania*	No	N/A	No	N/A	
2	Algeria*	No	N/A	Yes	N/A	
3	Andorra	No	N/A	Yes	N/A	
4	Argentina	No	N/A	Yes	N/A	
5	Armenia	No	N/A	Yes	N/A	
6	Australia	Yes	PPT alone	N/A	N/A	
7	Austria	Yes	PPT alone	N/A	N/A	
8	Azerbaijan*	No	N/A	Yes	N/A	
9	Bahrain	No	N/A	No	N/A	
10	Bangladesh*	No	N/A	Yes	N/A	
11	Belarus*	No	N/A	No	N/A	
12	Belgium	No	N/A	Yes	N/A	
13	Benin	No	N/A	Yes	N/A	
14	Bolivia*	No	N/A	No	N/A	
15	Bosnia and Herzegovina*	No	N/A	Yes	N/A	
16	Botswana	No	N/A	No	N/A	

17	Brazil	No	N/A	Yes	N/A	
18	Bulgaria	No	N/A	Yes	N/A	
19	Burkina Faso	No	N/A	Yes	N/A	
20	Cameroon	No	N/A	Yes	N/A	
21	Canada	No	N/A	Yes	N/A	
22	Central African Republic*	No	N/A	No	N/A	
23	Chile	No	N/A	Yes	N/A	
24	China (People's Republic of)	No	N/A	Yes	N/A	
25	Congo	No	N/A	No	N/A	
26	Cote d'Ivoire	No	N/A	Yes	N/A	
27	Croatia	No	N/A	Yes	N/A	
28	Cyprus*	No	N/A	Yes	N/A	
29	Czech Republic	No	N/A	Yes	N/A	
30	Ecuador*	No	N/A	No	N/A	
31	Egypt	No	N/A	Yes	N/A	
32	Estonia	No	N/A	Yes	N/A	
33	Ethiopia*	No	N/A	No	N/A	
34	Finland	No	N/A	Yes	N/A	
35	Gabon	No	N/A	Yes	N/A	
36	Georgia	No	N/A	Yes	N/A	
37	Germany	No	N/A	Yes	N/A	
38	Ghana*	No	N/A	No	N/A	
39	Greece	No	N/A	Yes	N/A	
40	Guinea*	No	N/A	No	N/A	
41	Hong Kong (China)	No	N/A	Yes	N/A	
42	Hungary	No	N/A	Yes	N/A	
43	Iceland	No	N/A	Yes	N/A	
44	India	No	N/A	Yes	N/A	
45	Indonesia	No	N/A	Yes	N/A	
46	Iran*	No	N/A	No	N/A	
47	Ireland	No	N/A	Yes	N/A	
48	Israel	Yes	PPT alone	N/A	N/A	
49	Italy	No	N/A	Yes	N/A	
50	Jamaica	No	N/A	Yes	N/A	
51	Japan	Yes	PPT and LOB	N/A	N/A	
52	Jordan*	No	N/A	Yes	N/A	
53	Kazakhstan	No	N/A	Yes	N/A	
54	Kenya	No	N/A	Yes	N/A	
55	Korea	No	N/A	Yes	N/A	
56	Kosovo*	No	N/A	No	N/A	
57	Kuwait*	No	N/A	Yes	N/A	
58	Kyrgyzstan*	No	N/A	No	N/A	
59	Latvia	No	N/A	Yes	N/A	
60	Lebanon*	No	N/A	Yes	N/A	
61	Libya*	No	N/A	No	N/A	
62	Lithuania	Yes	PPT alone	N/A	N/A	
63	Luxembourg	No	N/A	Yes	N/A	
64	North Macedonia	No	N/A	No	N/A	
65	Madagascar*	No	N/A	No	N/A	
66	Malawi*	No	N/A	No	N/A	
67	Malaysia	No	N/A	Yes	N/A	
68	Mali*	No	N/A	No	N/A	

69	Malta	No	N/A	Yes	N/A	
70	Mauritania*	No	N/A	Yes	N/A	
71	Mauritius	No	N/A	Yes	N/A	
72	Mexico	No	N/A	Yes	N/A	
73	Monaco	No	N/A	Yes	N/A	
74	Mongolia	No	N/A	Yes	N/A	
75	Montenegro*	No	N/A	No	N/A	
76	Morocco	No	N/A	Yes	N/A	
77	Namibia*	No	N/A	No	N/A	
78	Netherlands	No	N/A	Yes	N/A	
79	New Zealand	Yes	PPT alone	N/A	N/A	
80	Niger*	No	N/A	No	N/A	
81	Nigeria	No	N/A	Yes	N/A	
82	Norway	No	N/A	Yes	N/A	
83	Oman	No	N/A	Yes	N/A	
84	Pakistan	No	N/A	Yes	N/A	
85	Panama	No	N/A	Yes	N/A	
86	Philippines*	No	N/A	Yes	N/A	
87	Poland	Yes	PPT alone	N/A	N/A	
88	Portugal	No	N/A	Yes	N/A	
89	Qatar	No	N/A	Yes	N/A	
90	Romania	No	N/A	Yes	N/A	
91	Russia	No	N/A	Yes	N/A	
92	Saudi Arabia	No	N/A	Yes	N/A	
93	Senegal	No	N/A	Yes	N/A	
94	Serbia	Yes	PPT alone	N/A	N/A	
95	Singapore	No	N/A	Yes	N/A	
96	Slovak Republic	Yes	PPT alone	N/A	N/A	
97	Slovenia	Yes	PPT alone	N/A	N/A	
98	South Africa	No	N/A	Yes	N/A	
99	Spain	No	N/A	Yes	N/A	
100	Sri Lanka	No	N/A	Yes	N/A	
101	Sweden	No	N/A	Yes	N/A	
102	Switzerland	No	N/A	Yes	N/A	
103	Syrian Arab Republic*	No	N/A	No	N/A	
104	Thailand	No	N/A	Yes	N/A	
105	Togo*	No	N/A	No	N/A	
106	Trinidad and Tobago	No	N/A	No	N/A	
107	Tunisia	No	N/A	Yes	N/A	
108	Turkey	No	N/A	Yes	N/A	
109	Turkmenistan*	No	N/A	No	N/A	
110	Ukraine	No	N/A	Yes	N/A	
111	United Arab Emirates	No	N/A	Yes	N/A	
112	United Kingdom	Yes	PPT alone	N/A	N/A	
113	United States	No	N/A	Yes	N/A	
114	Uzbekistan*	No	N/A	No	N/A	
115	Venezuela*	No	N/A	No	N/A	
116	Viet Nam	No	N/A	Yes	N/A	
117	Zambia	No	N/A	Yes	N/A	
118	Zimbabwe*	No	N/A	Yes	N/A	

Gabon

A. Progress in the implementation of the minimum standard

Gabon has four tax agreements in force, as reported in its response to the Peer Review questionnaire.

Gabon signed the MLI in 2017, listing four tax agreements.

Gabon is implementing the minimum standard through the inclusion of the preamble statement and the PPT.[58]

The agreements that will be modified by the MLI will come into compliance with the minimum standard once the provisions of the MLI take effect.

B. Implementation issues

No jurisdiction has raised any concerns about their agreements with Gabon.

Summary of the jurisdiction response – Gabon

	Treaty partners	Compliance with the standard	If compliant, the alternative implemented	Signature of a complying instrument	The alternative implemented through the complying instrument (if not the MLI)	Comments
1	Belgium	No	N/A	Yes	N/A	
2	Canada	No	N/A	Yes	N/A	
3	France	No	N/A	Yes	N/A	
4	Morocco	No	N/A	Yes	N/A	

Georgia

A. Progress in the implementation of the minimum standard

Georgia has 56 tax agreements in force, as reported in its response to the Peer Review questionnaire.

Georgia signed the MLI in 2017, listing 34 tax agreements.

Georgia is implementing the minimum standard through the inclusion of the preamble statement and the PPT.[59]

The agreements that will be modified by the MLI will come into compliance with the minimum standard once the provisions of the MLI take effect.

Georgia has indicated in the response to the Peer Review questionnaire that bilateral negotiations would be used for its agreement with Poland.

B. Implementation issues

No jurisdiction has raised any concerns about their agreements with Georgia.

Summary of the jurisdiction response – Georgia

	Treaty partners	Compliance with the standard	If compliant, the alternative implemented	Signature of a complying instrument	The alternative implemented through the complying instrument (if not the MLI)	Comments
1	Armenia	No	N/A	No	N/A	
2	Austria	No	N/A	No	N/A	
3	Azerbaijan*	No	N/A	No	N/A	
4	Bahrain	No	N/A	No	N/A	
5	Belarus*	No	N/A	No	N/A	
6	Belgium	No	N/A	Yes	N/A	
7	Bulgaria	No	N/A	Yes	N/A	
8	China (People's Republic of)	No	N/A	Yes	N/A	
9	Croatia	No	N/A	Yes	N/A	
10	Cyprus*	No	N/A	Yes	N/A	
11	Czech Republic	No	N/A	Yes	N/A	
12	Denmark	No	N/A	No	N/A	
13	Egypt	No	N/A	No	N/A	
14	Estonia	No	N/A	Yes	N/A	
15	Finland	No	N/A	Yes	N/A	
16	France	No	N/A	Yes	N/A	
17	Germany	No	N/A	No	N/A	
18	Greece	No	N/A	Yes	N/A	
19	Hungary	No	N/A	Yes	N/A	
20	Iceland	No	N/A	Yes	N/A	
21	India	No	N/A	Yes	N/A	

22	Iran*	No	N/A	No	N/A	
23	Ireland	No	N/A	Yes	N/A	
24	Israel	No	N/A	Yes	N/A	
25	Italy	No	N/A	Yes	N/A	
26	Japan	No	N/A	No	N/A	
27	Kazakhstan	No	N/A	No	N/A	
28	Korea	No	N/A	Yes	N/A	
29	Kuwait*	No	N/A	No	N/A	
30	Latvia	No	N/A	Yes	N/A	
31	Liechtenstein	No	N/A	Yes	N/A	
32	Lithuania	No	N/A	Yes	N/A	
33	Luxembourg	No	N/A	Yes	N/A	
34	Malta	No	N/A	No	N/A	
35	Moldova*	No	N/A	No	N/A	
36	Netherlands	No	N/A	Yes	N/A	
37	Norway	No	N/A	Yes	N/A	
38	Poland	No	N/A	No	N/A	
39	Portugal	No	N/A	Yes	N/A	
40	Qatar	No	N/A	No	N/A	
41	Romania	No	N/A	Yes	N/A	
42	San Marino	No	N/A	Yes	N/A	
43	Saudi Arabia	No	N/A	No	N/A	
44	Serbia	No	N/A	Yes	N/A	
45	Singapore	No	N/A	Yes	N/A	
46	Slovak Republic	No	N/A	Yes	N/A	
47	Slovenia	No	N/A	Yes	N/A	
48	Spain	No	N/A	Yes	N/A	
49	Sweden	No	N/A	Yes	N/A	
50	Switzerland	No	N/A	No	N/A	
51	Turkey	No	N/A	Yes	N/A	
52	Turkmenistan*	No	N/A	No	N/A	
53	Ukraine	No	N/A	No	N/A	
54	United Arab Emirates	No	N/A	No	N/A	
55	United Kingdom	No	N/A	Yes	N/A	
56	Uzbekistan*	No	N/A	No	N/A	

Germany

A. Progress in the implementation of the minimum standard

Germany has 96 tax agreements in force, as reported in its response to the Peer Review questionnaire. Two of those agreements, the agreements with Australia and Japan, comply with the minimum standard.

Germany signed the MLI in 2017, listing 35 tax agreements.[60]

Germany is implementing the minimum standard through the inclusion of the preamble statement and the PPT.[61]

The agreements that will be modified by the MLI will come into compliance with the minimum standard once the provisions of the MLI take effect.

Germany indicated in its response to the Peer Review questionnaire that most of its agreements contain a provision based on paragraph 1 of Article 28 of the German Treaty Negotiation Basis which enables Contracting States to apply domestic anti-abuse provisions such as Section 50d of the German Income Tax Act (Anti Conduit Rule) or Section 42 of the German Fiscal Code (GAAR).

Germany further indicated that bilateral negotiations would be used for its agreements with Argentina, Belgium, Bulgaria, Canada, Costa Rica, Cyprus, Denmark, Ecuador*, Egypt, Estonia, Finland, Greece, Iceland, India, Indonesia, Iran*, Israel, Ireland, Kyrgyzstan*, Latvia, Norway, Poland, Portugal, Singapore, South Africa, Sri Lanka, Sweden, Switzerland, Tajikistan*, Trinidad and Tobago, Ukraine and the United Kingdom.

B. Implementation issues

No jurisdiction has raised any concerns about their agreements with Germany.

Summary of the jurisdiction response – Germany

	Treaty partners	Compliance with the standard	If compliant, the alternative implemented	Signature of a complying instrument	The alternative implemented through the complying instrument (if not the MLI)	Comments
1	Albania*	No	N/A	No	N/A	
2	Algeria*	No	N/A	No	N/A	
3	Argentina	No	N/A	No	N/A	
4	Armenia	No	N/A	No	N/A	
5	Australia	Yes	PPT alone	N/A	N/A	
6	Austria	No	N/A	Yes	N/A	
7	Azerbaijan*	No	N/A	No	N/A	
8	Bangladesh*	No	N/A	No	N/A	
9	Belarus*	No	N/A	No	N/A	
10	Belgium	No	N/A	No	N/A	
11	Bolivia*	No	N/A	No	N/A	
12	Bosnia and Herzegovina*	No	N/A	No	N/A	

13	Bulgaria	No	N/A	Yes	N/A	
14	Canada	No	N/A	No	N/A	
15	China (People's Republic of)	No	N/A	Yes	N/A	
16	Chinese Taipei*	No	N/A	No	N/A	
17	Costa Rica	No	N/A	Yes	N/A	
18	Cote d'Ivoire	No	N/A	No	N/A	
19	Croatia	No	N/A	Yes	N/A	
20	Cyprus*	No	N/A	Yes	N/A	
21	Czech Republic	No	N/A	Yes	N/A	
22	Denmark	No	N/A	Yes	N/A	
23	Ecuador*	No	N/A	No	N/A	
24	Egypt	No	N/A	No	N/A	
25	Estonia	No	N/A	Yes	N/A	
26	Finland	No	N/A	Yes	N/A	
27	France	No	N/A	Yes	N/A	
28	Georgia	No	N/A	No	N/A	
29	Ghana*	No	N/A	No	N/A	
30	Greece	No	N/A	No	N/A	
31	Hungary	No	N/A	Yes	N/A	
32	Iceland	No	N/A	No	N/A	
33	India	No	N/A	No	N/A	
34	Indonesia	No	N/A	No	N/A	
35	Iran*	No	N/A	No	N/A	
36	Ireland	No	N/A	Yes	N/A	
37	Israel	No	N/A	Yes	N/A	
38	Italy	No	N/A	Yes	N/A	
39	Jamaica	No	N/A	No	N/A	
40	Japan	Yes	PPT and LOB	N/A	N/A	
41	Kazakhstan	No	N/A	No	N/A	
42	Kenya	No	N/A	No	N/A	
43	Korea	No	N/A	Yes	N/A	
44	Kosovo*	No	N/A	No	N/A	
45	Kuwait*	No	N/A	No	N/A	
46	Kyrgyzstan*	No	N/A	No	N/A	
47	Latvia	No	N/A	Yes	N/A	
48	Liberia	No	N/A	No	N/A	
49	Liechtenstein	No	N/A	Yes	N/A	
50	Lithuania	No	N/A	Yes	N/A	
51	Luxembourg	No	N/A	Yes	N/A	
52	North Macedonia	No	N/A	No	N/A	
53	Malaysia	No	N/A	No	N/A	
54	Malta	No	N/A	Yes	N/A	
55	Mauritius	No	N/A	Yes	N/A	
56	Mexico	No	N/A	Yes	N/A	
57	Moldova*	No	N/A	No	N/A	
58	Mongolia	No	N/A	No	N/A	
59	Montenegro*	No	N/A	No	N/A	
60	Morocco	No	N/A	No	N/A	
61	Namibia*	No	N/A	No	N/A	
62	Netherlands	No	N/A	Yes	N/A	
63	New Zealand	No	N/A	Yes	N/A	
64	Norway	No	N/A	No	N/A	
65	Pakistan	No	N/A	No	N/A	

66	Philippines*	No	N/A	No	N/A	
67	Poland	No	N/A	No	N/A	
68	Portugal	No	N/A	No	N/A	
69	Romania	No	N/A	Yes	N/A	
70	Russia	No	N/A	Yes	N/A	
71	Serbia	No	N/A	No	N/A	
72	Singapore	No	N/A	No	N/A	
73	Slovak Republic	No	N/A	Yes	N/A	
74	Slovenia	No	N/A	Yes	N/A	
75	South Africa	No	N/A	No	N/A	
76	Spain	No	N/A	Yes	N/A	
77	Sri Lanka	No	N/A	No	N/A	
78	Sweden	No	N/A	No	N/A	
79	Switzerland	No	N/A	No	N/A	
80	Syrian Arab Republic*	No	N/A	No	N/A	
81	Tajikistan*	No	N/A	No	N/A	
82	Thailand	No	N/A	No	N/A	
83	Trinidad and Tobago	No	N/A	No	N/A	
84	Tunisia	No	N/A	No	N/A	
85	Turkey	No	N/A	Yes	N/A	
86	Turkmenistan*	No	N/A	No	N/A	
87	Ukraine	No	N/A	No	N/A	
88	United Arab Emirates	No	N/A	Yes	N/A	
89	United Kingdom	No	N/A	Yes	N/A	
90	United States	No	N/A	Yes	N/A	
91	Uruguay	No	N/A	No	N/A	
92	Uzbekistan*	No	N/A	No	N/A	
93	Venezuela*	No	N/A	No	N/A	
94	Viet Nam	No	N/A	No	N/A	
95	Zambia	No	N/A	No	N/A	
96	Zimbabwe*	No	N/A	No	N/A	

Greece

A. Progress in the implementation of the minimum standard

Greece has 57 tax agreements in force, as reported in its response to the Peer Review questionnaire.

Greece signed the MLI in 2017, listing 57 tax agreements.

Greece is implementing the minimum standard in its tax agreements through the inclusion of the preamble statement and the PPT.[62]

The agreements that will be modified by the MLI will come into compliance with the minimum standard once the provisions of the MLI take effect.

B. Implementation issues

No jurisdiction has raised any concerns about their agreements with Greece.

Summary of the jurisdiction response – Greece

	Treaty partners	Compliance with the standard	If compliant, the alternative implemented	Signature of a complying instrument	The alternative implemented through the complying instrument (if not the MLI)	Comments
1	Albania*	No	N/A	Yes	N/A	
2	Armenia	No	N/A	Yes	N/A	
3	Austria	No	N/A	Yes	N/A	
4	Azerbaijan*	No	N/A	Yes	N/A	
5	Belgium	No	N/A	Yes	N/A	
6	Bosnia and Herzegovina*	No	N/A	Yes	N/A	
7	Bulgaria	No	N/A	Yes	N/A	
8	Canada	No	N/A	Yes	N/A	
9	China (People's Republic of)	No	N/A	Yes	N/A	
10	Croatia	No	N/A	Yes	N/A	
11	Cyprus*	No	N/A	Yes	N/A	
12	Czech Republic	No	N/A	Yes	N/A	
13	Denmark	No	N/A	Yes	N/A	
14	Egypt	No	N/A	Yes	N/A	
15	Estonia	No	N/A	Yes	N/A	
16	Finland	No	N/A	Yes	N/A	
17	France	No	N/A	Yes	N/A	
18	Georgia	No	N/A	Yes	N/A	
19	Germany	No	N/A	Yes	N/A	
20	Hungary	No	N/A	Yes	N/A	
21	Iceland	No	N/A	Yes	N/A	
22	India	No	N/A	Yes	N/A	
23	Ireland	No	N/A	Yes	N/A	
24	Israel	No	N/A	Yes	N/A	

25	Italy	No	N/A	Yes	N/A	
26	Korea	No	N/A	Yes	N/A	
27	Kuwait*	No	N/A	Yes	N/A	
28	Latvia	No	N/A	Yes	N/A	
29	Lithuania	No	N/A	Yes	N/A	
30	Luxembourg	No	N/A	Yes	N/A	
31	Malta	No	N/A	Yes	N/A	
32	Mexico	No	N/A	Yes	N/A	
33	Moldova*	No	N/A	Yes	N/A	
34	Morocco	No	N/A	Yes	N/A	
35	Netherlands	No	N/A	Yes	N/A	
36	Norway	No	N/A	Yes	N/A	
37	Poland	No	N/A	Yes	N/A	
38	Portugal	No	N/A	Yes	N/A	
39	Qatar	No	N/A	Yes	N/A	
40	Romania	No	N/A	Yes	N/A	
41	Russia	No	N/A	Yes	N/A	
42	San Marino	No	N/A	Yes	N/A	
43	Saudi Arabia	No	N/A	Yes	N/A	
44	Serbia	No	N/A	Yes	N/A	
45	Slovak Republic	No	N/A	Yes	N/A	
46	Slovenia	No	N/A	Yes	N/A	
47	South Africa	No	N/A	Yes	N/A	
48	Spain	No	N/A	Yes	N/A	
49	Sweden	No	N/A	Yes	N/A	
50	Switzerland	No	N/A	Yes	N/A	
51	Tunisia	No	N/A	Yes	N/A	
52	Turkey	No	N/A	Yes	N/A	
53	Ukraine	No	N/A	Yes	N/A	
54	United Arab Emirates	No	N/A	Yes	N/A	
55	United Kingdom	No	N/A	Yes	N/A	
56	United States	No	N/A	Yes	N/A	
57	Uzbekistan*	No	N/A	Yes	N/A	

Greenland

A. Progress in the implementation of the minimum standard

Greenland has four tax agreements in force, as reported in its response to the Peer Review questionnaire. Greenland has not signed the MLI.

Greenland indicated in its response to the Peer Review questionnaire that bilateral negotiations would be used with respect to its agreements.

B. Implementation issues

No jurisdiction has raised any concerns about their agreements with Greenland.

Summary of the jurisdiction response – Greenland

	Treaty partners	Compliance with the standard	If compliant, the alternative implemented	Signature of a complying instrument	The alternative implemented through the complying instrument (if not the MLI)	Comments
1	Denmark	No	N/A	No	N/A	Greenland and Denmark has negotiated an amendment to the DTA which will make it comply with the minimum standard. Expected to enter into force before 2020.
2	Faroe Islands	No	N/A	No	N/A	Greenland and The Faroe Islands has negotiated an amendment to the DTA which will make it comply with the minimum standard. Expected to enter into force before

						2020.
3	Iceland	No	N/A	No	N/A	Greenland and Iceland has agreed to start the negotiation of amendments to the DTA. The negotiations are expected to begin in the autumn of 2019, and will be aimed at securing compliance with the minimum standards.
4	Norway	No	N/A	No	N/A	Greenland and Norway has agreed to start the negotiation of amendments to the DTA. The negotiations are expected to begin in the autumn of 2019, and will be aimed at securing compliance with the minimum standards.

Grenada

A. Progress in the implementation of the minimum standard

Grenada has four tax agreements in force, as reported in its response to the Peer Review questionnaire, including the multilateral agreement among the members of the CARICOM concluded with ten treaty partners (the CARICOM Agreement).[63]

None of Grenada's agreements comply with the minimum standard or are subject to a complying instrument.

B. Implementation issues

Grenada is encouraged to implement the minimum standard in its agreements.

Grenada is encouraged to bring the CARICOM Agreement up to date by commencing talks among all the treaty partners.[64]

Summary of the jurisdiction response – Grenada

	Treaty partners	Compliance with the standard	If compliant, the alternative implemented	Signature of a complying instrument	The alternative implemented through the complying instrument (if not the MLI)	Comments
1	Antigua and Barbuda	No	N/A	No	N/A	CARICOM
2	Barbados	No	N/A	No	N/A	CARICOM
3	Belize	No	N/A	No	N/A	CARICOM
4	Dominica	No	N/A	No	N/A	CARICOM
5	Guyana*	No	N/A	No	N/A	CARICOM
6	Jamaica	No	N/A	No	N/A	CARICOM
7	Saint Kitts and Nevis	No	N/A	No	N/A	CARICOM
8	Saint Lucia	No	N/A	No	N/A	CARICOM
9	Saint Vincent and the Grenadines	No	N/A	No	N/A	CARICOM
10	South Africa	No	N/A	No	N/A	
11	Switzerland	No	N/A	No	N/A	
12	Trinidad and Tobago	No	N/A	No	N/A	CARICOM
13	United Kingdom	No	N/A	No	N/A	

Guernsey

A. Progress in the implementation of the minimum standard

Guernsey has 13 tax agreements in force, as reported in its response to the Peer Review questionnaire. Its agreement with the United Kingdom complies with the minimum standard.

Guernsey signed the MLI in 2017 and deposited its instrument of ratification on 12 February 2019, listing nine tax agreements. The MLI entered into force for Guernsey on 1 October 2018.

Guernsey is implementing the minimum standard through the inclusion of the preamble statement and the PPT.[65]

The agreements modified by the MLI come into compliance with the minimum standard once the provisions of the MLI take effect. Other agreements listed under the MLI are expected to become compliant with the minimum standard by the end of 2019.

Guernsey indicated in its response to the Peer Review questionnaire that bilateral negotiations would be used with respect to its agreement with Qatar and the other Crown Dependencies (the Isle of Man and Jersey).

B. Implementation issues

No jurisdiction has raised any concerns about their agreements with Guernsey.

Summary of the jurisdiction response – Guernsey

	Treaty partners	Compliance with the standard	If compliant, the alternative implemented	Signature of a complying instrument	The alternative implemented through the complying instrument (if not the MLI)	Comments
1	Cyprus*	No	N/A	Yes	N/A	
2	Hong Kong (China)	No	N/A	Yes	N/A	
3	Isle of Man	No	N/A	No	N/A	Under bilateral renegotiation
4	Jersey	No	N/A	No	N/A	Under bilateral renegotiation
5	Liechtenstein	No	N/A	Yes	N/A	
6	Luxembourg	No	N/A	Yes	N/A	Entry into force for Luxembourg will be 1 August 2019
7	Malta	No	N/A	Yes	N/A	Entry into force for Malta was 1 April 2019; for Guernsey

						1 June 2019
8	Mauritius	No	N/A	Yes	N/A	
9	Monaco	No	N/A	Yes	N/A	Entry into force for Monaco was 1 May 2019; for Guernsey 1 June 2019
10	Qatar	No	N/A	No	N/A	Under bilateral renegotiation
11	Seychelles	No	N/A	Yes	N/A	
12	Singapore	No	N/A	Yes	N/A	Entry into force for Singapore was 1 April 2019; for Guernsey 1 June 2019
13	United Kingdom	Yes	PPT alone	No	N/A	New agreement in force from 7 January 2019, replacing earlier agreement. The express statement in the preamble and the Principal Purpose Test (PPT) alone (text equivalent to paragraph 9 of Article 29 of the 2017 OECD Model Tax Convention)

Haiti

A. Progress in the implementation of the minimum standard

Haiti has no tax agreements, as reported in its response to the Peer Review questionnaire.

B. Implementation issues

No jurisdiction has raised any concerns about Haiti.

Hong Kong (China)

A. Progress in the implementation of the minimum standard

Hong Kong (China) has 39 tax agreements in force, as reported in its response to the Peer Review questionnaire. Two of those agreements, the agreements with Belarus* and Finland, comply with the minimum standard.

Hong Kong (China) joined the MLI in 2017, listing 36 tax agreements.[66]

Hong Kong (China) is implementing the minimum standard through the inclusion of the preamble statement and the PPT.[67]

The agreements that will be modified by the MLI will come into compliance with the minimum standard once the provisions of the MLI take effect.

B. Implementation issues

No jurisdiction has raised any concerns about their agreements with Hong Kong (China).

Summary of the jurisdiction response – Hong Kong, China

	Treaty partners	Compliance with the standard	If compliant, the alternative implemented	Signature of a complying instrument	The alternative implemented through the complying instrument (if not the MLI)	Comments
1	Austria	No	N/A	Yes	N/A	
2	Belarus*	Yes	PPT alone	N/A	N/A	
3	Belgium	No	N/A	Yes	N/A	
4	Brunei Darussalam	No	N/A	Yes	N/A	
5	Canada	No	N/A	Yes	N/A	
6	Czech Republic	No	N/A	Yes	N/A	
7	Finland	Yes	PPT alone	N/A	N/A	
8	France	No	N/A	Yes	N/A	
9	Guernsey	No	N/A	Yes	N/A	
10	Hungary	No	N/A	Yes	N/A	
11	India	No	N/A	No	N/A	To be added to the list of agreements that Hong Kong wishes to cover under the MLI or through bilateral negotiations of an amending protocol
12	Indonesia	No	N/A	Yes	N/A	
13	Ireland	No	N/A	Yes	N/A	
14	Italy	No	N/A	Yes	N/A	
15	Japan	No	N/A	Yes	N/A	
16	Jersey	No	N/A	Yes	N/A	

17	Korea	No	N/A	Yes	N/A	
18	Kuwait*	No	N/A	Yes	N/A	
19	Latvia	No	N/A	Yes	N/A	
20	Liechtenstein	No	N/A	Yes	N/A	
21	Luxembourg	No	N/A	Yes	N/A	
22	Malaysia	No	N/A	Yes	N/A	
23	Malta	No	N/A	Yes	N/A	
24	Mexico	No	N/A	Yes	N/A	
25	Netherlands	No	N/A	Yes	N/A	
26	New Zealand	No	N/A	Yes	N/A	
27	Pakistan	No	N/A	Yes	N/A	Partial compliance (just lacks the new preamble)
28	Portugal	No	N/A	Yes	N/A	
29	Qatar	No	N/A	Yes	N/A	
30	Romania	No	N/A	Yes	N/A	
31	Russia	No	N/A	Yes	N/A	
32	Saudi Arabia	No	N/A	No	N/A	To be added to the list of agreements that Hong Kong wishes to cover under the MLI or through bilateral negotiations of an amending protocol
33	South Africa	No	N/A	Yes	N/A	
34	Spain	No	N/A	Yes	N/A	
35	Switzerland	No	N/A	Yes	N/A	Switzerland has not listed this agreement in its MLI position and has proposed bilateral negotiations of an amending protocol instead
36	Thailand	No	N/A	Yes	N/A	
37	United Arab Emirates	No	N/A	Yes	N/A	
38	United Kingdom	No	N/A	Yes	N/A	
39	Viet Nam	No	N/A	Yes	N/A	

Hungary

A. Progress in the implementation of the minimum standard

Hungary has 81 tax agreements, as reported in its response to the Peer Review questionnaire.

Hungary signed the MLI in 2017, listing 66 tax agreements.

Hungary is implementing the minimum standard through the inclusion of the preamble statement and the PPT.[68]

The agreements that will be modified by the MLI will come into compliance with the minimum standard once the provisions of the MLI take effect.

Hungary indicated in its response to the Peer Review questionnaire that the agreements not listed under the MLI were concluded with treaty partners that were not ad hoc Group members at the time of Hungary's signature. Hungary further indicated that it is not concerned by treaty shopping with respect to those agreements.

B. Implementation issues

No jurisdiction has raised any concerns about their agreements with Hungary.

Summary of the jurisdiction response – Hungary

	Treaty partners	Compliance with the standard	If compliant, the alternative implemented	Signature of a complying instrument	The alternative implemented through the complying instrument (if not the MLI)	Comments
1	Albania*	No	N/A	No	N/A	
2	Armenia	No	N/A	No	N/A	
3	Australia	No	N/A	Yes	N/A	
4	Austria	No	N/A	Yes	N/A	
5	Azerbaijan*	No	N/A	Yes	N/A	
6	Bahrain	No	N/A	No	N/A	
7	Belarus*	No	N/A	No	N/A	
8	Belgium	No	N/A	Yes	N/A	
9	Bosnia Herzegovina*	No	N/A	No	N/A	
10	Brazil	No	N/A	Yes	N/A	
11	Bulgaria	No	N/A	Yes	N/A	
12	Canada	No	N/A	Yes	N/A	
13	China (People's Republic of)	No	N/A	Yes	N/A	
14	Chinese Taipei*	No	N/A	No	N/A	
15	Croatia	No	N/A	Yes	N/A	
16	Cyprus*	No	N/A	Yes	N/A	
17	Czech Republic	No	N/A	Yes	N/A	
18	Denmark	No	N/A	Yes	N/A	
19	Egypt	No	N/A	Yes	N/A	

20	Estonia	No	N/A	Yes	N/A	
21	Finland	No	N/A	Yes	N/A	
22	France	No	N/A	Yes	N/A	
23	Georgia	No	N/A	Yes	N/A	
24	Germany	No	N/A	Yes	N/A	
25	Greece	No	N/A	Yes	N/A	
26	Hong Kong	No	N/A	Yes	N/A	
27	Iceland	No	N/A	Yes	N/A	
28	India	No	N/A	Yes	N/A	
29	Indonesia	No	N/A	Yes	N/A	
30	Iran*	No	N/A	No	N/A	
31	Ireland	No	N/A	Yes	N/A	
32	Israel	No	N/A	Yes	N/A	
33	Italy	No	N/A	Yes	N/A	
34	Japan	No	N/A	Yes	N/A	
35	Kazakhstan	No	N/A	Yes	N/A	
36	Kosovo*	No	N/A	No	N/A	
37	Kuwait*	No	N/A	No	N/A	
38	Latvia	No	N/A	Yes	N/A	
39	Liechtenstein	No	N/A	Yes	N/A	
40	Lithuania	No	N/A	Yes	N/A	
41	Luxembourg	No	N/A	Yes	N/A	
42	North Macedonia	No	N/A	No	N/A	
43	Malaysia	No	N/A	Yes	N/A	
44	Malta	No	N/A	Yes	N/A	
45	Mexico	No	N/A	Yes	N/A	
46	Moldova*	No	N/A	Yes	N/A	
47	Mongolia	No	N/A	Yes	N/A	
48	Montenegro*	No	N/A	No	N/A	
49	Morocco	No	N/A	Yes	N/A	
50	Netherlands	No	N/A	Yes	N/A	
51	Norway	No	N/A	Yes	N/A	
52	Oman	No	N/A	No	N/A	
53	Pakistan	No	N/A	Yes	N/A	
54	Philippines*	No	N/A	Yes	N/A	
55	Poland	No	N/A	Yes	N/A	
56	Portugal	No	N/A	Yes	N/A	
57	Qatar	No	N/A	Yes	N/A	
58	Romania	No	N/A	Yes	N/A	
59	Russia	No	N/A	Yes	N/A	
60	San Marino	No	N/A	Yes	N/A	
61	Saudi Arabia	No	N/A	Yes	N/A	
62	Serbia	No	N/A	Yes	N/A	
63	Singapore	No	N/A	Yes	N/A	
64	Slovak republic	No	N/A	Yes	N/A	
65	Slovenia	No	N/A	Yes	N/A	
66	South Africa	No	N/A	Yes	N/A	
67	Korea	No	N/A	Yes	N/A	
68	Spain	No	N/A	Yes	N/A	
69	Sweden	No	N/A	Yes	N/A	
70	Switzerland	No	N/A	Yes	N/A	
71	Thailand	No	N/A	Yes	N/A	
72	Tunisia	No	N/A	Yes	N/A	

73	Turkey	No	N/A	Yes	N/A	
74	Turkmenistan*	No	N/A	No	N/A	
75	Ukraine	No	N/A	Yes	N/A	
76	United Arab Emirates	No	N/A	No	N/A	
77	United Kingdom	No	N/A	Yes	N/A	
78	United States	No	N/A	Yes	N/A	
79	Uruguay	No	N/A	Yes	N/A	
80	Uzbekistan*	No	N/A	No	N/A	
81	Vietnam	No	N/A	Yes	N/A	

Iceland

A. Progress in the implementation of the minimum standard

Iceland has 41 tax agreements in force, as reported in its response to the Peer Review questionnaire, including the multilateral Nordic Convention concluded with Denmark, the Faroe Islands, Finland, Norway and Sweden (the "Nordic Convention").[69] Two of its agreements, the agreements with Japan and Liechtenstein, comply with the minimum standard.

Iceland signed the MLI in 2017, listing 35 tax agreements.

Iceland is generally implementing the minimum standard through the inclusion of the preamble statement and the PPT.[70]

The agreements that will be modified by the MLI will come into compliance with the minimum standard once the provisions of the MLI take effect.

Iceland indicated in its response to the Peer Review questionnaire that bilateral negotiations would be used with respect to its agreement with Austria, Germany and Greenland.

The Parties to the Nordic Convention signed a complying instrument in 2018.

B. Implementation issues

No jurisdiction has raised any concerns about their agreements with Iceland.

Summary of the jurisdiction response – Iceland

	Treaty partners	Compliance with the standard	If compliant, the alternative implemented	Signature of a complying instrument	The alternative implemented through the complying instrument (if not the MLI)	Comments
1	Albania*	No	N/A	Yes	N/A	
2	Austria	No	N/A	No	N/A	Bilateral
3	Barbados	No	N/A	Yes	N/A	
4	Belgium	No	N/A	Yes	N/A	
5	Canada	No	N/A	Yes	N/A	
6	China (People's Republic of)	No	N/A	Yes	N/A	
7	Croatia	No	N/A	Yes	N/A	
8	Cyprus*	No	N/A	Yes	N/A	
9	Czech Republic	No	N/A	Yes	N/A	
10	Denmark	No	N/A	Yes	PPT alone	Nordic Conventio n Protocol signed 28.8.2018
11	Estonia	No	N/A	Yes	N/A	
12	Faroe Islands	No	N/A	Yes	PPT alone	Nordic Conventio

						n Protocol signed 28.8.2018
13	Finland	No	N/A	Yes	PPT alone	Nordic Conventio n Protocol signed 28.8.2018
14	France	No	N/A	Yes	N/A	
15	Georgia	No	N/A	Yes	N/A	
16	Germany	No	N/A	No	N/A	Bilateral
17	Greece	No	N/A	Yes	N/A	
18	Greenland	No	N/A	No	N/A	Bilateral
19	Hungary	No	N/A	Yes	N/A	
20	India	No	N/A	Yes	N/A	
21	Ireland	No	N/A	Yes	N/A	
22	Italy	No	N/A	Yes	N/A	
23	Japan	Yes	PPT and LOB	N/A	N/A	In force 31.10.201 8
24	Korea	No	N/A	Yes	N/A	
25	Latvia	No	N/A	Yes	N/A	
26	Liechtenstein	Yes	PPT alone	N/A	N/A	
27	Lithuania	No	N/A	Yes	N/A	
28	Luxembourg	No	N/A	Yes	N/A	
29	Malta	No	N/A	Yes	N/A	
30	Mexico	No	N/A	Yes	N/A	
31	Netherlands	No	N/A	Yes	N/A	
32	Norway	No	N/A	Yes	PPT alone	Nordic Conventio n Protocol signed 28.8.2018
33	Poland	No	N/A	Yes	N/A	
34	Portugal	No	N/A	Yes	N/A	
35	Romania	No	N/A	Yes	N/A	
36	Russia	No	N/A	Yes	N/A	
37	Slovak Republic	No	N/A	Yes	N/A	
38	Slovenia	No	N/A	Yes	N/A	
39	Spain	No	N/A	Yes	N/A	
40	Sweden	No	N/A	Yes	PPT alone	Nordic Conventio n Protocol signed 28.8.2018
41	Switzerland	No	N/A	Yes	N/A	
42	Ukraine	No	N/A	Yes	N/A	
43	United Kingdom	No	N/A	Yes	N/A	
44	United States	No	N/A	Yes	N/A	
45	Viet Nam	No	N/A	Yes	N/A	

India

A. Progress in the implementation of the minimum standard

India has 95 tax agreements in force, as reported in its response to the Peer Review questionnaire. Two of those agreements, the agreements with China and Iran*, comply with the minimum standard.

India signed the MLI in 2017 and deposited its instrument of ratification on 25 June 2019, listing 93 tax agreements. The MLI entered into force for India on 1 October 2019.

India is implementing the minimum standard through the inclusion of the preamble statement and the PPT combined with the LOB.[71]

The agreements that will be modified by the MLI will come into compliance with the minimum standard once the provisions of the MLI take effect.

B. Implementation issues

No jurisdiction has raised any concerns about their agreements with India.

Summary of the jurisdiction response – India

	Treaty partners	Compliance with the standard	If compliant, the alternative implemented	Signature of a complying instrument	The alternative implemented through the complying instrument (if not the MLI)	Comments
1	Albania*	No	N/A	Yes	N/A	
2	Armenia	No	N/A	Yes	N/A	
3	Australia	No	N/A	Yes	N/A	
4	Austria	No	N/A	Yes	N/A	
5	Bangladesh*	No	N/A	Yes	N/A	
6	Belarus*	No	N/A	Yes	N/A	
7	Belgium	No	N/A	Yes	N/A	
8	Bhutan*	No	N/A	Yes	N/A	
9	Botswana	No	N/A	Yes	N/A	
10	Brazil	No	N/A	Yes	N/A	
11	Bulgaria	No	N/A	Yes	N/A	
12	Canada	No	N/A	Yes	N/A	
13	China (People's Republic of)	Yes	PPT alone	N/A	N/A	
14	Colombia	No	N/A	Yes	N/A	
15	Croatia	No	N/A	Yes	N/A	
16	Cyprus*	No	N/A	Yes	N/A	
17	Czech Republic	No	N/A	Yes	N/A	
18	Denmark	No	N/A	Yes	N/A	
19	Egypt	No	N/A	Yes	N/A	
20	Estonia	No	N/A	Yes	N/A	
21	Ethiopia*	No	N/A	Yes	N/A	

22	Fiji*	No	N/A	Yes	N/A	
23	Finland	No	N/A	Yes	N/A	
24	France	No	N/A	Yes	N/A	
25	Georgia	No	N/A	Yes	N/A	
26	Germany	No	N/A	Yes	N/A	
27	Greece	No	N/A	Yes	N/A	
28	Hong Kong (China)	No	N/A	Yes	N/A	
29	Hungary	No	N/A	Yes	N/A	
30	Iceland	No	N/A	Yes	N/A	
31	Indonesia	No	N/A	Yes	N/A	
32	Iran*	Yes	PPT alone	N/A	N/A	
33	Ireland	No	N/A	Yes	N/A	
34	Israel	No	N/A	Yes	N/A	
35	Italy	No	N/A	Yes	N/A	
36	Japan	No	N/A	Yes	N/A	
37	Jordan*	No	N/A	Yes	N/A	
38	Kazakhstan	No	N/A	Yes	N/A	
39	Kenya	No	N/A	Yes	N/A	
40	Korea	No	N/A	Yes	N/A	
41	Kuwait*	No	N/A	Yes	N/A	
42	Kyrgyzstan*	No	N/A	Yes	N/A	
43	Latvia	No	N/A	Yes	N/A	
44	Libya*	No	N/A	Yes	N/A	
45	Lithuania	No	N/A	Yes	N/A	
46	Luxembourg	No	N/A	Yes	N/A	
47	North Macedonia	No	N/A	Yes	N/A	
48	Malaysia	No	N/A	Yes	N/A	
49	Malta	No	N/A	Yes	N/A	
50	Mauritius	No	N/A	Yes	N/A	
51	Mexico	No	N/A	Yes	N/A	
52	Mongolia	No	N/A	Yes	N/A	
53	Montenegro*	No	N/A	Yes	N/A	
54	Morocco	No	N/A	Yes	N/A	
55	Mozambique*	No	N/A	Yes	N/A	
56	Myanmar*	No	N/A	Yes	N/A	
57	Namibia*	No	N/A	Yes	N/A	
58	Nepal*	No	N/A	Yes	N/A	
59	Netherlands	No	N/A	Yes	N/A	
60	New Zealand	No	N/A	Yes	N/A	
61	Norway	No	N/A	Yes	N/A	
62	Oman	No	N/A	Yes	N/A	
63	Philippines*	No	N/A	Yes	N/A	
64	Poland	No	N/A	Yes	N/A	
65	Portugal	No	N/A	Yes	N/A	
66	Qatar	No	N/A	Yes	N/A	
67	Romania	No	N/A	Yes	N/A	
68	Russia	No	N/A	Yes	N/A	
69	Saudi Arabia	No	N/A	Yes	N/A	
70	Serbia	No	N/A	Yes	N/A	
71	Singapore	No	N/A	Yes	N/A	
72	Slovak Republic	No	N/A	Yes	N/A	
73	Slovenia	No	N/A	Yes	N/A	
74	South Africa	No	N/A	Yes	N/A	

75	Spain	No	N/A	Yes	N/A	
76	Sri Lanka	No	N/A	Yes	N/A	
77	Sudan*	No	N/A	Yes	N/A	
78	Sweden	No	N/A	Yes	N/A	
79	Switzerland	No	N/A	Yes	N/A	
80	Syrian Arab Republic*	No	N/A	Yes	N/A	
81	Tajikistan*	No	N/A	Yes	N/A	
82	Tanzania*	No	N/A	Yes	N/A	
83	Thailand	No	N/A	Yes	N/A	
84	Trinidad and Tobago	No	N/A	Yes	N/A	
85	Turkey	No	N/A	Yes	N/A	
86	Turkmenistan*	No	N/A	Yes	N/A	
87	Uganda*	No	N/A	Yes	N/A	
88	Ukraine	No	N/A	Yes	N/A	
89	United Arab Emirates	No	N/A	Yes	N/A	
90	United Kingdom	No	N/A	Yes	N/A	
91	United States	No	N/A	Yes	N/A	
92	Uruguay	No	N/A	Yes	N/A	
93	Uzbekistan*	No	N/A	Yes	N/A	
94	Viet Nam	No	N/A	Yes	N/A	
95	Zambia	No	N/A	Yes	N/A	

Indonesia

A. Progress in the implementation of the minimum standard

Indonesia has 68 tax agreements in force, as reported in its response to the Peer Review questionnaire.

Indonesia signed the MLI in 2017, listing 47 tax agreements.[72]

Indonesia is implementing the minimum standard through the inclusion of the preamble statement and the PPT.[73]

The agreements that will be modified by the MLI will come into compliance with the minimum standard once the provisions of the MLI take effect.

B. Implementation issues

No jurisdiction has raised any concerns about their agreements with Indonesia.

Summary of the jurisdiction response – Indonesia

	Treaty partners	Compliance with the standard	If compliant, the alternative implemented	Signature of a complying instrument	The alternative implemented through the complying instrument (if not the MLI)	Comments
1	Algeria*	No	N/A	No	N/A	
2	Armenia	No	N/A	Yes	N/A	
3	Australia	No	N/A	Yes	N/A	
4	Austria	No	N/A	No	N/A	
5	Bangladesh*	No	N/A	No	N/A	
6	Belarus*	No	N/A	No	N/A	
7	Belgium	No	N/A	Yes	N/A	
8	Brunei Darussalam	No	N/A	Yes	N/A	Brunei Darussalam is not signatory to the MLI
9	Bulgaria	No	N/A	Yes	N/A	
10	Canada	No	N/A	Yes	N/A	
11	China (People's Republic of)	No	N/A	Yes	N/A	
12	Chinese Taipei*	No	N/A	No	N/A	
13	Croatia	No	N/A	Yes	N/A	
14	Czech Republic	No	N/A	Yes	N/A	
15	Democratic People's Republic of Korea*	No	N/A	No	N/A	
16	Denmark	No	N/A	Yes	N/A	
17	Egypt	No	N/A	Yes	N/A	
18	Finland	No	N/A	Yes	N/A	
19	France	No	N/A	Yes	N/A	
20	Germany	No	N/A	No	N/A	
21	Hong Kong (China)	No	N/A	Yes	N/A	
22	Hungary	No	N/A	Yes	N/A	

23	India	No	N/A	Yes	N/A	
24	Iran*	No	N/A	No	N/A	
25	Italy	No	N/A	Yes	N/A	
26	Japan	No	N/A	Yes	N/A	
27	Jordan*	No	N/A	No	N/A	
28	Korea	No	N/A	Yes	N/A	
29	Kuwait*	No	N/A	No	N/A	
30	Lao People's Democratic Republic*	No	N/A	Yes	N/A	Lao People's Democratic Republic* is not signatory to the MLI
31	Luxembourg	No	N/A	Yes	N/A	
32	Malaysia	No	N/A	Yes	N/A	
33	Mexico	No	N/A	Yes	N/A	
34	Mongolia	No	N/A	No	N/A	
35	Morocco	No	N/A	No	N/A	
36	Netherlands	No	N/A	Yes	N/A	
37	New Zealand	No	N/A	Yes	N/A	
38	Norway	No	N/A	Yes	N/A	Norway has not listed Indonesia
39	Pakistan	No	N/A	Yes	N/A	
40	Papua New Guinea	No	N/A	No	N/A	
41	Philippines*	No	N/A	Yes	N/A	Philippines* is not signatory to the MLI
42	Poland	No	N/A	Yes	N/A	
43	Portugal	No	N/A	Yes	N/A	
44	Qatar	No	N/A	Yes	N/A	
45	Romania	No	N/A	Yes	N/A	
46	Russia	No	N/A	Yes	N/A	
47	Saudi Arabia	No	N/A	No	N/A	
48	Seychelles	No	N/A	Yes	N/A	
49	Singapore	No	N/A	Yes	N/A	
50	Slovak Republic	No	N/A	Yes	N/A	
51	South Africa	No	N/A	Yes	N/A	
52	Spain	No	N/A	Yes	N/A	
53	Sri Lanka	No	N/A	No	N/A	
54	Sudan*	No	N/A	No	N/A	
55	Suriname*	No	N/A	No	N/A	
56	Sweden	No	N/A	Yes	N/A	
57	Switzerland	No	N/A	Yes	N/A	Switzerland has not listed Indonesia
58	Syrian Arab Republic*	No	N/A	No	N/A	
59	Thailand	No	N/A	Yes	N/A	Thailand is not signatory to the MLI
60	Tunisia	No	N/A	No	N/A	
61	Turkey	No	N/A	Yes	N/A	
62	Ukraine	No	N/A	No	N/A	
63	United Arab Emirates	No	N/A	Yes	N/A	
64	United Kingdom	No	N/A	Yes	N/A	
65	United States	No	N/A	Yes	N/A	United States is not signatory to the MLI
66	Uzbekistan*	No	N/A	No	N/A	
67	Venezuela*	No	N/A	No	N/A	
68	Viet Nam	No	N/A	Yes	N/A	Viet Nam is not signatory to the MLI

Ireland

A. Progress in the implementation of the minimum standard

Ireland has 73 tax agreements in force, as reported in its response to the Peer Review questionnaire.

Ireland signed the MLI in 2017, listing 70 tax agreements.[74] The MLI entered into force for Ireland on 1 May 2019.

Ireland is implementing the minimum standard through the inclusion of the preamble statement and the PPT.[75]

The agreements that will be modified by the MLI will come into compliance with the minimum standard once the provisions of the MLI take effect. Several agreements are expected to become compliant with the minimum standard by the end of 2019.

Ireland also signed bilateral complying instruments with respect to two of its agreements, the agreements with the Netherlands and Switzerland.

Ireland indicated in its response to the Peer Review questionnaire that bilateral negotiations would be used with respect to its agreement with Germany.

B. Implementation issues

No jurisdiction has raised any concerns about their agreements with Ireland.

Summary of the jurisdiction response – Ireland

	Treaty partners	Compliance with the standard	If compliant, the alternative implemented	Signature of a complying instrument	The alternative implemented through the complying instrument (if not the MLI)	Comments
1	Albania*	No	N/A	Yes	N/A	
2	Armenia	No	N/A	Yes	N/A	
3	Australia	No	N/A	Yes	N/A	
4	Austria	No	N/A	Yes	N/A	
5	Bahrain	No	N/A	Yes	N/A	
6	Belarus*	No	N/A	Yes	N/A	
7	Belgium	No	N/A	Yes	N/A	
8	Bosnia and Herzegovina*	No	N/A	Yes	N/A	
9	Botswana	No	N/A	Yes	N/A	
10	Bulgaria	No	N/A	Yes	N/A	
11	Canada	No	N/A	Yes	N/A	
12	Chile	No	N/A	Yes	N/A	
13	China (People's Republic of)	No	N/A	Yes	N/A	
14	Croatia	No	N/A	Yes	N/A	
15	Cyprus*	No	N/A	Yes	N/A	

16	Czech Republic	No	N/A	Yes	N/A	
17	Denmark	No	N/A	Yes	N/A	
18	Egypt	No	N/A	Yes	N/A	
19	Estonia	No	N/A	Yes	N/A	
20	Ethiopia*	No	N/A	Yes	N/A	
21	Finland	No	N/A	Yes	N/A	
22	France	No	N/A	Yes	N/A	
23	Georgia	No	N/A	Yes	N/A	
24	Germany	No	N/A	No	N/A	Protocol implementing the minimum standard is awaiting signature.
25	Greece	No	N/A	Yes	N/A	
26	Hong Kong (China)	No	N/A	Yes	N/A	
27	Hungary	No	N/A	Yes	N/A	
28	Iceland	No	N/A	Yes	N/A	
29	India	No	N/A	Yes	N/A	
30	Israel	No	N/A	Yes	N/A	
31	Italy	No	N/A	Yes	N/A	
32	Japan	No	N/A	Yes	N/A	
33	Kazakhstan	No	N/A	Yes	N/A	Partial compliance with minimum standard. PPT included; preamble missing.
34	Korea	No	N/A	Yes	N/A	
35	Kuwait*	No	N/A	Yes	N/A	
36	Latvia	No	N/A	Yes	N/A	
37	Lithuania	No	N/A	Yes	N/A	
38	Luxembourg	No	N/A	Yes	N/A	
39	North Macedonia	No	N/A	Yes	N/A	
40	Malaysia	No	N/A	Yes	N/A	
41	Malta	No	N/A	Yes	N/A	
42	Mexico	No	N/A	Yes	N/A	
43	Moldova*	No	N/A	Yes	N/A	
44	Montenegro*	No	N/A	Yes	N/A	
45	Morocco	No	N/A	Yes	N/A	
46	Netherlands	No	N/A	Yes	PPT alone	It is anticipated that new treaty incorporating the minimum standard will be signed in June 2019.
47	New Zealand	No	N/A	Yes	N/A	
48	Norway	No	N/A	Yes	N/A	
49	Pakistan	No	N/A	Yes	N/A	
50	Panama	No	N/A	Yes	N/A	
51	Poland	No	N/A	Yes	N/A	

52	Portugal	No	N/A	Yes	N/A	
53	Qatar	No	N/A	Yes	N/A	
54	Romania	No	N/A	Yes	N/A	
55	Russia	No	N/A	Yes	N/A	
56	Saudi Arabia	No	N/A	Yes	N/A	
57	Serbia	No	N/A	Yes	N/A	
58	Singapore	No	N/A	Yes	N/A	
59	Slovak Republic	No	N/A	Yes	N/A	
60	Slovenia	No	N/A	Yes	N/A	
61	South Africa	No	N/A	Yes	N/A	
62	Spain	No	N/A	Yes	N/A	
63	Sweden	No	N/A	Yes	N/A	
64	Switzerland	No	N/A	Yes	PPT alone	It is anticipated that Protocol incorporating the minimum standard will be signed in June 2019.
65	Thailand	No	N/A	Yes	N/A	
66	Turkey	No	N/A	Yes	N/A	
67	Ukraine	No	N/A	Yes	N/A	
68	United Arab Emirates	No	N/A	Yes	N/A	
69	United Kingdom	No	N/A	Yes	N/A	
70	United States	No	N/A	Yes	N/A	
71	Uzbekistan*	No	N/A	Yes	N/A	
72	Viet Nam	No	N/A	Yes	N/A	
73	Zambia	No	N/A	Yes	N/A	

Isle of Man

A. Progress in the implementation of the minimum standard

The Isle of Man has ten tax agreements in force, as reported in its response to the Peer Review questionnaire. Its agreement with the United Kingdom complies with the minimum standard.

The Isle of Man signed the MLI in 2017, and deposited its instrument of ratification on 27 October 2017, listing eight tax agreements. The MLI has entered into force for the Isle of Man on 1 July 2018.

The Isle of Man is implementing the minimum standard through the inclusion of the preamble statement and the PPT.[76]

The agreements that will be modified by the MLI will come into compliance with the minimum standard once the provisions of the MLI take effect. Some agreements listed under the MLI are expected to become compliant with the minimum standard by the end of 2019.

The Isle of Man indicated in its response to the Peer Review questionnaire that bilateral negotiations would be used for its arrangements with other Crown Dependencies.

B. Implementation issues

No jurisdiction has raised any concerns about their agreements with the Isle of Man.

Summary of the jurisdiction response – Isle of Man

	Treaty partners	Compliance with the standard	If compliant, the alternative implemented	Signature of a complying instrument	The alternative implemented through the complying instrument (if not the MLI)	Comments
1	Bahrain	No	N/A	Yes	N/A	
2	Estonia	No	N/A	Yes	N/A	
3	Guernsey	No	N/A	No	N/A	Bilateral negotiations ongoing
4	Jersey	No	N/A	No	N/A	Bilateral negotiations ongoing
5	Luxembourg	No	N/A	Yes	N/A	
6	Malta	No	N/A	Yes	N/A	
7	Qatar	No	N/A	Yes	N/A	
8	Seychelles	No	N/A	Yes	N/A	
9	Singapore	No	N/A	Yes	N/A	
10	United Kingdom	Yes	PPT alone	N/A	N/A	

Israel

A. Progress in the implementation of the minimum standard

Israel has 55 tax agreements in force, as reported in its response to the Peer Review questionnaire. Seven of those agreements, the agreements with Austria, France, Japan, Lithuania, Poland, Slovak Republic and Slovenia, comply with the minimum standard.

Israel signed the MLI in 2017 and deposited its instrument of ratification on 13 September 2018, listing of 52 tax agreements.[77] The MLI entered into force for Israel on 1 January 2019.

Israel is implementing the minimum standard through the inclusion of the preamble statement and the PPT.[78]

The agreements modified by the MLI come into compliance with the minimum standard once the provisions of the MLI take effect. Other agreements listed under the MLI are expected to become compliant with the minimum standard by the end of 2019. Israel indicated in its response to the Peer Review questionnaire that bilateral negotiations would be used for its agreements with Germany and Switzerland.

B. Implementation issues

No jurisdiction has raised any concerns about their agreements with Israel.

Summary of the jurisdiction response – Israel

	Treaty partners	Compliance with the standard	If compliant, the alternative implemented	Signature of a complying instrument	The alternative implemented through the complying instrument (if not the MLI)	Comments
1	Armenia	No	N/A	Yes	N/A	
2	Austria	Yes	PPT alone	N/A	N/A	
3	Azerbaijan*	No	N/A	Yes	N/A	
4	Belarus*	No	N/A	Yes	N/A	
5	Belgium	No	N/A	Yes	N/A	
6	Brazil	No	N/A	Yes	N/A	
7	Bulgaria	No	N/A	Yes	N/A	
8	Canada	No	N/A	Yes	N/A	
9	China (People's Republic of)	No	N/A	Yes	N/A	
10	Chinese Taipei*	No	N/A	Yes	N/A	
11	Croatia	No	N/A	Yes	N/A	
12	Czech Republic	No	N/A	Yes	N/A	
13	Denmark	No	N/A	Yes	N/A	
14	Estonia	No	N/A	Yes	N/A	
15	Ethiopia*	No	N/A	Yes	N/A	
16	Finland	No	N/A	Yes	N/A	
17	France	Yes	PPT alone	N/A	N/A	
18	Georgia	No	N/A	Yes	N/A	

19	Germany	No	N/A	No	N/A	
20	Greece	No	N/A	Yes	N/A	
21	Hungary	No	N/A	Yes	N/A	
22	India	No	N/A	Yes	N/A	
23	Ireland	No	N/A	Yes	N/A	
24	Italy	No	N/A	Yes	N/A	
25	Jamaica	No	N/A	Yes	N/A	
26	Japan	Yes	PPT alone	N/A	N/A	
27	Korea	No	N/A	Yes	N/A	
28	Latvia	No	N/A	Yes	N/A	
29	Lithuania	Yes	PPT alone	N/A	N/A	
30	Luxembourg	No	N/A	Yes	N/A	
31	Malta	No	N/A	Yes	N/A	
32	Mexico	No	N/A	Yes	N/A	
33	Moldova*	No	N/A	Yes	N/A	
34	Netherlands	No	N/A	Yes	N/A	
35	Norway	No	N/A	Yes	N/A	
36	Panama	No	N/A	Yes	N/A	
37	Philippines*	No	N/A	Yes	N/A	
38	Poland	Yes	PPT alone	N/A	N/A	
39	Portugal	No	N/A	Yes	N/A	
40	Romania	No	N/A	Yes	N/A	
41	Russia	No	N/A	Yes	N/A	
42	Singapore	No	N/A	Yes	N/A	
43	Slovak Republic	Yes	PPT alone	N/A	N/A	
44	Slovenia	Yes	PPT alone	N/A	N/A	
45	South Africa	No	N/A	Yes	N/A	
46	Spain	No	N/A	Yes	N/A	
47	Sweden	No	N/A	Yes	N/A	
48	Switzerland	No	N/A	No	N/A	
49	Thailand	No	N/A	Yes	N/A	
50	Turkey	No	N/A	Yes	N/A	
51	Ukraine	No	N/A	Yes	N/A	
52	United Kingdom	No	N/A	Yes	PPT alone	
53	United States	No	N/A	Yes	N/A	
54	Uzbekistan*	No	N/A	Yes	N/A	
55	Viet Nam	No	N/A	Yes	N/A	

Italy

A. Progress in the implementation of the minimum standard

Italy has 99 tax agreements in force, as reported in its response to the Peer Review questionnaire. Its agreement with Chile complies with the minimum standard.

Italy signed the MLI in 2017, listing 80 tax agreements.[79]

Italy is implementing the minimum standard through the inclusion of the preamble statement and the PPT.[80]

The agreements that will be modified by the MLI will come into compliance with the minimum standard once the provisions of the MLI take effect.

Italy indicated in its response to the Peer Review questionnaire that the agreements not listed under the MLI were concluded with treaty partners that were not ad hoc Group members at the time of Italy's signature of the MLI.

B. Implementation issues

No jurisdiction has raised any concerns about their agreements with Italy.

Summary of the jurisdiction response – Italy

	Treaty partners	Compliance with the standard	If compliant, the alternative implemented	Signature of a complying instrument	The alternative implemented through the complying instrument (if not the MLI)	Comments
1	Albania*	No	N/A	No	N/A	This agreement is likely to be included in the Italian CTA revised list which has not been updated at the current date.
2	Algeria*	No	N/A	No	N/A	This agreement is likely to be included in the Italian CTA revised list which has not been updated at the current date.
3	Argentina	No	N/A	Yes	N/A	

4	Armenia	No	N/A	Yes	N/A	
5	Australia	No	N/A	Yes	N/A	
6	Austria	No	N/A	Yes	N/A	
7	Azerbaijan*	No	N/A	Yes	N/A	
8	Bangladesh*	No	N/A	Yes	N/A	
9	Barbados	No	N/A	Yes	N/A	
10	Belarus*	No	N/A	No	N/A	For the time being, Italy has included in the CTA list only Jurisdictions that were members of the Ad Hoc Group on MLI at the date of the signature of MLI by Italy.
11	Belgium	No	N/A	Yes	N/A	
12	Bosnia and Herzegovina*	No	N/A	Yes	N/A	
13	Brazil	No	N/A	Yes	N/A	
14	Bulgaria	No	N/A	Yes	N/A	
15	Canada	No	N/A	Yes	N/A	
16	Chile	Yes	PPT alone	N/A	N/A	
17	China (People's Republic of)	No	N/A	Yes	PPT alone	
18	Congo	No	N/A	No	N/A	For the time being, Italy has included in the CTA list only Jurisdictions that were members of the Ad Hoc Group on MLI at the date of the signature of MLI by Italy.
19	Cote d'Ivoire	No	N/A	Yes	N/A	
20	Croatia	No	N/A	Yes	N/A	
21	Cyprus*	No	N/A	Yes	N/A	
22	Czech Republic	No	N/A	Yes	N/A	
23	Denmark	No	N/A	Yes	N/A	
24	Ecuador*	No	N/A	No	N/A	For the time being, Italy has included in the CTA list only Jurisdictions that were members of the Ad Hoc Group on

						MLI at the date of the signature of MLI by Italy.
25	Egypt	No	N/A	Yes	N/A	
26	Estonia	No	N/A	Yes	N/A	
27	Ethiopia*	No	N/A	No	N/A	For the time being, Italy has included in the CTA list only Jurisdictions that were members of the Ad Hoc Group on MLI at the date of the signature of MLI by Italy.
28	Finland	No	N/A	Yes	N/A	
29	France	No	N/A	Yes	N/A	
30	Georgia	No	N/A	Yes	N/A	
31	Germany	No	N/A	Yes	N/A	
32	Ghana*	No	N/A	No	N/A	For the time being, Italy has included in the CTA list only Jurisdictions that were members of the Ad Hoc Group on MLI at the date of the signature of MLI by Italy.
33	Greece	No	N/A	Yes	N/A	
34	Hong Kong (China)	No	N/A	Yes	N/A	
35	Hungary	No	N/A	Yes	N/A	
36	Iceland	No	N/A	Yes	N/A	
37	India	No	N/A	Yes	N/A	
38	Indonesia	No	N/A	Yes	N/A	
39	Ireland	No	N/A	Yes	N/A	
40	Israel	No	N/A	Yes	N/A	
41	Japan	No	N/A	Yes	N/A	
42	Jordan*	No	N/A	Yes	N/A	
43	Kazakhstan	No	N/A	Yes	N/A	
44	Korea	No	N/A	Yes	N/A	
45	Kuwait*	No	N/A	Yes	N/A	The other Jurisdiction has not notified this Agreement as a Covered Tax

						Agreement for the purpose of MLI,
46	Kyrgyzstan*	No	N/A	No	N/A	For the time being, Italy has included in the CTA list only Jurisdictions that were members of the Ad Hoc Group on MLI at the date of the signature of MLI by Italy.
47	Latvia	No	N/A	Yes	N/A	
48	Lebanon*	No	N/A	Yes	N/A	
49	Lithuania	No	N/A	Yes	N/A	
50	Luxembourg	No	N/A	Yes	N/A	
51	North Macedonia	No	N/A	No	N/A	For the time being, Italy has included in the CTA list only Jurisdictions that were members of the Ad Hoc Group on MLI at the date of the signature of MLI by Italy.
52	Malaysia	No	N/A	Yes	N/A	
53	Malta	No	N/A	Yes	N/A	
54	Mauritius	No	N/A	Yes	N/A	
55	Mexico	No	N/A	Yes	N/A	
56	Moldova*	No	N/A	Yes	N/A	
57	Montenegro*	No	N/A	No	N/A	For the time being, Italy has included in the CTA list only Jurisdictions that were members of the Ad Hoc Group on MLI at the date of the signature of MLI by Italy.
58	Morocco	No	N/A	Yes	N/A	
59	Mozambique*	No	N/A	No	N/A	For the time being, Italy has

						included in the CTA list only Jurisdictions that were members of the Ad Hoc Group on MLI at the date of the signature of MLI by Italy.
60	Netherlands	No	N/A	Yes	N/A	
61	New Zealand	No	N/A	Yes	N/A	
62	Norway	No	N/A	Yes	N/A	The other Jurisdiction has not notified this agreement as a Covered Tax Agreement for the purpose of MLI.
63	Oman	No	N/A	No	N/A	This agreement is likely to be included in the Italian CTA revised list which has not been updated at the current date.
64	Pakistan	No	N/A	Yes	N/A	
65	Panama	No	N/A	No	N/A	This agreement is likely to be included in the Italian CTA revised list which has not been updated at the current date.
66	Philippines*	No	N/A	Yes	N/A	
67	Poland	No	N/A	Yes	N/A	
68	Portugal	No	N/A	Yes	N/A	
69	Qatar	No	N/A	Yes	N/A	
70	Romania	No	N/A	Yes	N/A	
71	Russia	No	N/A	Yes	N/A	
72	San Marino	No	N/A	Yes	N/A	
73	Saudi Arabia	No	N/A	Yes	N/A	
74	Senegal	No	N/A	Yes	N/A	
75	Serbia	No	N/A	Yes	N/A	
76	Singapore	No	N/A	Yes	N/A	

77	Slovak Republic	No	N/A	Yes	N/A	
78	Slovenia	No	N/A	Yes	N/A	
79	South Africa	No	N/A	Yes	N/A	
80	Spain	No	N/A	Yes	N/A	
81	Sri Lanka	No	N/A	Yes	N/A	
82	Sweden	No	N/A	Yes	N/A	
83	Switzerland	No	N/A	Yes	N/A	
84	Syrian Arab Republic*	No	N/A	No	N/A	For the time being, Italy has included in the CTA list only Jurisdictions that were members of the Ad Hoc Group on MLI at the date of the signature of MLI by Italy.
85	Tajikistan*	No	N/A	No	N/A	For the time being, Italy has included in the CTA list only Jurisdictions that were members of the Ad Hoc Group on MLI at the date of the signature of MLI by Italy.
86	Tanzania*	No	N/A	Yes	N/A	
87	Thailand	No	N/A	Yes	N/A	
88	Trinidad and Tobago	No	N/A	No	N/A	For the time being, Italy has included in the CTA list only Jurisdictions that were members of the Ad Hoc Group on MLI at the date of the signature of MLI by Italy.
89	Tunisia	No	N/A	Yes	N/A	
90	Turkey	No	N/A	Yes	N/A	
91	Uganda*	No	N/A	Yes	N/A	
92	Ukraine	No	N/A	Yes	N/A	
93	United Arab Emirates	No	N/A	Yes	N/A	
94	United Kingdom	No	N/A	Yes	N/A	

95	United States	No	N/A	Yes	N/A	The Agreement already contains an LOB. However the preamble is missing but it could be included subject to the signature of the MLI by the other Jurisdiction.
96	Uzbekistan*	No	N/A	No	N/A	For the time being, Italy has included in the CTA list only Jurisdictions that were members of the Ad Hoc Group on MLI at the date of the signature of MLI by Italy.
97	Venezuela*	No	N/A	No	N/A	For the time being, Italy has included in the CTA list only Jurisdictions that were members of the Ad Hoc Group on MLI at the date of the signature of MLI by Italy.
98	Viet Nam	No	N/A	Yes	N/A	
99	Zambia	No	N/A	Yes	N/A	

Jamaica

A. Progress in the implementation of the minimum standard

Jamaica has 14 tax agreements in force, as reported in its response to the Peer Review questionnaire, including the multilateral agreement among the members of the CARICOM concluded with ten treaty partners (the CARICOM Agreement).[81]

Jamaica signed the MLI in 2018, listing 14 tax agreements.

Jamaica is implementing the minimum standard through the inclusion of the preamble statement and the PPT combined with the LOB.[82]

The agreements that will be modified by the MLI will come into compliance with the minimum standard once the provisions of the MLI take effect.

B. Implementation issues

Jamaica is encouraged to bring the CARICOM Agreement up to date by commencing talks among all the treaty partners.[83]

Summary of the jurisdiction response – Jamaica

	Treaty partners	Compliance with the standard	If compliant, the alternative implemented	Signature of a complying instrument	The alternative implemented through the complying instrument (if not the MLI)	Comments
1	Antigua and Barbuda	No	N/A	Yes	N/A	CARICOM
2	Barbados	No	N/A	Yes	N/A	CARICOM
3	Belize	No	N/A	Yes	N/A	CARICOM
4	Canada	No	N/A	Yes	N/A	
5	China (People's Republic of)	No	N/A	Yes	N/A	
6	Denmark	No	N/A	Yes	N/A	
7	Dominica	No	N/A	Yes	N/A	CARICOM
8	France	No	N/A	Yes	N/A	
9	Germany	No	N/A	Yes	N/A	
10	Grenada*	No	N/A	Yes	N/A	CARICOM
11	Guyana*	No	N/A	Yes	N/A	CARICOM
12	Israel	No	N/A	Yes	N/A	
13	Mexico		N/A	Yes	N/A	
14	Norway	No	N/A	Yes	N/A	
15	Saint Kitts and Nevis	No	N/A	Yes	N/A	CARICOM
16	Saint Lucia	No	N/A	Yes	N/A	CARICOM
17	Saint Vincent and the Grenadines	No	N/A	Yes	N/A	CARICOM
18	Spain	No	N/A	Yes	N/A	

19	Sweden	No	N/A	Yes	N/A	
20	Switzerland	No	N/A	Yes	N/A	
21	Trinidad and Tobago	No	N/A	Yes	N/A	CARICOM
22	United Kingdom	No	N/A	Yes	N/A	
23	United States	No	N/A	Yes	N/A	

Japan

A. Progress in the implementation of the minimum standard

Japan has 71 tax agreements in force, as reported in its response to the Peer Review questionnaire. Eighteen of those agreements, the agreements with Australia, Austria, Belgium, Chile, Denmark, Estonia, France, Germany, Iceland, Israel, Latvia, Lithuania, New Zealand, Poland, Russia, Slovak Republic, Slovenia and United Kingdom, comply with the minimum standard.

Japan signed the MLI in 2017, and deposited its instrument of ratification on 26 September 2018, listing of 39 tax agreements.[84] The MLI entered into force for Japan on 1 January 2019.

Japan is implementing the minimum standard through the inclusion of the preamble statement and the PPT for its compliant agreements with Chile, Israel, Poland, Slovak Republic and Slovenia. Japan is implementing the minimum standard through the inclusion of the preamble statement and the PPT combined with the LOB for its compliant agreements with Australia, Austria, Belgium, Denmark, Estonia, France, Germany, Iceland, Latvia, Lithuania, New Zealand, Russia and United Kingdom.[85]

The agreements modified by the MLI come into compliance with the minimum standard once the provisions of the MLI take effect. Other agreements listed under the MLI are expected to become compliant with the minimum standard by the end of 2019.

Japan also signed a bilateral complying instrument with respect to one of its agreements, the agreement with Spain.

Japan indicated in its response to the Peer Review questionnaire that the agreements not listed under the MLI were concluded with treaty partners that had not joined the MLI or had joined the MLI but not listed the agreements with Japan. Japan also indicated that it would list such agreements if the treaty partners join the MLI and list the agreements with Japan.

B. Implementation issues

No jurisdiction has raised any concerns about their agreements with Japan.

Summary of the jurisdiction response – Japan

	Treaty partners	Compliance with the standard	If compliant, the alternative implemented	Signature of a complying instrument	The alternative implemented through the complying instrument (if not the MLI)	Comments
1	Armenia	No	N/A	No	N/A	
2	Australia	Yes	PPT and LOB	N/A	N/A	
3	Austria	Yes	PPT and LOB	N/A	N/A	
4	Azerbaijan*	No	N/A	No	N/A	
5	Bangladesh*	No	N/A	No	N/A	
6	Belarus*	No	N/A	No	N/A	
7	Belgium	Yes	PPT and LOB	N/A	N/A	
8	Brazil	No	N/A	No	N/A	
9	Brunei Darussalam	No	N/A	No	N/A	

10	Bulgaria	No	N/A	Yes	N/A	
11	Canada	No	N/A	Yes	N/A	
12	Chile	Yes	PPT alone	N/A	N/A	
13	China (People's Republic of)	No	N/A	Yes	N/A	
14	Czech Republic	No	N/A	Yes	N/A	
15	Denmark	Yes	PPT and LOB	N/A	N/A	
16	Egypt	No	N/A	Yes	N/A	
17	Estonia	Yes	PPT and LOB	N/A	N/A	
18	Fiji*	No	N/A	Yes	N/A	
19	Finland	No	N/A	Yes	N/A	
20	France	Yes	PPT and LOB	N/A	N/A	
21	Georgia	No	N/A	No	N/A	
22	Germany	Yes	PPT and LOB	N/A	N/A	
23	Hong Kong (China)	No	N/A	Yes	N/A	
24	Hungary	No	N/A	Yes	N/A	
25	Iceland	Yes	PPT and LOB	N/A	N/A	
26	India	No	N/A	Yes	N/A	
27	Indonesia	No	N/A	Yes	N/A	
28	Ireland	No	N/A	Yes	N/A	
29	Israel	Yes	PPT alone	N/A	N/A	
30	Italy	No	N/A	Yes	N/A	
31	Kazakhstan	No	N/A	Yes	N/A	
32	Korea	No	N/A	Yes	N/A	
33	Kuwait*	No	N/A	Yes	N/A	
34	Kyrgyzstan*	No	N/A	No	N/A	
35	Latvia	Yes	PPT and LOB	N/A	N/A	
36	Lithuania	Yes	PPT and LOB	N/A	N/A	
37	Luxembourg	No	N/A	Yes	N/A	
38	Malaysia	No	N/A	Yes	N/A	
39	Mexico	No	N/A	Yes	N/A	
40	Moldova*	No	N/A	No	N/A	
41	Netherlands	No	N/A	Yes	N/A	
42	New Zealand	Yes	PPT and LOB	N/A	N/A	
43	Norway	No	N/A	Yes	N/A	
44	Oman	No	N/A	No	N/A	
45	Pakistan	No	N/A	Yes	N/A	
46	Philippines*	No	N/A	No	N/A	
47	Poland	Yes	PPT alone	N/A	N/A	
48	Portugal	No	N/A	Yes	N/A	
49	Qatar	No	N/A	No	N/A	
50	Romania	No	N/A	Yes	N/A	
51	Russian Federation	Yes	PPT and LOB	N/A	N/A	
52	Saudi Arabia	No	N/A	Yes	N/A	
53	Singapore	No	N/A	Yes	N/A	
54	Slovak Republic	Yes	PPT alone	N/A	N/A	
55	Slovenia	Yes	PPT alone	N/A	N/A	
56	South Africa	No	N/A	Yes	N/A	
57	Spain	No	N/A	Yes	PPT and LOB	
58	Sri Lanka	No	N/A	No	N/A	
59	Sweden	No	N/A	Yes	N/A	
60	Switzerland	No	N/A	No	N/A	

61	Tajikistan*	No	N/A	No	N/A	
62	Thailand	No	N/A	No	N/A	
63	Turkey	No	N/A	Yes	N/A	
64	Turkmenistan*	No	N/A	No	N/A	
65	Ukraine	No	N/A	Yes	N/A	
66	United Arab Emirates	No	N/A	Yes	N/A	
67	United Kingdom	Yes	PPT and LOB	N/A	N/A	
68	United States	No	N/A	No	N/A	
69	Uzbekistan*	No	N/A	No	N/A	
70	Viet Nam	No	N/A	No	N/A	
71	Zambia	No	N/A	No	N/A	

Jersey

A. Progress in the implementation of the minimum standard

Jersey has 15 tax agreements in force, as reported in its response to the Peer Review questionnaire. Two of those agreements, the agreements with Liechtenstein and the United Kingdom, comply with the minimum standard.

Jersey signed the MLI in 2017 and deposited its instrument of ratification of the MLI on 15 December 2018, listing ten tax agreements. The MLI has entered into force for Jersey on 1 July 2018.

Jersey is implementing the minimum standard through the inclusion of the preamble statement and the PPT.[86]

The agreements that will be modified by the MLI will come into compliance with the minimum standard once the provisions of the MLI take effect. Some agreements listed under the MLI are expected to become compliant with the minimum standard by the end of 2019.

B. Implementation issues

No jurisdiction has raised any concerns about their agreements with Jersey.

Summary of the jurisdiction response – Jersey

	Treaty partners	Compliance with the standard	If compliant, the alternative implemented	Signature of a complying instrument	The alternative implemented through the complying instrument (if not the MLI)	Comments
1	Cyprus*	No	N/A	Yes	N/A	
2	Estonia	No	N/A	Yes	N/A	
3	Guernsey	No	N/A	No	N/A	
4	Hong Kong (China)	No	N/A	Yes	N/A	
5	Isle of Man	No	N/A	No	N/A	
6	Liechtenstein	Yes	PPT alone	N/A	N/A	
7	Luxembourg	No	N/A	Yes	N/A	
8	Malta	No	N/A	Yes	N/A	
9	Mauritius	No	N/A	No	N/A	
10	Qatar	No	N/A	Yes	N/A	
11	Rwanda*	No	N/A	Yes	N/A	
12	Seychelles	No	N/A	Yes	N/A	
13	Singapore	No	N/A	Yes	N/A	
14	United Arab Emirates	No	N/A	Yes	N/A	
15	United Kingdom	Yes	PPT alone	N/A	N/A	

Kazakhstan

A. Progress in the implementation of the minimum standard

Kazakhstan has 54 tax agreements in force, as reported in its response to the Peer Review questionnaire.

Kazakhstan signed the MLI in 2018, listing 54 tax agreements.

Kazakhstan is implementing the minimum standard through the inclusion of the preamble statement and the PPT combined with the LOB.[87]

The agreements that will be modified by the MLI will come into compliance with the minimum standard once the provisions of the MLI take effect.

B. Implementation issues

No jurisdiction has raised any concerns about their agreements with Kazakhstan.

Summary of the jurisdiction response – Kazakhstan

	Treaty partners	Compliance with the standard	If compliant, the alternative implemented	Signature of a complying instrument	The alternative implemented through the complying instrument (if not the MLI)	Comments
1	Armenia	No	N/A	Yes	N/A	
2	Austria	No	N/A	Yes	N/A	
3	Azerbaijan*	No	N/A	Yes	N/A	
4	Belarus*	No	N/A	Yes	N/A	
5	Belgium	No	N/A	Yes	N/A	
6	Bulgaria	No	N/A	Yes	N/A	
7	Canada	No	N/A	Yes	N/A	
8	China (People's Republic of)	No	N/A	Yes	N/A	
9	Croatia	No	N/A	Yes	N/A	
10	Czech Republic	No	N/A	Yes	N/A	
11	Estonia	No	N/A	Yes	N/A	
12	Finland	No	N/A	Yes	N/A	
13	France	No	N/A	Yes	N/A	
14	Georgia	No	N/A	Yes	N/A	
15	Germany	No	N/A	Yes	N/A	
16	Hungary	No	N/A	Yes	N/A	
17	India	No	N/A	Yes	N/A	
18	Iran*	No	N/A	Yes	N/A	
19	Ireland	No	N/A	Yes	N/A	
20	Italy	No	N/A	Yes	N/A	
21	Japan	No	N/A	Yes	N/A	
22	Korea	No	N/A	Yes	N/A	
23	Kyrgyzstan*	No	N/A	Yes	N/A	

24	Latvia	No	N/A	Yes	N/A	
25	Lithuania	No	N/A	Yes	N/A	
26	Luxembourg	No	N/A	Yes	N/A	
27	North Macedonia	No	N/A	Yes	N/A	
28	Malaysia	No	N/A	Yes	N/A	
29	Moldova*	No	N/A	Yes	N/A	
30	Mongolia	No	N/A	Yes	N/A	
31	Netherlands	No	N/A	Yes	N/A	
32	Norway	No	N/A	Yes	N/A	
33	Pakistan	No	N/A	Yes	N/A	
34	Poland	No	N/A	Yes	N/A	
35	Qatar	No	N/A	Yes	N/A	
36	Romania	No	N/A	Yes	N/A	
37	Russia	No	N/A	Yes	N/A	
38	Saudi Arabia	No	N/A	Yes	N/A	
39	Serbia	No	N/A	Yes	N/A	
40	Singapore	No	N/A	Yes	N/A	
41	Slovak Republic	No	N/A	Yes	N/A	
42	Slovenia	No	N/A	Yes	N/A	
43	Spain	No	N/A	Yes	N/A	
44	Sweden	No	N/A	Yes	N/A	
45	Switzerland	No	N/A	Yes	N/A	
46	Tajikistan*	No	N/A	Yes	N/A	
47	Turkey	No	N/A	Yes	N/A	
48	Turkmenistan*	No	N/A	Yes	N/A	
49	Ukraine	No	N/A	Yes	N/A	
50	United Arab Emirates	No	N/A	Yes	N/A	
51	United Kingdom	No	N/A	Yes	N/A	
52	United States	No	N/A	Yes	N/A	
53	Uzbekistan*	No	N/A	Yes	N/A	
54	Viet Nam	No	N/A	Yes	N/A	

Kenya

A. Progress in the implementation of the minimum standard

Kenya has 15 tax agreements in force, as reported in its response to the Peer Review questionnaire.

None of Kenya's agreements comply with the minimum standard or are subject to a complying instrument.

B. Implementation issues

No jurisdiction has raised any concerns about their agreements with Kenya.

Kenya is encouraged to implement the minimum standard in its agreements.

Summary of the jurisdiction response – Kenya

	Treaty partners	Compliance with the standard	If compliant, the alternative implemented	Signature of a complying instrument	The alternative implemented through the complying instrument (if not the MLI)	Comments
1	Canada	No	N/A	No	N/A	
2	Denmark	No	N/A	No	N/A	
3	France	No	N/A	No	N/A	
4	Germany	No	N/A	No	N/A	
5	India	No	N/A	No	N/A	
6	Iran*	No	N/A	No	N/A	
7	Korea	No	N/A	No	N/A	
8	Norway	No	N/A	No	N/A	
9	Qatar	No	N/A	No	N/A	
10	Seychelles	No	N/A	No	N/A	
11	South Africa	No	N/A	No	N/A	
12	Sweden	No	N/A	No	N/A	
13	United Arab Emirates	No	N/A	No	N/A	
14	United Kingdom	No	N/A	No	N/A	
15	Zambia	No	N/A	No	N/A	

Korea

A. Progress in the implementation of the minimum standard

Korea has 93 tax agreements in force, as reported in its response to the Peer Review questionnaire.

Korea signed the MLI in 2017, listing 63 tax agreements.

Korea is implementing the minimum standard through the inclusion of the preamble statement and the PPT.[88]

The agreements that will be modified by the MLI will come into compliance with the minimum standard once the provisions of the MLI take effect.

Korea also signed a bilateral complying instrument with the Czech Republic, Singapore, Switzerland, Turkmenistan*, the United Arab Emirates, and Uzbekistan*.

Korea indicated in its response to the Peer Review questionnaire that bilateral negotiations would be used for its agreements with Albania*, Austria, Belarus*, Brazil, Brunei Darussalam, Ecuador*, Ethiopia*, Germany, Iran*, Kyrgyzstan*, Lao*, Myanmar*, Nepal*, Norway, Tajikistan*, Turkey, Venezuela* and Viet Nam.

B. Implementation issues

No jurisdiction has raised any concerns about their agreements with Korea.

Summary of the jurisdiction response – Korea

	Treaty partners	Compliance with the standard	If compliant, the alternative implemented	Signature of a complying instrument	The alternative implemented through the complying instrument (if not the MLI)	Comments
1	Albania*	No	N/A	No	N/A	
2	Algeria*	No	N/A	No	N/A	to be additionally covered by MLI when MLI is ratified
3	Australia	No	N/A	No	N/A	to be additionally covered by MLI when MLI is ratified
4	Austria	No	N/A	No	N/A	Bilateral negotiation completed
5	Azerbaijan*	No	N/A	Yes	N/A	
6	Bahrain	No	N/A	No	N/A	to be additionally covered by

						MLI when MLI is ratified
7	Bangladesh*	No	N/A	Yes	N/A	
8	Belarus*	No	N/A	No	N/A	
9	Belgium	No	N/A	Yes	N/A	
10	Brazil	No	N/A	No	N/A	
11	Brunei Darussalam	No	N/A	No	N/A	to be additionally covered by MLI when MLI is ratified
12	Bulgaria	No	N/A	Yes	N/A	
13	Canada	No	N/A	Yes	N/A	
14	Chile	No	N/A	Yes	N/A	
15	China (People's Republic of)	No	N/A	Yes	N/A	
16	Colombia	No	N/A	Yes	N/A	
17	Croatia	No	N/A	Yes	N/A	
18	Czech Republic	No	N/A	Yes	PPT alone	
19	Denmark	No	N/A	Yes	N/A	
20	Ecuador*	No	N/A	No	N/A	
21	Egypt	No	N/A	Yes	N/A	
22	Estonia	No	N/A	Yes	N/A	
23	Ethiopia*	No	N/A	No	N/A	
24	Fiji*	No	N/A	Yes	N/A	
25	Finland	No	N/A	Yes	N/A	
26	France	No	N/A	Yes	N/A	
27	Gabon	No	N/A	Yes	N/A	
28	Georgia	No	N/A	Yes	N/A	
29	Germany	No	N/A	Yes	N/A	to be removed from MLI CTA list when MLI is ratified Bilateral negotiation completed
30	Greece	No	N/A	Yes	N/A	
31	Hong Kong (China)	No	N/A	Yes	N/A	
32	Hungary	No	N/A	Yes	N/A	
33	Iceland	No	N/A	Yes	N/A	
34	India	No	N/A	Yes	N/A	
35	Indonesia	No	N/A	Yes	N/A	
36	Iran*	No	N/A	No	N/A	
37	Ireland	No	N/A	Yes	N/A	
38	Israel	No	N/A	Yes	N/A	
39	Italy	No	N/A	Yes	N/A	
40	Japan	No	N/A	Yes	N/A	
41	Jordan*	No	N/A	Yes	N/A	
42	Kazakhstan	No	N/A	Yes	N/A	
43	Kenya	No	N/A	No	N/A	to be additionally covered by MLI when

						MLI is ratified
44	Kuwait*	No	N/A	Yes	N/A	
45	Kyrgyzstan*	No	N/A	No	N/A	
46	Lao People's Democratic Republic*	No	N/A	No	N/A	
47	Latvia	No	N/A	Yes	N/A	
48	Lithuania	No	N/A	Yes	N/A	
49	Luxembourg	No	N/A	Yes	N/A	
50	Malaysia	No	N/A	No	N/A	to be additionally covered by MLI when MLI is ratified
51	Malta	No	N/A	Yes	N/A	
52	Mexico	No	N/A	Yes	N/A	
53	Mongolia	No	N/A	Yes	N/A	
54	Morocco	No	N/A	Yes	N/A	
55	Myanmar*	No	N/A	No	N/A	
56	Nepal*	No	N/A	No	N/A	
57	Netherlands	No	N/A	Yes	N/A	
58	New Zealand	No	N/A	Yes	N/A	
59	Norway	No	N/A	Yes	N/A	
60	Oman	No	N/A	No	N/A	to be additionally covered by MLI when MLI is ratified
61	Pakistan	No	N/A	Yes	N/A	
62	Panama	No	N/A	No	N/A	to be additionally covered by MLI when MLI is ratified
63	Papua New Guinea	No	N/A	Yes	N/A	
64	Peru	No	N/A	No	N/A	to be additionally covered by MLI when MLI is ratified
65	Philippines*	No	N/A	Yes	N/A	
66	Poland	No	N/A	Yes	N/A	
67	Portugal	No	N/A	Yes	N/A	
68	Qatar	No	N/A	Yes	N/A	
69	Romania	No	N/A	Yes	N/A	
70	Russia	No	N/A	Yes	N/A	
71	Saudi Arabia	No	N/A	Yes	N/A	
72	Serbia	No	N/A	Yes	N/A	
73	Singapore	No	N/A	Yes	PPT alone	
74	Slovak Republic	No	N/A	Yes	N/A	
75	Slovenia	No	N/A	Yes	N/A	
76	South Africa	No	N/A	Yes	N/A	
77	Spain	No	N/A	Yes	N/A	
78	Sri Lanka	No	N/A	Yes	N/A	

79	Sweden	No	N/A	Yes	N/A	
80	Switzerland	No	N/A	Yes	PPT alone	to be removed from MLI CTA list when MLI is ratified
81	Tajikistan*	No	N/A	No	N/A	
82	Thailand	No	N/A	Yes	N/A	
83	Tunisia	No	N/A	Yes	N/A	
84	Turkey	No	N/A	No	N/A	Bilateral negotiation completed
85	Turkmenistan*	No	N/A	Yes	PPT alone	
86	Ukraine	No	N/A	Yes	N/A	
87	United Arab Emirates	No	N/A	Yes	PPT alone	to be additionally covered by MLI when MLI is ratified
88	United Kingdom	No	N/A	Yes	N/A	
89	United States	No	N/A	No	N/A	to be additionally covered by MLI when MLI is ratified
90	Uruguay	No	N/A	Yes	N/A	
91	Uzbekistan*	No	N/A	Yes	PPT alone	
92	Venezuela*	No	N/A	No	N/A	
93	Viet Nam	No	N/A	No	N/A	to be additionally covered by MLI when MLI is ratified

Latvia

A. Progress in the implementation of the minimum standard

Latvia has 62 tax agreements in force, as reported in its response to the Peer Review questionnaire. Two of those agreements, the agreements with Japan and Switzerland, comply with the minimum standard.

Latvia signed the MLI in 2017, listing 47 tax agreements.

Latvia is generally implementing the minimum standard through the inclusion of the preamble statement and the PPT.[89]

The agreements that will be modified by the MLI will come into compliance with the minimum standard once the provisions of the MLI take effect.

Latvia indicated in its response to the Peer Review questionnaire that it would expand its list of covered tax agreements under the MLI. Latvia further indicated that that bilateral negotiation would be used with respect to its agreement with Germany, Japan and Switzerland.

B. Implementation issues

No jurisdiction has raised any concerns about their agreements with Latvia.

Summary of the jurisdiction response – Latvia

	Treaty partners	Compliance with the standard	If compliant, the alternative implemented	Signature of a complying instrument	The alternative implemented through the complying instrument (if not the MLI)	Comments
1	Albania*	No	N/A	No	N/A	
2	Armenia	No	N/A	No	N/A	
3	Austria	No	N/A	Yes	N/A	
4	Azerbaijan*	No	N/A	Yes	N/A	
5	Belarus*	No	N/A	No	N/A	
6	Belgium	No	N/A	Yes	N/A	
7	Bulgaria	No	N/A	Yes	N/A	
8	Canada	No	N/A	Yes	N/A	
9	China (People's Republic of)	No	N/A	Yes	N/A	
10	Croatia	No	N/A	Yes	N/A	
11	Cyprus*	No	N/A	Yes	N/A	
12	Czech Republic	No	N/A	Yes	N/A	
13	Denmark	No	N/A	Yes	N/A	
14	Estonia	No	N/A	Yes	N/A	
15	Finland	No	N/A	Yes	N/A	
16	France	No	N/A	Yes	N/A	
17	Georgia	No	N/A	Yes	N/A	
18	Germany	No	N/A	Yes	N/A	
19	Greece	No	N/A	Yes	N/A	
20	Hong Kong	No	N/A	Yes	N/A	

	(China)					
21	Hungary	No	N/A	Yes	N/A	
22	Iceland	No	N/A	Yes	N/A	
23	India	No	N/A	Yes	N/A	
24	Ireland	No	N/A	Yes	N/A	
25	Israel	No	N/A	Yes	N/A	
26	Italy	No	N/A	Yes	N/A	
27	Japan	Yes	PPT and LOB	N/A	N/A	
28	Kazakhstan	No	N/A	Yes	N/A	
29	Korea	No	N/A	Yes	N/A	
30	Kuwait*	No	N/A	No	N/A	
31	Kyrgyzstan*	No	N/A	No	N/A	
32	Lithuania	No	N/A	Yes	N/A	
33	Luxembourg	No	N/A	Yes	N/A	
34	North Macedonia	No	N/A	No	N/A	
35	Malta	No	N/A	Yes	N/A	
36	Mexico	No	N/A	Yes	N/A	
37	Moldova*	No	N/A	Yes	N/A	
38	Montenegro*	No	N/A	Yes	N/A	
39	Morocco	No	N/A	No	N/A	
40	Netherlands	No	N/A	Yes	N/A	
41	Norway	No	N/A	Yes	N/A	
42	Poland	No	N/A	Yes	N/A	
43	Portugal	No	N/A	Yes	N/A	
44	Qatar	No	N/A	Yes	N/A	
45	Romania	No	N/A	Yes	N/A	
46	Russia	No	N/A	Yes	N/A	
47	Serbia	No	N/A	Yes	N/A	
48	Singapore	No	N/A	Yes	N/A	
49	Slovak Republic	No	N/A	Yes	N/A	
50	Slovenia	No	N/A	Yes	N/A	
51	Spain	No	N/A	Yes	N/A	
52	Sweden	No	N/A	Yes	N/A	
53	Switzerland	Yes	PPT alone	N/A	N/A	
54	Tajikistan*	No	N/A	No	N/A	
55	Turkey	No	N/A	Yes	N/A	
56	Turkmenistan*	No	N/A	No	N/A	
57	Ukraine	No	N/A	Yes	N/A	
58	United Arab Emirates	No	N/A	No	N/A	
59	United Kingdom	No	N/A	Yes	N/A	
60	United States	No	N/A	No	N/A	
61	Uzbekistan*	No	N/A	No	N/A	
62	Viet Nam	No	N/A	No	N/A	

Liberia

A. Progress in the implementation of the minimum standard

Liberia has one tax agreement in force with Germany, as reported in its response to the Peer Review questionnaire.

Liberia's agreement does not comply with the minimum standard and is not subject to any complying instrument.

B. Implementation issues

No jurisdiction has raised any concerns about their agreements with Liberia.

Liberia is encouraged to implement the minimum standard in its agreement.

Summary of the jurisdiction response – Liberia

	Treaty partners	Compliance with the standard	If compliant, the alternative implemented	Signature of a complying instrument	The alternative implemented through the complying instrument (if not the MLI)	Comments
1	Germany	No	N/A	No	N/A	

Liechtenstein

A. Progress in the implementation of the minimum standard

Liechtenstein has 19 tax agreements in force, as reported in its response to the Peer Review questionnaire. Four of those agreements, the agreements with Austria, Iceland, Jersey and Monaco, comply with the minimum standard.

Liechtenstein signed the MLI in 2017, listing 15 tax agreements.

Liechtenstein is implementing the minimum standard through the inclusion of the preamble statement and the PPT.[90]

The agreements that will be modified by the MLI will come into compliance with the minimum standard once the provisions of the MLI take effect.

B. Implementation issues

No jurisdiction has raised any concerns about their agreements with Liechtenstein.

Summary of the jurisdiction response – Liechtenstein

	Treaty partners	Compliance with the standard	If compliant, the alternative implemented	Signature of a complying instrument	The alternative implemented through the complying instrument (if not the MLI)	Comments
1	Andorra	No	N/A	Yes	N/A	
2	Austria	Yes	PPT alone	N/A	N/A	
3	Czech Republic	No	N/A	Yes	N/A	
4	Georgia	No	N/A	Yes	N/A	
5	Germany	No	N/A	Yes	N/A	
6	Guernsey	No	N/A	Yes	N/A	
7	Hong Kong (China)	No	N/A	Yes	N/A	
8	Hungary	No	N/A	Yes	N/A	
9	Iceland	Yes	PPT alone	N/A	N/A	
10	Jersey	Yes	PPT alone	N/A	N/A	
11	Luxembourg	No	N/A	Yes	N/A	
12	Malta	No	N/A	Yes	N/A	
13	Monaco	Yes	PPT alone	N/A	N/A	
14	San Marino	No	N/A	Yes	N/A	
15	Singapore	No	N/A	Yes	N/A	
16	Switzerland	No	N/A	Yes	N/A	
17	United Arab Emirates	No	N/A	Yes	N/A	
18	United Kingdom	No	N/A	Yes	N/A	
19	Uruguay	No	N/A	Yes	N/A	

Lithuania

A. Progress in the implementation of the minimum standard

Lithuania has 56 tax agreements in force, as reported in its response to the Peer Review questionnaire. Nine of those agreements, the agreements with Austria, France, Israel, Japan, Poland, Serbia, the Slovak Republic, Slovenia and the United Kingdom, comply with the minimum standard.

Lithuania signed the MLI in 2017 and deposited its instrument of ratification on 11 September 2018, listing 55 tax agreements. The MLI entered into force for the Lithuania on 1 January 2019.

Lithuania is generally implementing the minimum standard through the inclusion of the preamble statement and the PPT.[91]

The agreements modified by the MLI come into compliance with the minimum standard once the provisions of the MLI take effect. Other agreements listed under the MLI are expected to become compliant with the minimum standard by the end of 2019. B. Implementation issues

No jurisdiction has raised any concerns about their agreements with Lithuania.

Summary of the jurisdiction response – Lithuania

	Treaty partners	Compliance with the standard	If compliant, the alternative implemented	Signature of a complying instrument	The alternative implemented through the complying instrument (if not the MLI)	Comments
1	Armenia	No	N/A	Yes	N/A	
2	Austria	Yes	PPT alone	N/A	N/A	
3	Azerbaijan*	No	N/A	Yes	N/A	
4	Belarus*	No	N/A	Yes	N/A	
5	Belgium	No	N/A	Yes	N/A	Preamble missing, partial compliance in respect of PPT.
6	Bulgaria	No	N/A	Yes	N/A	
7	Canada	No	N/A	Yes	N/A	Preamble missing, partial compliance in respect of PPT.
8	China (People's Republic of)	No	N/A	Yes	N/A	
9	Croatia	No	N/A	Yes	N/A	
10	Cyprus*	No	N/A	Yes	N/A	
11	Czech Republic	No	N/A	Yes	N/A	
12	Denmark	No	N/A	Yes	N/A	
13	Estonia	No	N/A	Yes	N/A	Preamble missing,

						partial compliance in respect of PPT.
14	Finland	No	N/A	Yes	N/A	
15	France	Yes	PPT alone	N/A	N/A	
16	Georgia	No	N/A	Yes	N/A	
17	Germany	No	N/A	Yes	N/A	
18	Greece	No	N/A	Yes	N/A	
19	Hungary	No	N/A	Yes	N/A	
20	Iceland	No	N/A	Yes	N/A	
21	India	No	N/A	Yes	N/A	Preamble missing, partial compliance in respect of PPT.
22	Ireland	No	N/A	Yes	N/A	
23	Israel	Yes	PPT alone	N/A	N/A	
24	Italy	No	N/A	Yes	N/A	Preamble missing, partial compliance in respect of PPT.
25	Japan	Yes	PPT and LOB	N/A	N/A	The agreement was signed on 13 July 2017 and entered into effect on 1 January 2019.
26	Kazakhstan	No	N/A	Yes	N/A	Preamble missing, partial compliance in respect of PPT.
27	Korea	No	N/A	Yes	N/A	
28	Kuwait*	No	N/A	Yes	N/A	
29	Kyrgyzstan*	No	N/A	Yes	N/A	
30	Latvia	No	N/A	Yes	N/A	Preamble missing, partial compliance in respect of PPT.
31	Luxembourg	No	N/A	Yes	N/A	
32	North Macedonia	No	N/A	Yes	N/A	Preamble missing, partial compliance in respect of PPT.
33	Malta	No	N/A	Yes	N/A	Preamble missing, partial compliance

						in respect of PPT.
34	Mexico	No	N/A	Yes	N/A	Preamble missing, partial compliance in respect of PPT.
35	Moldova*	No	N/A	Yes	N/A	
36	Morocco	No	N/A	Yes	N/A	
37	Netherlands	No	N/A	Yes	N/A	
38	Norway	No	N/A	Yes	N/A	
39	Poland	Yes	PPT alone	N/A	N/A	
40	Portugal	No	N/A	Yes	N/A	
41	Romania	No	N/A	Yes	N/A	
42	Russia	No	N/A	Yes	N/A	Preamble missing, partial compliance in respect of PPT.
43	Serbia	Yes	PPT alone	N/A	N/A	
44	Singapore	No	N/A	Yes	N/A	Preamble missing, partial compliance in respect of PPT.
45	Slovak Republic	Yes	PPT alone	N/A	N/A	
46	Slovenia	Yes	PPT alone	N/A	N/A	
47	Spain	No	N/A	Yes	N/A	
48	Sweden	No	N/A	Yes	N/A	
49	Switzerland	No	N/A	Yes	N/A	
50	Turkey	No	N/A	Yes	N/A	
51	Turkmenistan*	No	N/A	Yes	N/A	
52	Ukraine	No	N/A	Yes	N/A	Preamble missing, partial compliance in respect of PPT.
53	United Arab Emirates	No	N/A	Yes	N/A	Preamble missing, partial compliance in respect of PPT.
54	United Kingdom	Yes	PPT alone	N/A	N/A	
55	United States	No	N/A	Yes	N/A	Preamble missing, partial compliance in respect of LOB.
56	Uzbekistan*	No	N/A	Yes	N/A	Preamble missing, partial compliance in respect of PPT.

Luxembourg

A. Progress in the implementation of the minimum standard

Luxembourg has 82 tax agreements in force, as reported in its response to the Peer Review questionnaire. Two of those agreements, the agreements with Cyprus* and Senegal, comply with the minimum standard.

Luxembourg signed the MLI in 2017 and deposited its instrument of ratification on 9 April 2019, listing 81 agreements. The MLI entered into force for Luxembourg on 1 August 2019.

Luxembourg is implementing the minimum standard through the inclusion of the preamble statement and the PPT.[92]

The agreements that will be modified by the MLI will come into compliance with the minimum standard once the provisions of the MLI take effect.

B. Implementation issues

No jurisdiction has raised any concerns about their agreements with Luxembourg.

Summary of the jurisdiction response – Luxembourg

	Treaty partners	Compliance with the standard	If compliant, the alternative implemented	Signature of a complying instrument	The alternative implemented through the complying instrument (if not the MLI)	Comments
1	Andorra	No	N/A	Yes	N/A	
2	Armenia	No	N/A	Yes	N/A	
3	Austria	No	N/A	Yes	N/A	
4	Azerbaijan*	No	N/A	Yes	N/A	
5	Bahrain	No	N/A	Yes	N/A	
6	Barbados	No	N/A	Yes	N/A	
7	Belgium	No	N/A	Yes	N/A	
8	Brazil	No	N/A	Yes	N/A	
9	Brunei Darussalam	No	N/A	Yes	N/A	
10	Bulgaria	No	N/A	Yes	N/A	
11	Canada	No	N/A	Yes	N/A	
12	China (People's Republic of)	No	N/A	Yes	N/A	
13	Chinese Taipei*	No	N/A	Yes	N/A	
14	Croatia	No	N/A	Yes	N/A	
15	Cyprus*	Yes	PPT alone	N/A	N/A	
16	Czech Republic	No	N/A	Yes	N/A	
17	Denmark	No	N/A	Yes	N/A	
18	Estonia	No	N/A	Yes	N/A	
19	Finland	No	N/A	Yes	N/A	
20	France	No	N/A	Yes	N/A	Nouvelle Convention signée le

						20/3/2018 en cours de ratification
21	Georgia	No	N/A	Yes	N/A	
22	Germany	No	N/A	Yes	N/A	
23	Greece	No	N/A	Yes	N/A	
24	Guernsey	No	N/A	Yes	N/A	
25	Hong Kong (China)	No	N/A	Yes	N/A	
26	Hungary	No	N/A	Yes	N/A	
27	Iceland	No	N/A	Yes	N/A	
28	India	No	N/A	Yes	N/A	
29	Indonesia	No	N/A	Yes	N/A	
30	Ireland	No	N/A	Yes	N/A	
31	Isle of Man	No	N/A	Yes	N/A	
32	Israel	No	N/A	Yes	N/A	
33	Italy	No	N/A	Yes	N/A	
34	Japan	No	N/A	Yes	N/A	
35	Jersey	No	N/A	Yes	N/A	
36	Kazakhstan	No	N/A	Yes	N/A	
37	Korea	No	N/A	Yes	N/A	
38	Lao People's Democratic Republic*	No	N/A	Yes	N/A	
39	Latvia	No	N/A	Yes	N/A	
40	Liechtenstein	No	N/A	Yes	N/A	
41	Lithuania	No	N/A	Yes	N/A	
42	North Macedonia	No	N/A	Yes	N/A	
43	Malaysia	No	N/A	Yes	N/A	
44	Malta	No	N/A	Yes	N/A	
45	Mauritius	No	N/A	Yes	N/A	
46	Mexico	No	N/A	Yes	N/A	
47	Moldova*	No	N/A	Yes	N/A	
48	Monaco	No	N/A	Yes	N/A	
49	Morocco	No	N/A	Yes	N/A	
50	Netherlands	No	N/A	Yes	N/A	
51	Norway	No	N/A	Yes	N/A	
52	Panama	No	N/A	Yes	N/A	
53	Poland	No	N/A	Yes	N/A	
54	Portugal	No	N/A	Yes	N/A	
55	Qatar	No	N/A	Yes	N/A	
56	Romania	No	N/A	Yes	N/A	
57	Russia	No	N/A	Yes	N/A	
58	San Marino	No	N/A	Yes	N/A	
59	Saudi Arabia	No	N/A	Yes	N/A	
60	Senegal	Yes	PPT alone	N/A	N/A	
61	Serbia	No	N/A	Yes	N/A	
62	Seychelles	No	N/A	Yes	N/A	
63	Singapore	No	N/A	Yes	N/A	
64	Slovak Republic	No	N/A	Yes	N/A	
65	Slovenia	No	N/A	Yes	N/A	
66	South Africa	No	N/A	Yes	N/A	
67	Spain	No	N/A	Yes	N/A	
68	Sri Lanka	No	N/A	Yes	N/A	
69	Sweden	No	N/A	Yes	N/A	

70	Switzerland	No	N/A	Yes	N/A	
71	Tajikistan*	No	N/A	Yes	N/A	
72	Thailand	No	N/A	Yes	N/A	
73	Trinidad and Tobago	No	N/A	Yes	N/A	
74	Tunisia	No	N/A	Yes	N/A	
75	Turkey	No	N/A	Yes	N/A	
76	Ukraine	No	N/A	Yes	N/A	
77	United Arab Emirates	No	N/A	Yes	N/A	
78	United Kingdom	No	N/A	Yes	N/A	
79	United States	No	N/A	Yes	N/A	
80	Uruguay	No	N/A	Yes	N/A	
81	Uzbekistan*	No	N/A	Yes	N/A	
82	Viet Nam	No	N/A	Yes	N/A	

Macau (China)

A. Progress in the implementation of the minimum standard

Macau (China) has four tax agreements in force, as reported in its response to the Peer Review questionnaire.

None of Macau (China)'s agreements comply with the minimum standard or are subject to a complying instrument.

B. Implementation issues

No jurisdiction has raised any concerns about their agreements with Macau (China).

Macau (China) is encouraged to implement the minimum standard in its agreements.

Summary of the jurisdiction response – Macau (China)

	Treaty partners	Compliance with the standard	If compliant, the alternative implemented	Signature of a complying instrument	The alternative implemented through the complying instrument (if not the MLI)	Comments
1	Cabo Verde	No	N/A	No	N/A	
2	Mozambique*	No	N/A	No	N/A	
3	Portugal	No	N/A	No	N/A	
4	Viet Nam	No	N/A	No	N/A	

Malaysia

A. Progress in the implementation of the minimum standard

Malaysia has 72 tax agreements in force, as reported in its response to the Peer Review questionnaire.

Malaysia signed the MLI in 2018, listing 72 tax agreements.[93]

Malaysia is implementing the minimum standard through the inclusion of the preamble statement and the PPT.[94]

The agreements that will be modified by the MLI will come into compliance with the minimum standard once the provisions of the MLI take effect. Malaysia indicated in its response to the Peer Review questionnaire that bilateral negotiations would be used with respect to its agreement with Austria, Bahrain, Brunei Darussalam, Germany, Mongolia, Morocco, Norway, Sri Lanka, Switzerland, Thailand and Viet Nam.

B. Implementation issues

No jurisdiction has raised any concerns about their agreements with Malaysia.

Summary of the jurisdiction response – Malaysia

	Treaty partners	Compliance with the standard	If compliant, the alternative implemented	Signature of a complying instrument	The alternative implemented through the complying instrument (if not the MLI)	Comments
1	Albania*	No	N/A	Yes	N/A	
2	Australia	No	N/A	Yes	N/A	
3	Austria	No	N/A	Yes	N/A	
4	Bahrain	No	N/A	Yes	N/A	
5	Bangladesh*	No	N/A	Yes	N/A	
6	Belgium	No	N/A	Yes	N/A	
7	Bosnia and Herzegovina*	No	N/A	Yes	N/A	
8	Brunei Darussalam	No	N/A	Yes	N/A	
9	Canada	No	N/A	Yes	N/A	
10	Chile	No	N/A	Yes	N/A	The treaty contains main purpose test in dividends, interest and royalties articles
11	China (People's Republic of)	No	N/A	Yes	N/A	
12	Croatia	No	N/A	Yes	N/A	
13	Czech Republic	No	N/A	Yes	N/A	
14	Denmark	No	N/A	Yes	N/A	

15	Egypt	No	N/A	Yes	N/A	
16	Fiji*	No	N/A	Yes	N/A	
17	Finland	No	N/A	Yes	N/A	
18	France	No	N/A	Yes	N/A	
19	Germany	No	N/A	Yes	N/A	
20	Hong Kong (China)	No	N/A	Yes	N/A	
21	Hungary	No	N/A	Yes	N/A	
22	India	No	N/A	Yes	N/A	Contains provision on the application of domestic anti abuse provision and main purpose test.
23	Indonesia	No	N/A	Yes	N/A	
24	Iran*	No	N/A	Yes	N/A	.
25	Ireland	No	N/A	Yes	N/A	
26	Italy	No	N/A	Yes	N/A	
27	Japan	No	N/A	Yes	N/A	
28	Jordan*	No	N/A	Yes	N/A	
29	Kazakhstan	No	N/A	Yes	N/A	Contains main purpose test in interest and royalties articles.
30	Korea	No	N/A	Yes	N/A	
31	Kuwait*	No	N/A	Yes	N/A	
32	Kyrgyzstan*	No	N/A	Yes	N/A	.
33	Lao People's Democratic Republic*	No	N/A	Yes	N/A	
34	Lebanon*	No	N/A	Yes	N/A	.
35	Luxembourg	No	N/A	Yes	N/A	
36	Malta	No	N/A	Yes	N/A	
37	Mauritius	No	N/A	Yes	N/A	
38	Mongolia	No	N/A	Yes	N/A	
39	Morocco	No	N/A	Yes	N/A	
40	Myanmar*	No	N/A	Yes	N/A	
41	Namibia*	No	N/A	Yes	N/A	
42	Netherlands	No	N/A	Yes	N/A	
43	New Zealand	No	N/A	Yes	N/A	
44	Norway	No	N/A	Yes	N/A	
45	Pakistan	No	N/A	Yes	N/A	
46	Papua New Guinea	No	N/A	Yes	N/A	Contains main purpose test in interest article.
47	Philippines*	No	N/A	Yes	N/A	
48	Poland	No	N/A	Yes	N/A	Malaysia and Poland signed a new tax agreement in 2013,

						which has not yet entered into force. This agreement, although not compliant with the Action 6 minimum standard, is listed in the Malaysia's MLI position. The new Poland agreement contains main purpose test in dividends, interest, royalties and technical fees articles.
49	Qatar	No	N/A	Yes	N/A	
50	Romania	No	N/A	Yes	N/A	
51	Russia	No	N/A	Yes	N/A	
52	San Marino	No	N/A	Yes	N/A	
53	Saudi Arabia	No	N/A	Yes	N/A	
54	Seychelles	No	N/A	Yes	N/A	
55	Singapore	No	N/A	Yes	N/A	
56	Slovak Republic	No	N/A	Yes	N/A	
57	South Africa	No	N/A	Yes	N/A	
58	Spain	No	N/A	Yes	N/A	
59	Sri Lanka	No	N/A	Yes	N/A	
60	Sudan*	No	N/A	Yes	N/A	
61	Sweden	No	N/A	Yes	N/A	
62	Switzerland	No	N/A	Yes	N/A	
63	Syrian Arab Republic*	No	N/A	Yes	N/A	
64	Thailand	No	N/A	Yes	N/A	
65	Turkey	No	N/A	Yes	N/A	
66	Turkmenistan*	No	N/A	Yes	N/A	
67	United Arab Emirates	No	N/A	Yes	N/A	
68	United Kingdom	No	N/A	Yes	N/A	Contains main purpose test in dividends, interest and royalties articles.
69	Uzbekistan*	No	N/A	Yes	N/A	
70	Venezuela*	No	N/A	Yes	N/A	
71	Viet Nam	No	N/A	Yes	N/A	
72	Zimbabwe*	No	N/A	Yes	N/A	

Maldives

A. Progress in the implementation of the minimum standard

The Maldives has one tax agreement in force, as reported in its response to the Peer Review questionnaire.

The Maldives' agreement does not comply with the minimum standard and is not subject to a complying instrument.

B. Implementation issues

No jurisdiction has raised any concerns about the Maldives.

The Maldives is encouraged to implement the minimum standard in its agreement.

Summary of the jurisdiction response – Maldives

	Treaty partners	Compliance with the standard	If compliant, the alternative implemented	Signature of a complying instrument	The alternative implemented through the complying instrument (if not the MLI)	Comments
1	United Arab Emirates	No	N/A	No	N/A	

Malta

A. Progress in the implementation of the minimum standard

Malta has 76 tax agreements in force, as reported in its response to the Peer Review questionnaire.

Malta signed the MLI in 2017 and deposited its instrument of ratification on 18 December 2018, listing 72 tax agreements.[95] The MLI entered into force for Malta on 1 April 2019.

Malta is implementing the minimum standard through the inclusion of the preamble statement and the PPT.[96]

The agreements that will be modified by the MLI will come into compliance with the minimum standard once the provisions of the MLI take effect. Some agreements listed under the MLI are expected to become compliant with the minimum standard by the end of 2019.[97]

B. Implementation issues

No jurisdiction has raised any concerns about their agreements with Malta.

Summary of the jurisdiction response – Malta

	Treaty partners	Compliance with the standard	If compliant, the alternative implemented	Signature of a complying instrument	The alternative implemented through the complying instrument (if not the MLI)	Comments
1	Albania*	No	N/A	Yes	N/A	
2	Andorra	No	N/A	Yes	N/A	
3	Australia	No	N/A	Yes	N/A	
4	Austria	No	N/A	Yes	N/A	
5	Azerbaijan*	No	N/A	Yes	N/A	
6	Bahrain	No	N/A	Yes	N/A	
7	Barbados	No	N/A	Yes	N/A	
8	Belgium	No	N/A	Yes	N/A	
9	Botswana	No	N/A	No	N/A	Entered into force on 13.11.18
10	Bulgaria	No	N/A	No	N/A	
11	Canada	No	N/A	Yes	N/A	
12	China (People's Republic of)	No	N/A	Yes	N/A	
13	Croatia	No	N/A	Yes	N/A	
14	Cyprus*	No	N/A	Yes	N/A	
15	Czech Republic	No	N/A	Yes	N/A	
16	Denmark	No	N/A	Yes	N/A	
17	Egypt	No	N/A	Yes	N/A	
18	Estonia	No	N/A	Yes	N/A	
19	Finland	No	N/A	Yes	N/A	

20	France	No	N/A	Yes	N/A	
21	Georgia	No	N/A	Yes	N/A	
22	Germany	No	N/A	Yes	N/A	
23	Greece	No	N/A	Yes	N/A	
24	Guernsey	No	N/A	Yes	N/A	
25	Hong Kong (China)	No	N/A	Yes	N/A	
26	Hungary	No	N/A	Yes	N/A	
27	Iceland	No	N/A	Yes	N/A	
28	India	No	N/A	Yes	N/A	
29	Ireland	No	N/A	Yes	N/A	
30	Isle of Man	No	N/A	Yes	N/A	
31	Israel	No	N/A	Yes	N/A	
32	Italy	No	N/A	Yes	N/A	
33	Jersey	No	N/A	Yes	N/A	
34	Jordan*	No	N/A	Yes	N/A	
35	Korea	No	N/A	Yes	N/A	
36	Kuwait*	No	N/A	Yes	N/A	
37	Latvia	No	N/A	Yes	N/A	
38	Lebanon*	No	N/A	Yes	N/A	
39	Libya*	No	N/A	Yes	N/A	
40	Liechtenstein	No	N/A	Yes	N/A	
41	Lithuania	No	N/A	Yes	N/A	
42	Luxembourg	No	N/A	Yes	N/A	
43	Malaysia	No	N/A	Yes	N/A	
44	Mauritius	No	N/A	Yes	N/A	
45	Mexico	No	N/A	Yes	N/A	
46	Moldova*	No	N/A	Yes	N/A	
47	Monaco	No	N/A	No	N/A	Entered into force on 16.05.19
48	Montenegro*	No	N/A	Yes	N/A	
49	Morocco	No	N/A	Yes	N/A	
50	Netherlands	No	N/A	Yes	N/A	
51	Norway	No	N/A	Yes	N/A	
52	Pakistan	No	N/A	Yes	N/A	
53	Poland	No	N/A	Yes	N/A	
54	Portugal	No	N/A	Yes	N/A	
55	Qatar	No	N/A	Yes	N/A	
56	Romania	No	N/A	Yes	N/A	
57	Russia	No	N/A	Yes	N/A	
58	San Marino	No	N/A	Yes	N/A	
59	Saudi Arabia	No	N/A	Yes	N/A	
60	Serbia	No	N/A	Yes	N/A	
61	Singapore	No	N/A	Yes	N/A	
62	Slovak Republic	No	N/A	Yes	N/A	
63	Slovenia	No	N/A	Yes	N/A	
64	South Africa	No	N/A	Yes	N/A	
65	Spain	No	N/A	Yes	N/A	
66	Sweden	No	N/A	Yes	N/A	
67	Switzerland	No	N/A	Yes	N/A	
68	Syrian Arab Republic*	No	N/A	Yes	N/A	

69	Tunisia	No	N/A	Yes	N/A	
70	Turkey	No	N/A	Yes	N/A	
71	Ukraine	No	N/A	Yes	N/A	
72	United Arab Emirates	No	N/A	Yes	N/A	
73	United Kingdom	No	N/A	Yes	N/A	
74	United States	No	N/A	No	N/A	
75	Uruguay	No	N/A	Yes	N/A	
76	Viet Nam	No	N/A	Yes	N/A	

Mauritius

A. Progress in the implementation of the minimum standard

Mauritius has 45 tax agreements in force, as reported in its response to the Peer Review questionnaire.

Mauritius signed the MLI in 2017, listing 41 tax agreements.[98]

Mauritius is implementing the minimum standard in its tax agreements through the inclusion of the preamble statement and the PPT.[99]

The agreements that will be modified by the MLI will come into compliance with the minimum standard once the provisions of the MLI take effect.

Mauritius indicated in its response to the Peer Review questionnaire that it would expand its list of covered tax agreements under the MLI. Mauritius further indicated that bilateral negotiations would be used with respect to its agreement with India.

B. Implementation issues

No jurisdiction has raised any concerns about their agreements with Mauritius.

Summary of the jurisdiction response – Mauritius

	Treaty partners	Compliance with the standard	If compliant, the alternative implemented	Signature of a complying instrument	The alternative implemented through the complying instrument (if not the MLI)	Comments
1	Bangladesh*	No	N/A	Yes	N/A	
2	Barbados	No	N/A	Yes	N/A	
3	Belgium	No	N/A	Yes	N/A	
4	Botswana	No	N/A	Yes	N/A	
5	Cabo Verde	No	N/A	No	N/A	
6	China (People's Republic of)	No	N/A	Yes	N/A	
7	Congo	No	N/A	Yes	N/A	
8	Croatia	No	N/A	Yes	N/A	
9	Cyprus*	No	N/A	Yes	N/A	
10	Egypt	No	N/A	Yes	N/A	
11	France	No	N/A	Yes	N/A	
12	Germany	No	N/A	Yes	N/A	
13	Ghana*	No	N/A	No	N/A	
14	Guernsey	No	N/A	Yes	N/A	
15	India	No	N/A	No	N/A	
16	Italy	No	N/A	Yes	N/A	
17	Jersey	No	N/A	No	N/A	
18	Kuwait*	No	N/A	Yes	N/A	
19	Lesotho*	No	N/A	Yes	N/A	
20	Luxembourg	No	N/A	Yes	N/A	

21	Madagascar*	No	N/A	Yes	N/A	
22	Malaysia	No	N/A	Yes	N/A	
23	Malta	No	N/A	Yes	N/A	
24	Monaco	No	N/A	Yes	N/A	
25	Mozambique*	No	N/A	Yes	N/A	
26	Namibia*	No	N/A	Yes	N/A	
27	Nepal*	No	N/A	Yes	N/A	
28	Oman	No	N/A	Yes	N/A	
29	Pakistan	No	N/A	Yes	N/A	
30	Qatar	No	N/A	Yes	N/A	
31	Rwanda*	No	N/A	Yes	N/A	
32	Senegal	No	N/A	Yes	N/A	
33	Seychelles	No	N/A	Yes	N/A	
34	Singapore	No	N/A	Yes	N/A	
35	South Africa	No	N/A	Yes	N/A	
36	Sri Lanka	No	N/A	Yes	N/A	
37	Eswatini*	No	N/A	Yes	N/A	
38	Sweden	No	N/A	Yes	N/A	
39	Thailand	No	N/A	Yes	N/A	
40	Tunisia	No	N/A	Yes	N/A	
41	Uganda*	No	N/A	Yes	N/A	
42	United Arab Emirates	No	N/A	Yes	N/A	
43	United Kingdom	No	N/A	Yes	N/A	
44	Zambia	No	N/A	Yes	N/A	
45	Zimbabwe*	No	N/A	Yes	N/A	

Mexico

A. Progress in the implementation of the minimum standard

Mexico has 60 tax agreements in force, as reported in its response to the Peer Review questionnaire. Three of those agreements, the agreements with Argentina, the Philippines* and Spain, comply with the minimum standard.

Mexico signed the MLI in 2017, listing 60 tax agreements.[100]

Mexico is implementing the minimum standard through the inclusion of the preamble statement and the PPT combined with the LOB.[101]

The agreements that will be modified by the MLI will come into compliance with the minimum standard once the provisions of the MLI take effect.

B. Implementation issues

No jurisdiction has raised any concerns about their agreements with Mexico.

Summary of the jurisdiction response – Mexico

	Treaty partners	Compliance with the standard	If compliant, the alternative implemented	Signature of a complying instrument	The alternative implemented through the complying instrument (if not the MLI)	Comments
1	Argentina	Yes	PPT and LOB	N/A	N/A	
2	Australia	No	N/A	Yes	N/A	
3	Austria	No	N/A	Yes	N/A	
4	Bahrain	No	N/A	Yes	N/A	
5	Barbados	No	N/A	Yes	N/A	
6	Belgium	No	N/A	Yes	N/A	
7	Brazil	No	N/A	Yes	N/A	
8	Canada	No	N/A	Yes	N/A	
9	Chile	No	N/A	Yes	N/A	
10	China (People's Republic of)	No	N/A	Yes	N/A	
11	Colombia	No	N/A	Yes	N/A	
12	Costa Rica	No	N/A	Yes	N/A	
13	Czech Republic	No	N/A	Yes	N/A	
14	Denmark	No	N/A	Yes	N/A	
15	Ecuador*	No	N/A	Yes	N/A	
16	Estonia	No	N/A	Yes	N/A	
17	Finland	No	N/A	Yes	N/A	
18	France	No	N/A	Yes	N/A	
19	Germany	No	N/A	Yes	N/A	
20	Greece	No	N/A	Yes	N/A	
21	Hong Kong (China)	No	N/A	Yes	N/A	

22	Hungary	No	N/A	Yes	N/A	
23	Iceland	No	N/A	Yes	N/A	
24	India	No	N/A	Yes	N/A	
25	Indonesia	No	N/A	Yes	N/A	
26	Ireland	No	N/A	Yes	N/A	
27	Israel	No	N/A	Yes	N/A	
28	Italy	No	N/A	Yes	N/A	
29	Jamaica	No	N/A	Yes	N/A	
30	Japan	No	N/A	Yes	N/A	
31	Korea	No	N/A	Yes	N/A	
32	Kuwait*	No	N/A	Yes	N/A	
33	Latvia	No	N/A	Yes	N/A	
34	Lithuania	No	N/A	Yes	N/A	
35	Luxembourg	No	N/A	Yes	N/A	
36	Malta	No	N/A	Yes	N/A	
37	Netherlands	No	N/A	Yes	N/A	
38	New Zealand	No	N/A	Yes	N/A	
39	Norway	No	N/A	Yes	N/A	
40	Panama	No	N/A	Yes	N/A	
41	Peru	No	N/A	Yes	N/A	
42	Philippines*	Yes	PPT alone	N/A	N/A	
43	Poland	No	N/A	Yes	N/A	
44	Portugal	No	N/A	Yes	N/A	
45	Qatar	No	N/A	Yes	N/A	
46	Romania	No	N/A	Yes	N/A	
47	Russia	No	N/A	Yes	N/A	
48	Saudi Arabia	No	N/A	Yes	N/A	
49	Singapore	No	N/A	Yes	N/A	
50	Slovak Republic	No	N/A	Yes	N/A	
51	South Africa	No	N/A	Yes	N/A	
52	Spain	Yes	PPT alone	N/A	N/A	
53	Sweden	No	N/A	Yes	N/A	
54	Switzerland	No	N/A	Yes	N/A	
55	Turkey	No	N/A	Yes	N/A	
56	Ukraine	No	N/A	Yes	N/A	
57	United Arab Emirates	No	N/A	Yes	N/A	
58	United Kingdom	No	N/A	Yes	N/A	
59	United States	No	N/A	Yes	N/A	
60	Uruguay	No	N/A	Yes	N/A	

Monaco

A. Progress in the implementation of the minimum standard

Monaco has ten tax agreements in force, as reported in its response to the Peer Review questionnaire. Its agreement with Liechtenstein complies with the minimum standard.

Monaco signed the MLI in 2017 and deposited its instrument of ratification on 10 January 2019, listing eight tax agreements.[102] The MLI entered into force for Monaco on 1 May 2019.

Monaco is implementing the minimum standard through the inclusion of the preamble statement and the PPT.[103]

The agreements that will be modified by the MLI will come into compliance with the minimum standard once the provisions of the MLI take effect. Some agreements listed under the MLI are expected to become compliant with the minimum standard by the end of 2019.

B. Implementation issues

No jurisdiction has raised any concerns about their agreements with Monaco.

Summary of the jurisdiction response – Monaco

	Treaty partners	Compliance with the standard	If compliant, the alternative implemented	Signature of a complying instrument	The alternative implemented through the complying instrument (if not the MLI)	Comments
1	France	No	N/A	Yes	N/A	
2	Guernsey	No	N/A	Yes	N/A	
3	Liechtenstein	Yes	PPT alone	N/A	N/A	
4	Luxembourg	No	N/A	Yes	N/A	
5	Mali*	No	N/A	Yes	N/A	
6	Malta	No	N/A	No	N/A	
7	Mauritius	No	N/A	Yes	N/A	
8	Qatar	No	N/A	Yes	N/A	
9	Saint Kitts and Nevis	No	N/A	Yes	N/A	
10	Seychelles	No	N/A	Yes	N/A	

Mongolia

A. Progress in the implementation of the minimum standard

Mongolia has 25 tax agreements in force as reported in its response to the Peer Review questionnaire.

None of Mongolia's agreements comply with the minimum standard or are subject to a complying instrument.

B. Implementation issues

No jurisdiction has raised any concerns about their agreements with Mongolia.

Mongolia is encouraged to implement the minimum standard in its agreements.

Summary of the jurisdiction response – Mongolia

	Treaty partners	Compliance with the standard	If compliant, the alternative implemented	Signature of a complying instrument	The alternative implemented through the complying instrument (if not the MLI)	Comments
1	Austria	No	N/A	No	N/A	
2	Belarus*	No	N/A	No	N/A	
3	Belgium	No	N/A	No	N/A	
4	Bulgaria	No	N/A	No	N/A	
5	Canada	No	N/A	No	N/A	
6	China (People's Republic of)	No	N/A	No	N/A	
7	Czech Republic	No	N/A	No	N/A	
8	Democratic People's Republic of Korea*	No	N/A	No	N/A	
9	France	No	N/A	No	N/A	
10	Germany	No	N/A	No	N/A	
11	Hungary	No	N/A	No	N/A	
12	India	No	N/A	No	N/A	
13	Indonesia	No	N/A	No	N/A	
14	Kazakhstan	No	N/A	No	N/A	
15	Korea	No	N/A	No	N/A	
16	Kyrgyzstan*	No	N/A	No	N/A	
17	Malaysia	No	N/A	No	N/A	
18	Poland	No	N/A	No	N/A	
19	Russia	No	N/A	No	N/A	
20	Singapore	No	N/A	No	N/A	
21	Switzerland	No	N/A	No	N/A	
22	Turkey	No	N/A	No	N/A	
23	Ukraine	No	N/A	No	N/A	
24	United Kingdom	No	N/A	No	N/A	
25	Viet Nam	No	N/A	No	N/A	

Montserrat

A. Progress in the implementation of the minimum standard

Montserrat has two tax agreements in force, as reported in its response to the Peer Review questionnaire.

Neither of Montserrat's agreements comply with the minimum standard or are subject to a complying instrument.

Montserrat indicated in its response to the Peer Review questionnaire that its agreement with the United Kingdom is an arrangement that cannot be modified with the MLI.

B. Implementation issues

No jurisdiction has raised any concerns about their agreements with Montserrat.

Montserrat is encouraged to implement the minimum standard in its agreements.

Summary of the jurisdiction response – Montserrat

	Treaty partners	Compliance with the standard	If compliant, the alternative implemented	Signature of a complying instrument	The alternative implemented through the complying instrument (if not the MLI)	Comments
1	Switzerland	No	N/A	No	N/A	
2	United Kingdom	No	N/A	No	N/A	

Morocco

A. Progress in the implementation of the minimum standard

Morocco has 53 tax agreements in force, as reported in its response to the Peer Review questionnaire, including the Arab Maghreb Union Income Agreement concluded with four treaty partners.[104]

Morocco signed the MLI in 2019, listing 53 tax agreements.[105]

Morocco is implementing the minimum standard through the inclusion of the preamble statement and the PPT.[106]

The agreements that will be modified by the MLI will come into compliance with the minimum standard once the provisions of the MLI take effect.

B. Implementation issues

No jurisdiction has raised any concerns about their agreements with Morocco.

Summary of the jurisdiction response – Morocco

	Treaty partners	Compliance with the standard	If compliant, the alternative implemented	Signature of a complying instrument	The alternative implemented through the complying instrument (if not the MLI)	Comments
1	Algeria*	No	N/A	Yes	N/A	
2	Austria	No	N/A	Yes	N/A	
3	Bahrain	No	N/A	Yes	N/A	
4	Belgium	No	N/A	Yes	N/A	
5	Bulgaria	No	N/A	Yes	N/A	
6	Canada	No	N/A	Yes	N/A	
7	China (People's Republic of)	No	N/A	Yes	N/A	
8	Côte d'Ivoire	No	N/A	Yes	N/A	
9	Croatia	No	N/A	Yes	N/A	
10	Czech Republic	No	N/A	Yes	N/A	
11	Denmark	No	N/A	Yes	N/A	
12	Egypt	No	N/A	Yes	N/A	
13	Finland	No	N/A	Yes	N/A	
14	France	No	N/A	Yes	N/A	
15	Gabon	No	N/A	Yes	N/A	
16	Germany	No	N/A	Yes	N/A	
17	Greece	No	N/A	Yes	N/A	
18	Guinea*	No	N/A	Yes	N/A	
19	Hungary	No	N/A	Yes	N/A	
20	India	No	N/A	Yes	N/A	
21	Indonesia	No	N/A	Yes	N/A	
22	Ireland	No	N/A	Yes	N/A	

23	Italy	No	N/A	Yes	N/A	
24	Jordan*	No	N/A	Yes	N/A	
25	Korea	No	N/A	Yes	N/A	
26	Kuwait*	No	N/A	Yes	N/A	
27	Latvia	No	N/A	Yes	N/A	
28	Lebanon*	No	N/A	Yes	N/A	
29	Libya*	No	N/A	Yes	N/A	
30	Luxembourg	No	N/A	Yes	N/A	
31	Malaysia	No	N/A	Yes	N/A	
32	Mali*	No	N/A	Yes	N/A	
33	Malta	No	N/A	Yes	N/A	
34	Mauritania*	No	N/A	Yes	N/A	
35	Netherlands	No	N/A	Yes	N/A	
36	North Macedonia	No	N/A	Yes	N/A	
37	Norway	No	N/A	Yes	N/A	
38	Oman	No	N/A	Yes	N/A	
39	Pakistan	No	N/A	Yes	N/A	
40	Poland	No	N/A	Yes	N/A	
41	Portugal	No	N/A	Yes	N/A	
42	Qatar	No	N/A	Yes	N/A	
43	Romania	No	N/A	Yes	N/A	
44	Russian Federation	No	N/A	Yes	N/A	
45	Senegal	No	N/A	Yes	N/A	
46	Singapore	No	N/A	Yes	N/A	
47	Spain	No	N/A	Yes	N/A	
48	Switzerland	No	N/A	Yes	N/A	
49	Syrian Arab Republic*	No	N/A	Yes	N/A	
50	Tunisia	No	N/A	Yes	N/A	
51	Turkey	No	N/A	Yes	N/A	
52	United Arab Emirates	No	N/A	Yes	N/A	
53	United Kingdom	No	N/A	Yes	N/A	
54	Ukraine	No	N/A	Yes	N/A	
55	United States	No	N/A	Yes	N/A	
56	Viet Nam	No	N/A	Yes	N/A	

Netherlands

A. Progress in the implementation of the minimum standard

The Netherlands has 95 tax agreements in force, as reported in its response to the Peer Review questionnaire. Three of those agreements, the agreements with Denmark, Ghana* and Uzbekistan*, comply with the minimum standard.

The Netherlands signed the MLI in 2017 and deposited its instrument of acceptance in 2019, listing 81 tax agreements. The MLI entered into force for the Netherlands on 1 July 2019.

The Netherlands is implementing the minimum standard through the inclusion of the preamble statement and the PPT.[107]

The agreements that will be modified by the MLI will come into compliance with the minimum standard once the provisions of the MLI take effect.

The Netherlands signed a bilateral complying instrument with respect to five of its agreements, the agreements with Algeria*, Denmark, Ghana*, Ukraine and Uzbekistan*.[108]

The Netherlands indicated in its response to the Peer Review questionnaire that bilateral negotiations would be used with respect to its agreements with Belgium, Brazil, Bulgaria, Ireland, Poland and Spain.

B. Implementation issues

No jurisdiction has raised any concerns about their agreements with the Netherlands.

Summary of the jurisdiction response – Netherlands

	Treaty partners	Compliance with the standard	If compliant, the alternative implemented	Signature of a complying instrument	The alternative implemented through the complying instrument (if not the MLI)	Comments
1	Albania*	No	N/A	Yes	N/A	
2	Algeria*	No	N/A	Yes	PPT alone	
3	Argentina	No	N/A	Yes	N/A	
4	Armenia	No	N/A	Yes	N/A	
5	Aruba	No	N/A	No	N/A	
6	Australia	No	N/A	Yes	N/A	
7	Austria	No	N/A	Yes	N/A	
8	Azerbaijan*	No	N/A	Yes	N/A	
9	Bahrain	No	N/A	Yes	N/A	
10	Bangladesh*	No	N/A	Yes	N/A	
11	Barbados	No	N/A	Yes	N/A	
12	Belarus*	No	N/A	Yes	N/A	
13	Belgium	No	N/A	No	N/A	
14	Bosnia and Herzegovina*	No	N/A	Yes	N/A	
15	Brazil	No	N/A	No	N/A	
16	Bulgaria	No	N/A	No	N/A	

17	Canada	No	N/A	Yes	N/A	
18	China (People's Republic of)	No	N/A	Yes	N/A	
19	Chinese Taipei*	No	N/A	No	N/A	
20	Croatia	No	N/A	Yes	N/A	
21	Curacao	No	N/A	No	N/A	
22	Czech Republic	No	N/A	Yes	N/A	
23	Denmark	Yes	PPT alone	N/A	N/A	
24	Egypt	No	N/A	Yes	N/A	
25	Estonia	No	N/A	Yes	N/A	
26	Ethiopia*	No	N/A	Yes	N/A	
27	Finland	No	N/A	Yes	N/A	
28	France	No	N/A	Yes	N/A	
29	Georgia	No	N/A	Yes	N/A	
30	Germany	No	N/A	Yes	N/A	
31	Ghana*	Yes	PPT alone	N/A	N/A	
32	Greece	No	N/A	Yes	N/A	
33	Hong Kong (China)	No	N/A	Yes	N/A	
34	Hungary	No	N/A	Yes	N/A	
35	Iceland	No	N/A	Yes	N/A	
36	India	No	N/A	Yes	N/A	
37	Indonesia	No	N/A	Yes	N/A	
38	Ireland	No	N/A	Yes	PPT alone	
39	Israel	No	N/A	Yes	N/A	
40	Italy	No	N/A	Yes	N/A	
41	Japan	No	N/A	Yes	N/A	
42	Jordan*	No	N/A	Yes	N/A	
43	Kazakhstan	No	N/A	Yes	N/A	
44	Kenya	No	N/A	Yes	N/A	
45	Korea	No	N/A	Yes	N/A	
46	Kuwait*	No	N/A	Yes	N/A	
47	Latvia	No	N/A	Yes	N/A	
48	Lithuania	No	N/A	Yes	N/A	
49	Luxembourg	No	N/A	Yes	N/A	
50	North Macedonia	No	N/A	Yes	N/A	
51	Malawi*	No	N/A	Yes	N/A	
52	Malaysia	No	N/A	Yes	N/A	
53	Malta	No	N/A	Yes	N/A	
54	Mexico	No	N/A	Yes	N/A	
55	Moldova*	No	N/A	Yes	N/A	
56	Montenegro*	No	N/A	Yes	N/A	
57	Morocco	No	N/A	Yes	N/A	
58	New Zealand	No	N/A	Yes	N/A	
59	Nigeria	No	N/A	Yes	N/A	
60	Norway	No	N/A	Yes	N/A	
61	Oman	No	N/A	Yes	N/A	
62	Pakistan	No	N/A	Yes	N/A	
63	Panama	No	N/A	Yes	N/A	
64	Philippines*	No	N/A	Yes	N/A	
65	Poland	No	N/A	No	N/A	
66	Portugal	No	N/A	Yes	N/A	
67	Qatar	No	N/A	Yes	N/A	
68	Romania	No	N/A	Yes	N/A	

69	Russia	No	N/A	Yes	N/A	
70	Saudi Arabia	No	N/A	Yes	N/A	
71	Serbia	No	N/A	Yes	N/A	
72	Singapore	No	N/A	Yes	N/A	
73	Sint Maarten*	No	N/A	No	N/A	
74	Slovak Republic	No	N/A	Yes	N/A	
75	Slovenia	No	N/A	Yes	N/A	
76	South Africa	No	N/A	Yes	N/A	
77	Spain	No	N/A	No	N/A	
78	Sri Lanka	No	N/A	Yes	N/A	
79	Suriname*	No	N/A	Yes	N/A	
80	Sweden	No	N/A	Yes	N/A	
81	Switzerland	No	N/A	Yes	PPT alone	
82	Tajikistan*	No	N/A	Yes	N/A	
83	Thailand	No	N/A	Yes	N/A	
84	Tunisia	No	N/A	Yes	N/A	
85	Turkey	No	N/A	Yes	N/A	
86	Uganda*	No	N/A	Yes	N/A	
87	Ukraine	No	N/A	Yes	PPT alone	
88	United Arab Emirates	No	N/A	Yes	N/A	
89	United Kingdom	No	N/A	Yes	N/A	
90	United States	No	N/A	Yes	N/A	
91	Uzbekistan*	Yes	PPT alone	N/A	N/A	
92	Venezuela*	No	N/A	Yes	N/A	
93	Viet Nam	No	N/A	Yes	N/A	
94	Zambia	No	N/A	Yes	N/A	
95	Zimbabwe*	No	N/A	Yes	N/A	

New Zealand

A. Progress in the implementation of the minimum standard

New Zealand has 40 tax agreements in force, as reported in its response to the Peer Review questionnaire. Six of those agreements, the agreements with Australia, France, Japan, Poland, Samoa* and the United Kingdom, comply with the minimum standard.

New Zealand signed the MLI in 2017 and deposited its instrument of ratification on the 27 June 2018, listing 37 tax agreements. The MLI entered into force for New Zealand on 1 October 2018.

New Zealand is implementing the minimum standard through the inclusion of the preamble statement and the PPT.[109]

The agreements modified by the MLI come into compliance with the minimum standard once the provisions of the MLI take effect. Other agreements listed under the MLI are expected to become compliant with the minimum standard by the end of 2019.

B. Implementation issues

No jurisdiction has raised any concerns about their agreements with New Zealand.

Summary of the jurisdiction response – New Zealand

	Treaty partners	Compliance with the standard	If compliant, the alternative implemented	Signature of a complying instrument	The alternative implemented through the complying instrument (if not the MLI)	Comments
1	Australia	Yes	PPT alone	N/A	N/A	
2	Austria	No	N/A	Yes	N/A	
3	Belgium	No	N/A	Yes	N/A	
4	Canada	No	N/A	Yes	N/A	
5	Chile	No	N/A	Yes	N/A	
6	China (People's Republic of)	No	N/A	Yes	PPT alone	
7	Chinese Taipei*	No	N/A	No	N/A	
8	Czech Republic	No	N/A	Yes	N/A	
9	Denmark	No	N/A	Yes	N/A	
10	Fiji*	No	N/A	Yes	N/A	
11	Finland	No	N/A	Yes	N/A	
12	France	Yes	PPT alone	N/A	N/A	
13	Germany	No	N/A	Yes	N/A	
14	Hong Kong (China)	No	N/A	Yes	N/A	
15	India	No	N/A	Yes	N/A	
16	Indonesia	No	N/A	Yes	N/A	
17	Ireland	No	N/A	Yes	N/A	
18	Italy	No	N/A	Yes	N/A	
19	Japan	Yes	PPT and LOB	N/A	N/A	The treaty already contained

						an LOB and this is unaffected by the MLI
20	Korea	No	N/A	Yes	N/A	
21	Malaysia	No	N/A	Yes	N/A	
22	Mexico	No	N/A	Yes	N/A	
23	Netherlands	No	N/A	Yes	N/A	
24	Norway	No	N/A	Yes	N/A	
25	Papua New Guinea	No	N/A	Yes	N/A	
26	Philippines*	No	N/A	Yes	N/A	
27	Poland	Yes	PPT alone	N/A	N/A	
28	Russia	No	N/A	Yes	N/A	
29	Samoa*	Yes	PPT alone	N/A	N/A	
30	Singapore	No	N/A	Yes	N/A	
31	South Africa	No	N/A	Yes	N/A	
32	Spain	No	N/A	Yes	N/A	
33	Sweden	No	N/A	Yes	N/A	
34	Switzerland	No	N/A	Yes	N/A	
35	Thailand	No	N/A	Yes	N/A	
36	Turkey	No	N/A	Yes	N/A	
37	United Arab Emirates	No	N/A	Yes	N/A	
38	United Kingdom	Yes	PPT alone	N/A	N/A	
39	United States	No	N/A	No	N/A	Contains an LOB as per US treaty policy
40	Viet Nam	No	N/A	Yes	N/A	

Nigeria

A. Progress in the implementation of the minimum standard

Nigeria has 15 tax agreements in force, as reported in its response to the Peer Review questionnaire.

Nigeria signed the MLI in 2017, listing all 15 tax agreements.

Nigeria is implementing the minimum standard through the inclusion of the preamble statement and the PPT.

The agreements that will be modified by the MLI will come into compliance with the minimum standard once the provisions of the MLI take effect.[110]

B. Implementation issues

No jurisdiction has raised any concerns about their agreements with Nigeria.

Summary of the jurisdiction response – Nigeria

	Treaty partners	Compliance with the standard	If compliant, the alternative implemented	Signature of a complying instrument	The alternative implemented through the complying instrument (if not the MLI)	Comments
1	Belgium	No	N/A	Yes	N/A	
2	Canada	No	N/A	Yes	N/A	
3	China (People's Republic of)	No	N/A	Yes	N/A	
4	Czech Republic	No	N/A	Yes	N/A	
5	France	No	N/A	Yes	N/A	
6	Netherlands	No	N/A	Yes	N/A	
7	Pakistan	No	N/A	Yes	N/A	
8	Philippines*	No	N/A	Yes	N/A	
9	Romania	No	N/A	Yes	N/A	
10	Slovak Republic	No	N/A	Yes	N/A	
11	South Africa	No	N/A	Yes	N/A	
12	Spain	No	N/A	Yes	N/A	
13	Singapore	No	N/A	Yes	N/A	
14	Sweden	No	N/A	Yes	N/A	
15	United Kingdom	No	N/A	Yes	N/A	

The Republic of North Macedonia

A. Progress in the implementation of the minimum standard

The Republic of North Macedonia has 47 tax agreements in force, as reported in its response to the Peer Review questionnaire.

None of the Republic of North Macedonia's agreements comply with the minimum standard or are subject to a complying instrument.

B. Implementation issues

No jurisdiction has raised any concerns about the Republic of North Macedonia.

The Republic of North Macedonia is encouraged to implement the minimum standard in its agreements.

Summary of the jurisdiction response – The Republic of North Macedonia

	Treaty partners	Compliance with the standard	If compliant, the alternative implemented	Signature of a complying instrument	The alternative implemented through the complying instrument (if not the MLI)	Comments
1	Albania*	No	N/A	No	N/A	
2	Austria	No	N/A	No	N/A	
3	Azerbaijan*	No	N/A	No	N/A	
4	Belarus*	No	N/A	No	N/A	
5	Belgium	No	N/A	No	N/A	partial compliance with respect to PPT
6	Bosnia and Herzegovina*	No	N/A	No	N/A	
7	Bulgaria	No	N/A	No	N/A	
8	China (People's Republic of)	No	N/A	No	N/A	
9	Chinese Taipei*	No	N/A	No	N/A	
10	Croatia	No	N/A	No	N/A	
11	Czech Republic	No	N/A	No	N/A	
12	Denmark	No	N/A	No	N/A	
13	Estonia	No	N/A	No	N/A	
14	Finland	No	N/A	No	N/A	
15	France	No	N/A	No	N/A	
16	Germany	No	N/A	No	N/A	
17	Hungary	No	N/A	No	N/A	
18	India	No	N/A	No	N/A	partial compliance with respect to PPT

19	Iran*	No	N/A	No	N/A	
20	Ireland	No	N/A	No	N/A	
21	Italy	No	N/A	No	N/A	
22	Kazakhstan	No	N/A	No	N/A	
23	Kosovo*	No	N/A	No	N/A	
24	Kuwait*	No	N/A	No	N/A	
25	Latvia	No	N/A	No	N/A	
26	Lithuania	No	N/A	No	N/A	partial compliance with respect to PPT
27	Luxembourg	No	N/A	No	N/A	
28	Moldova*	No	N/A	No	N/A	
29	Montenegro*[111]	No	N/A	No	N/A	
30	Morocco	No	N/A	No	N/A	
31	Netherlands	No	N/A	No	N/A	
32	Norway	No	N/A	No	N/A	
33	Poland	No	N/A	No	N/A	
34	Qatar	No	N/A	No	N/A	
35	Romania	No	N/A	No	N/A	
36	Russian Federation	No	N/A	No	N/A	
37	Saudi Arabia	No	N/A	No	N/A	
38	Serbia[112]	No	N/A	No	N/A	
39	Slovak Republic	No	N/A	No	N/A	
40	Slovenia	No	N/A	No	N/A	
41	Spain	No	N/A	No	N/A	
42	Sweden	No	N/A	No	N/A	
43	Switzerland	No	N/A	No	N/A	Protocol concluded to meet minimum standard (preamble and PPT) and is awaiting signature
44	Turkey	No	N/A	No	N/A	
45	Ukraine	No	N/A	No	N/A	PPT with respect to interest and royalty articles
46	United Arab Emirates	No	N/A	No	N/A	
47	United Kingdom	No	N/A	No	N/A	PPT with respect to dividend, interest, royalty and other income articles

Norway

A. Progress in the implementation of the minimum standard

Norway has 84 tax agreements in force, as reported in its response to the Peer Review questionnaire, including the multilateral Nordic Convention concluded with Denmark, the Faroe Islands, Finland, Iceland and Sweden (the “Nordic Convention”).[113]

Norway signed the MLI in 2017, listing 28 tax agreements.

Norway is implementing the minimum standard through the inclusion of the preamble statement and the PPT.[114]

The agreements that will be modified by the MLI will come into compliance with the minimum standard once the provisions of the MLI take effect.

Norway indicated in its response to the Peer Review questionnaire that bilateral negotiations would be used with respect to its agreements with Belgium, Brazil, Canada, France, Germany, Israel, Korea, New Zealand, Singapore, Slovak Republic, Spain, Thailand and the United States.

The Parties to the Nordic Convention signed a complying instrument in 2018.

B. Implementation issues

No jurisdiction has raised any concerns about their agreements with Norway.

Summary of the jurisdiction response – Norway

	Treaty partners	Compliance with the standard	If compliant, the alternative implemented	Signature of a complying instrument	The alternative implemented through the complying instrument (if not the MLI)	Comments
1	Albania*	No	N/A	No	N/A	
2	Argentina	No	N/A	Yes	N/A	
3	Australia	No	N/A	Yes	N/A	
4	Austria	No	N/A	No	N/A	
5	Azerbaijan*	No	N/A	No	N/A	
6	Bangladesh*	No	N/A	No	N/A	
7	Barbados	No	N/A	No	N/A	
8	Belgium	No	N/A	No	N/A	
9	Benin	No	N/A	No	N/A	
10	Bosnia and Herzegovina*	No	N/A	No	N/A	
11	Brazil	No	N/A	No	N/A	
12	Bulgaria	No	N/A	Yes	N/A	
13	Canada	No	N/A	No	N/A	
14	Chile	No	N/A	Yes	N/A	
15	China (People's Republic of)	No	N/A	Yes	N/A	

16	Cote d'Ivoire	No	N/A	No	N/A	
17	Croatia	No	N/A	No	N/A	
18	Curacao	No	N/A	No	N/A	
19	Cyprus*	No	N/A	Yes	N/A	
20	Czech Republic	No	N/A	Yes	N/A	
21	Denmark	No	N/A	Yes	PPT alone	The Nordic Convention
22	Egypt	No	N/A	No	N/A	
23	Estonia	No	N/A	Yes	N/A	
24	Faroe Islands	No	N/A	Yes	PPT alone	The Nordic Convention
25	Finland	No	N/A	Yes	PPT alone	The Nordic Convention
26	France	No	N/A	No	N/A	
27	Gambia*	No	N/A	No	N/A	
28	Georgia	No	N/A	Yes	N/A	
29	Germany	No	N/A	No	N/A	
30	Greece	No	N/A	Yes	N/A	
31	Greenland	No	N/A	No	N/A	
32	Hungary	No	N/A	No	N/A	
33	Iceland	No	N/A	Yes	PPT alone	The Nordic Convention
34	India	No	N/A	Yes	N/A	
35	Indonesia	No	N/A	No	N/A	
36	Ireland	No	N/A	Yes	N/A	
37	Israel	No	N/A	No	N/A	
38	Italy	No	N/A	No	N/A	
39	Jamaica	No	N/A	No	N/A	
40	Japan	No	N/A	Yes	N/A	
41	Kazakhstan	No	N/A	No	N/A	
42	Kenya	No	N/A	No	N/A	
43	Korea	No	N/A	No	N/A	
44	Latvia	No	N/A	Yes	N/A	
45	Lithuania	No	N/A	Yes	N/A	
46	Luxembourg	No	N/A	Yes	N/A	
47	North Macedonia	No	N/A	No	N/A	
48	Malawi*	No	N/A	No	N/A	
49	Malaysia	No	N/A	No	N/A	
50	Malta	No	N/A	Yes	N/A	
51	Mexico	No	N/A	Yes	N/A	
52	Montenegro*	No	N/A	No	N/A	
53	Morocco	No	N/A	No	N/A	
54	Nepal*	No	N/A	No	N/A	
55	Netherlands	No	N/A	Yes	N/A	
56	New Zealand	No	N/A	No	N/A	
57	Pakistan	No	N/A	No	N/A	
58	Philippines*	No	N/A	No	N/A	
59	Poland	No	N/A	Yes	N/A	
60	Portugal	No	N/A	Yes	N/A	
61	Qatar	No	N/A	No	N/A	
62	Romania	No	N/A	Yes	N/A	
63	Russia	No	N/A	Yes	N/A	
64	Senegal	No	N/A	No	N/A	
65	Serbia	No	N/A	Yes	N/A	

66	Sierra Leone	No	N/A	No	N/A	
67	Singapore	No	N/A	No	N/A	
68	Sint Maarten*	No	N/A	No	N/A	
69	Slovak Republic	No	N/A	No	N/A	
70	Slovenia	No	N/A	Yes	N/A	
71	South Africa	No	N/A	Yes	N/A	
72	Spain	No	N/A	No	N/A	
73	Sri Lanka	No	N/A	No	N/A	
74	Sweden	No	N/A	Yes	PPT alone	The Nordic Convention
75	Switzerland	No	N/A	Yes	PPT alone	
76	Tanzania*	No	N/A	No	N/A	
77	Thailand	No	N/A	No	N/A	
78	Trinidad and Tobago	No	N/A	No	N/A	
79	Tunisia	No	N/A	No	N/A	
80	Turkey	No	N/A	Yes	N/A	
81	Uganda*	No	N/A	No	N/A	
82	Ukraine	No	N/A	No	N/A	
83	United Kingdom	No	N/A	Yes	N/A	
84	United States	No	N/A	No	N/A	
85	Venezuela*	No	N/A	No	N/A	
86	Viet Nam	No	N/A	No	N/A	
87	Zambia	No	N/A	No	N/A	
88	Zimbabwe*	No	N/A	No	N/A	

Oman

A. Progress in the implementation of the minimum standard

Oman has 35 tax agreements in force, as reported in its response to the Peer Review questionnaire.

None of Oman's agreements comply with the minimum standard or are subject to a complying instrument.

Oman indicated in its response to the Peer Review questionnaire that bilateral negotiations would be used with respect to its agreement with India.

B. Implementation issues

No jurisdiction has raised any concerns about their agreements with Oman.

Oman is encouraged to implement the minimum standard in its agreements.

Summary of the jurisdiction response – Oman

	Treaty partners	Compliance with the standard	If compliant, the alternative implemented	Signature of a complying instrument	The alternative implemented through the complying instrument (if not the MLI)	Comments
1	Algeria*	No	N/A	No	N/A	
2	Belarus*	No	N/A	No	N/A	
3	Brunei Darussalam	No	N/A	No	N/A	
4	Canada	No	N/A	No	N/A	
5	China (People's Republic of)	No	N/A	No	N/A	
6	Croatia	No	N/A	No	N/A	
7	France	No	N/A	No	N/A	
8	Hungary	No	N/A	No	N/A	
9	India	No	N/A	No	N/A	
10	Iran*	No	N/A	No	N/A	
11	Italy	No	N/A	No	N/A	
12	Japan	No	N/A	No	N/A	
13	Korea	No	N/A	No	N/A	
14	Lebanon*	No	N/A	No	N/A	
15	Mauritius	No	N/A	No	N/A	
16	Moldova*	No	N/A	No	N/A	
17	Morocco	No	N/A	No	N/A	
18	Netherlands	No	N/A	No	N/A	
19	Pakistan	No	N/A	No	N/A	
20	Portugal	No	N/A	No	N/A	
21	Seychelles	No	N/A	No	N/A	
22	Singapore	No	N/A	No	N/A	
23	Sri Lanka	No	N/A	No	N/A	

24	South Africa	No	N/A	No	N/A	
25	Spain	No	N/A	No	N/A	
26	Sudan*	No	N/A	No	N/A	
27	Switzerland	No	N/A	No	N/A	
28	Syrian Arab Republic*	No	N/A	No	N/A	
29	Thailand	No	N/A	No	N/A	
30	Tunisia	No	N/A	No	N/A	
31	Turkey	No	N/A	No	N/A	
32	United Kingdom	No	N/A	No	N/A	
33	Uzbekistan*	No	N/A	No	N/A	
34	Viet Nam	No	N/A	No	N/A	
35	Yemen*	No	N/A	No	N/A	

Pakistan

A. Progress in the implementation of the minimum standard

Pakistan has 65 tax agreements in force, as reported in its response to the Peer Review questionnaire.

Pakistan signed the MLI in 2017, listing 63 tax agreements.

Pakistan is implementing the minimum standard through the inclusion of the preamble statement and the PPT.[115]

The agreements that will be modified by the MLI will come into compliance with the minimum standard once the provisions of the MLI take effect.

B. Implementation issues

No jurisdiction has raised any concerns about their agreements with Pakistan.

Summary of the jurisdiction response – Pakistan

	Treaty partners	Compliance with the standard	If compliant, the alternative implemented	Signature of a complying instrument	The alternative implemented through the complying instrument (if not the MLI)	Comments
1	Austria	No	N/A	Yes	N/A	
2	Azerbaijan*	No	N/A	Yes	N/A	
3	Bahrain	No	N/A	Yes	N/A	
4	Bangladesh*	No	N/A	Yes	N/A	
5	Belarus*	No	N/A	Yes	N/A	
6	Belgium	No	N/A	Yes	N/A	
7	Bosnia and Herzegovina*	No	N/A	Yes	N/A	
8	Brunei Darussalam	No	N/A	No	N/A	We will include Brunei in the list of covered tax agreements while depositing the Instrument of Ratification of MLI.
9	Canada	No	N/A	Yes	N/A	
10	China (People's Republic of)	No	N/A	Yes	N/A	
11	Czech Republic	No	N/A	Yes	N/A	
12	Denmark	No	N/A	Yes	N/A	
13	Egypt	No	N/A	Yes	N/A	

14	Finland	No	N/A	Yes	N/A	
15	France	No	N/A	Yes	N/A	
16	Germany	No	N/A	Yes	N/A	
17	Hong Kong (China)	No	N/A	No	N/A	We will include Hong Kong in the list of covered tax agreements while depositing the Instrument of Ratification of MLI.
18	Hungary	No	N/A	Yes	N/A	
19	Indonesia	No	N/A	Yes	N/A	
20	Iran*	No	N/A	Yes	N/A	
21	Ireland	No	N/A	Yes	N/A	
22	Italy	No	N/A	Yes	N/A	
23	Japan	No	N/A	Yes	N/A	
24	Jordan*	No	N/A	Yes	N/A	
25	Kazakhstan	No	N/A	Yes	N/A	
26	Korea	No	N/A	Yes	N/A	
27	Kuwait*	No	N/A	Yes	N/A	
28	Kyrgyzstan*	No	N/A	Yes	N/A	
29	Lebanon*	No	N/A	Yes	N/A	
30	Libya*	No	N/A	Yes	N/A	
31	Malaysia	No	N/A	Yes	N/A	
32	Malta	No	N/A	Yes	N/A	
33	Mauritius	No	N/A	Yes	N/A	
34	Morocco	No	N/A	Yes	N/A	
35	Nepal*	No	N/A	Yes	N/A	
36	Netherlands	No	N/A	Yes	N/A	
37	Nigeria	No	N/A	Yes	N/A	
38	Norway	No	N/A	Yes	N/A	
39	Oman	No	N/A	Yes	N/A	
40	Philippines*	No	N/A	Yes	N/A	
41	Poland	No	N/A	Yes	N/A	
42	Portugal	No	N/A	Yes	N/A	
43	Qatar	No	N/A	Yes	N/A	
44	Romania	No	N/A	Yes	N/A	
45	Saudi Arabia	No	N/A	Yes	N/A	
46	Serbia	No	N/A	Yes	N/A	
47	Singapore	No	N/A	Yes	N/A	
48	South Africa	No	N/A	Yes	N/A	
49	Spain	No	N/A	Yes	N/A	
50	Sri Lanka	No	N/A	Yes	N/A	
51	Sweden	No	N/A	Yes	N/A	
52	Switzerland	No	N/A	Yes	N/A	
53	Syrian Arab Republic*	No	N/A	Yes	N/A	
54	Tajikistan*	No	N/A	Yes	N/A	
55	Thailand	No	N/A	Yes	N/A	
56	Tunisia	No	N/A	Yes	N/A	
57	Turkey	No	N/A	Yes	N/A	
58	Turkmenistan*	No	N/A	Yes	N/A	

59	Ukraine	No	N/A	Yes	N/A	
60	United Arab Emirates	No	N/A	Yes	N/A	
61	United Kingdom	No	N/A	Yes	N/A	
62	United States	No	N/A	Yes	N/A	
63	Uzbekistan*	No	N/A	Yes	N/A	
64	Viet Nam	No	N/A	Yes	N/A	
65	Yemen*	No	N/A	Yes	N/A	

Panama

A. Progress in the implementation of the minimum standard

Panama has 17 tax agreements in force, as reported in its response to the Peer Review questionnaire.

Panama signed the MLI in 2018, listing 17 tax agreements.

Panama is implementing the minimum standard through the inclusion of the preamble statement and the PPT.[116]

The agreements that will be modified by the MLI will come into compliance with the minimum standard once the provisions of the MLI take effect.

B. Implementation issues

No jurisdiction has raised any concerns about their agreements with Panama.

Summary of the jurisdiction response – Panama

	Treaty partners	Compliance with the standard	If compliant, the alternative implemented	Signature of a complying instrument	The alternative implemented through the complying instrument (if not the MLI)	Comments
1	Barbados	No	N/A	Yes	N/A	
2	Czech Republic	No	N/A	Yes	N/A	
3	France	No	N/A	Yes	N/A	
4	Ireland	No	N/A	Yes	N/A	
5	Israel	No	N/A	Yes	N/A	
6	Italy	No	N/A	Yes	N/A	
7	Korea	No	N/A	Yes	N/A	
8	Luxembourg	No	N/A	Yes	N/A	
9	Mexico	No	N/A	Yes	N/A	
10	Netherlands	No	N/A	Yes	N/A	
11	Portugal	No	N/A	Yes	N/A	
12	Qatar	No	N/A	Yes	N/A	
13	Singapore	No	N/A	Yes	N/A	
14	Spain	No	N/A	Yes	N/A	
15	United Arab Emirates	No	N/A	Yes	N/A	
16	United Kingdom	No	N/A	Yes	N/A	
17	Viet Nam	No	N/A	Yes	N/A	

Papua New Guinea

A. Progress in the implementation of the minimum standard

Papua New Guinea has ten tax agreements in force, as reported in its response to the Peer Review questionnaire.

Papua New Guinea signed the MLI in 2019, listing ten tax agreements.

Papua New Guinea is implementing the minimum standard through the inclusion of the preamble statement and the PPT.

The agreements that will be modified by the MLI will come into compliance with the minimum standard once the provisions of the MLI take effect.

B. Implementation issues

No jurisdiction has raised any concerns about their agreements with Papua New Guinea.

Summary of the jurisdiction response – Papua New Guinea

	Treaty partners	Compliance with the standard	If compliant, the alternative implemented	Signature of a complying instrument	The alternative implemented through the complying instrument (if not the MLI)	Comments
1	Australia	No	N/A	Yes	N/A	
2	Canada	No	N/A	Yes	N/A	
3	China (People's Republic of)	No	N/A	Yes	N/A	
4	Fiji*	No	N/A	Yes	N/A	
5	Indonesia	No	N/A	Yes	N/A	Indonesia has not listed our agreement in their MLI Position to be a CTA.
6	Korea	No	N/A	Yes	N/A	
7	Malaysia	No	N/A	Yes	N/A	
8	New Zealand	No	N/A	Yes	N/A	
9	Singapore	No	N/A	Yes	N/A	
10	United Kingdom	No	N/A	Yes	N/A	

Paraguay

A. Progress in the implementation of the minimum standard

Paraguay has two tax agreements in force, as reported in its response to the Peer Review questionnaire. Its agreement with Uruguay complies with the minimum standard. Paraguay has not signed the MLI.

B. Implementation issues

No jurisdiction has raised any concerns about their agreements with Paraguay.

Summary of the jurisdiction response – Paraguay

	Treaty partners	Compliance with the standard	If compliant, the alternative implemented	Signature of a complying instrument	The alternative implemented through the complying instrument (if not the MLI)	Comments
1	Chile	No	N/A	No	N/A	
2	Chinese Taipei*	No	N/A	No	N/A	
3	Uruguay	Yes	PPT and LOB	N/A	N/A	

Peru

A. Progress in the implementation of the minimum standard

Peru has eight tax agreements in force, as reported in its response to the Peer Review questionnaire, including the Decision 578 of the Andean Community Commission (Decision 578) for the members of the Andean Community.[117]

Peru signed the MLI in 2018, listing seven tax agreements.

Peru is implementing the minimum standard through the inclusion of the preamble statement and the PPT.[118]

The agreements that will be modified by the MLI will come into compliance with the minimum standard once the provisions of the MLI take effect.

Peru indicated in its response to the Peer Review questionnaire that the Andean Community Agreement has not been listed under the MLI as it is a decision of the Andean Community Commission.

B. Implementation issues

No jurisdiction has raised any concerns about their agreements with Peru.

Summary of the jurisdiction response – Peru

	Treaty partners	Compliance with the standard	If compliant, the alternative implemented	Signature of a complying instrument	The alternative implemented through the complying instrument (if not the MLI)	Comments
1	Bolivia*	No	N/A	No	N/A	Andean Community (Decision 578)
2	Brazil	No	N/A	Yes	N/A	
3	Canada	No	N/A	Yes	N/A	
4	Chile	No	N/A	Yes	N/A	
5	Colombia	No	N/A	No	N/A	Andean Community (Decision 578)
6	Ecuador*	No	N/A	No	N/A	Andean Community (Decision 578)
7	Korea	No	N/A	Yes	N/A	
8	Mexico	No	N/A	Yes	N/A	
9	Portugal	No	N/A	Yes	N/A	
10	Switzerland	No	N/A	Yes	N/A	

Poland

A. Progress in the implementation of the minimum standard

Poland has 82 tax agreements in force, as reported in its response to the Peer Review questionnaire. Eleven of those agreements, the agreements with Australia, Austria, France, Israel, Japan, Lithuania, New Zealand, Serbia, Slovak Republic, Slovenia, and the United Kingdom, comply with the minimum standard.

Poland signed the MLI in 2017 and deposited its instrument of ratification of the MLI on 23 January 2018, listing 76 tax agreements.[119] The MLI has entered into force for Poland on 1 July 2018.

Poland is implementing the minimum standard through the inclusion of the preamble statement and the PPT.[120]

The agreements modified by the MLI come into compliance with the minimum standard once the provisions of the MLI take effect. Other agreements listed under the MLI are expected to become compliant with the minimum standard once the MLI has been ratified by the other contracting jurisdiction. Poland indicated in its response to the Peer Review questionnaire that bilateral negotiations would be used with respect to its agreement with Georgia, Germany, Montenegro* and the United States.

B. Implementation issues

No jurisdiction has raised any concerns about their agreements with Poland.

Summary of the jurisdiction response – Poland

	Treaty partners	Compliance with the standard	If compliant, the alternative implemented	Signature of a complying instrument	The alternative implemented through the complying instrument (if not the MLI)	Comments
1	Albania*	No	N/A	Yes	N/A	
2	Armenia	No	N/A	Yes	N/A	
3	Australia	Yes	PPT alone	N/A	N/A	The express statement in the preamble and the PPT (equivalent to paragraph 9 of Article 29 of the 2017 OECD MTC)
4	Austria	Yes	PPT alone	N/A	N/A	The express statement in the preamble and the PPT (equivalent to paragraph 9 of Article 29 of the 2017

						OECD MTC)
5	Azerbaijan*	No	N/A	Yes	N/A	
6	Bangladesh*	No	N/A	Yes	N/A	
7	Belarus*	No	N/A	Yes	N/A	
8	Belgium	No	N/A	Yes	N/A	
9	Bosnia and Herzegovina*	No	N/A	Yes	N/A	
10	Bulgaria	No	N/A	Yes	N/A	
11	Canada	No	N/A	Yes	N/A	
12	Chile	No	N/A	Yes	N/A	
13	China (People's Republic of)	No	N/A	Yes	N/A	
14	Croatia	No	N/A	Yes	N/A	
15	Cyprus*	No	N/A	Yes	N/A	
16	Czech Republic	No	N/A	Yes	N/A	
17	Denmark	No	N/A	Yes	N/A	
18	Egypt	No	N/A	Yes	N/A	
19	Estonia	No	N/A	Yes	N/A	
20	Ethiopia*	No	N/A	Yes	N/A	
21	Finland	No	N/A	Yes	N/A	
22	France	Yes	PPT alone	N/A	N/A	The express statement in the preamble and the PPT alone (equivalent to paragraph 9 of Article 29 of the 2017 OECD MTC)
23	Georgia	No	N/A	No	N/A	
24	Germany	No	N/A	No	N/A	The Protocol will amend the text of the title of the DTA as well as the preamble. It will introduce also the PPT provision
25	Greece	No	N/A	Yes	N/A	
26	Hungary	No	N/A	Yes	N/A	
27	Iceland	No	N/A	Yes	N/A	
28	India	No	N/A	Yes	N/A	
29	Indonesia	No	N/A	Yes	N/A	
30	Iran*	No	N/A	Yes	N/A	
31	Ireland	No	N/A	Yes	N/A	
32	Israel	Yes	PPT alone	N/A	N/A	The express statement in the preamble and the PPT alone (equivalent to paragraph 9 of Article 29 of the 2017 OECD MTC)
33	Italy	No	N/A	Yes	N/A	
34	Japan	Yes	PPT alone	N/A	N/A	The express

						statement in the preamble and the PPT alone (equivalent to paragraph 9 of Article 29 of the 2017 OECD MTC)
35	Jordan*	No	N/A	Yes	N/A	
36	Kazakhstan	No	N/A	Yes	N/A	
37	Korea	No	N/A	Yes	N/A	
38	Kuwait*	No	N/A	Yes	N/A	
39	Kyrgyzstan*	No	N/A	Yes	N/A	
40	Latvia	No	N/A	Yes	N/A	
41	Lebanon*	No	N/A	Yes	N/A	
42	Lithuania	Yes	PPT alone	N/A	N/A	The express statement in the preamble and the PPT alone (equivalent to paragraph 9 of Article 29 of the 2017 OECD MTC)
43	Luxembourg	No	N/A	Yes	N/A	
44	North Macedonia	No	N/A	Yes	N/A	
45	Malaysia	No	N/A	No	N/A	
46	Malta	No	N/A	Yes	N/A	
47	Mexico	No	N/A	Yes	N/A	
48	Moldova*	No	N/A	Yes	N/A	
49	Mongolia	No	N/A	Yes	N/A	
50	Montenegro*	No	N/A	No	N/A	Invitation letter sent for bilateral negotiation
51	Morocco	No	N/A	Yes	N/A	
52	Netherlands	No	N/A	Yes	N/A	
53	New Zealand	Yes	PPT alone	N/A	N/A	The express statement in the preamble and the PPT alone (equivalent to paragraph 9 of Article 29 of the 2017 OECD MTC)
54	Norway	No	N/A	Yes	N/A	
55	Pakistan	No	N/A	Yes	N/A	
56	Philippines*	No	N/A	Yes	N/A	
57	Portugal	No	N/A	Yes	N/A	
58	Qatar	No	N/A	Yes	N/A	
59	Romania	No	N/A	Yes	N/A	
60	Russia	No	N/A	Yes	N/A	
61	Saudi Arabia	No	N/A	Yes	N/A	
62	Serbia	Yes	PPT alone	N/A	N/A	The express statement in

						the preamble and the PPT alone (equivalent to paragraph 9 of Article 29 of the 2017 OECD MTC)
63	Singapore	No	N/A	Yes	N/A	
64	Slovak Republic	Yes	PPT alone	N/A	N/A	The express statement in the preamble and the PPT alone (equivalent to paragraph 9 of Article 29 of the 2017 OECD MTC)
65	Slovenia	Yes	PPT alone	N/A	N/A	The express statement in the preamble and the PPT alone (equivalent to paragraph 9 of Article 29 of the 2017 OECD MTC)
66	South Africa	No	N/A	Yes	N/A	
67	Spain	No	N/A	Yes	N/A	
68	Sri Lanka	No	N/A	No	N/A	
69	Sweden	No	N/A	Yes	N/A	
70	Switzerland	No	N/A	Yes	N/A	
71	Syrian Arab Republic*	No	N/A	Yes	N/A	
72	Tajikistan*	No	N/A	Yes	N/A	
73	Thailand	No	N/A	Yes	N/A	
74	Tunisia	No	N/A	Yes	N/A	
75	Turkey	No	N/A	Yes	N/A	
76	Ukraine	No	N/A	Yes	N/A	
77	United Arab Emirates	No	N/A	Yes	N/A	
78	United Kingdom	Yes	PPT alone	N/A	N/A	The express statement in the preamble and the PPT alone (equivalent to paragraph 9 of Article 29 of the 2017 OECD MTC)
79	United States	No	N/A	No	N/A	Invitation letter sent for bilateral negotiation
80	Uzbekistan*	No	N/A	Yes	N/A	
81	Viet Nam	No	N/A	Yes	N/A	
82	Zimbabwe*	No	N/A	Yes	N/A	

Portugal

A. Progress in the implementation of the minimum standard

Portugal has 77 tax agreements in force, as reported in its response to the Peer Review questionnaire.

Portugal signed the MLI in 2017, listing 77 tax agreements.[121]

Portugal is implementing the minimum standard through the inclusion of the preamble statement and the PPT.[122]

The agreements that will be modified by the MLI will come into compliance with the minimum standard once the provisions of the MLI take effect.

B. Implementation issues

No jurisdiction has raised any concerns about their agreements with Portugal.

Summary of the jurisdiction response – Portugal

	Treaty partners	Compliance with the standard	If compliant, the alternative implemented	Signature of a complying instrument	The alternative implemented through the complying instrument (if not the MLI)	Comments
1	Algeria*	No	N/A	Yes	N/A	
2	Andorra	No	N/A	Yes	N/A	
3	Austria	No	N/A	Yes	N/A	
4	Bahrain	No	N/A	Yes	N/A	
5	Barbados	No	N/A	Yes	N/A	
6	Belgium	No	N/A	Yes	N/A	
7	Brazil	No	N/A	Yes	N/A	
8	Bulgaria	No	N/A	Yes	N/A	
9	Cabo Verde	No	N/A	Yes	N/A	
10	Canada	No	N/A	Yes	N/A	
11	Chile	No	N/A	Yes	N/A	
12	China (People's Republic of)	No	N/A	Yes	N/A	
13	Colombia	No	N/A	Yes	N/A	
14	Cote d'Ivoire	No	N/A	Yes	N/A	
15	Croatia	No	N/A	Yes	N/A	
16	Cuba*	No	N/A	Yes	N/A	
17	Cyprus*	No	N/A	Yes	N/A	
18	Czech Republic	No	N/A	Yes	N/A	
19	Denmark	No	N/A	Yes	N/A	
20	Estonia	No	N/A	Yes	N/A	
21	Ethiopia*	No	N/A	Yes	N/A	
22	France	No	N/A	Yes	N/A	

23	Georgia	No	N/A	Yes	N/A	
24	Germany	No	N/A	Yes	N/A	
25	Greece	No	N/A	Yes	N/A	
26	Guinea-Bissau*	No	N/A	Yes	N/A	
27	Hong Kong (China)	No	N/A	Yes	N/A	
28	Hungary	No	N/A	Yes	N/A	
29	Iceland	No	N/A	Yes	N/A	
30	India	No	N/A	Yes	N/A	
31	Indonesia	No	N/A	Yes	N/A	
32	Ireland	No	N/A	Yes	N/A	
33	Israel	No	N/A	Yes	N/A	
34	Italy	No	N/A	Yes	N/A	
35	Japan	No	N/A	Yes	N/A	
36	Korea	No	N/A	Yes	N/A	
37	Kuwait*	No	N/A	Yes	N/A	
38	Latvia	No	N/A	Yes	N/A	
39	Lithuania	No	N/A	Yes	N/A	
40	Luxembourg	No	N/A	Yes	N/A	
41	Macau (China)	No	N/A	Yes	N/A	
42	Malta	No	N/A	Yes	N/A	
43	Mexico	No	N/A	Yes	N/A	
44	Moldova*	No	N/A	Yes	N/A	
45	Montenegro*	No	N/A	Yes	N/A	
46	Morocco	No	N/A	Yes	N/A	
47	Mozambique*	No	N/A	Yes	N/A	
48	Netherlands	No	N/A	Yes	N/A	
49	Norway	No	N/A	Yes	N/A	
50	Oman	No	N/A	Yes	N/A	
51	Pakistan	No	N/A	Yes	N/A	
52	Panama	No	N/A	Yes	N/A	
53	Peru	No	N/A	Yes	N/A	
54	Poland	No	N/A	Yes	N/A	
55	Qatar	No	N/A	Yes	N/A	
56	Romania	No	N/A	Yes	N/A	
57	Russia	No	N/A	Yes	N/A	
58	San Marino	No	N/A	Yes	N/A	
59	Sao Tome and Principe*	No	N/A	Yes	N/A	
60	Saudi Arabia	No	N/A	Yes	N/A	
61	Senegal	No	N/A	Yes	N/A	
62	Singapore	No	N/A	Yes	N/A	
63	Slovak Republic	No	N/A	Yes	N/A	
64	Slovenia	No	N/A	Yes	N/A	
65	South Africa	No	N/A	Yes	N/A	
66	Spain	No	N/A	Yes	N/A	
67	Sweden	No	N/A	Yes	PPT alone	
68	Switzerland	No	N/A	Yes	N/A	
69	Tunisia	No	N/A	Yes	N/A	
70	Turkey	No	N/A	Yes	N/A	
71	Ukraine	No	N/A	Yes	N/A	
72	United Arab Emirates	No	N/A	Yes	N/A	
73	United Kingdom	No	N/A	Yes	N/A	

74	United States	No	N/A	Yes	N/A	
75	Uruguay	No	N/A	Yes	N/A	
76	Venezuela*	No	N/A	Yes	N/A	
77	Viet Nam	No	N/A	Yes	N/A	

Qatar

A. Progress in the implementation of the minimum standard

Qatar has 77 tax agreements in force, as reported in its response to the Peer Review questionnaire. Its agreement with Ghana* complies with the minimum standard

Qatar signed the MLI in 2018, listing 76 tax agreements.[123]

Qatar is implementing the minimum standard through the inclusion of the preamble statement and the PPT.[124]

The agreements that will be modified by the MLI will come into compliance with the minimum standard once the provisions of the MLI take effect.

B. Implementation issues

No jurisdiction has raised any concerns about their agreements with Qatar.

Summary of the jurisdiction response – Qatar

	Treaty partners	Compliance with the standard	If compliant, the alternative implemented	Signature of a complying instrument	The alternative implemented through the complying instrument (if not the MLI)	Comments
1	Albania*	No	N/A	Yes	N/A	
2	Algeria*	No	N/A	Yes	N/A	
3	Armenia	No	N/A	Yes	N/A	
4	Austria	No	N/A	Yes	N/A	Amending instrument ensuring compliance with standards under negotiation
5	Azerbaijan*	No	N/A	Yes	N/A	
6	Barbados	No	N/A	Yes	N/A	
7	Belarus*	No	N/A	Yes	N/A	
8	Bermuda	No	N/A	Yes	N/A	
9	Bosnia and Herzegovina*	No	N/A	Yes	N/A	
10	Brunei Darussalam	No	N/A	Yes	N/A	
11	Bulgaria	No	N/A	Yes	N/A	
12	Chad*	No	N/A	Yes	N/A	
13	China (People's Republic of)	No	N/A	Yes	N/A	
14	Croatia	No	N/A	Yes	N/A	
15	Cuba*	No	N/A	Yes	N/A	
16	Cyprus*	No	N/A	Yes	N/A	
17	Ecuador*	No	N/A	Yes	N/A	
18	Fiji*	No	N/A	Yes	N/A	

19	France	No	N/A	Yes	N/A	
20	Ghana*	Yes	PPT alone	N/A	N/A	Expected to be in force on 30 June 2019
21	Georgia	No	N/A	Yes	N/A	
22	Greece	No	N/A	Yes	N/A	
23	Guernsey	No	N/A	Yes	N/A	Amending instrument ensuring compliance with standards initialled
24	Hong Kong (China)	No	N/A	Yes	N/A	
25	Hungary	No	N/A	Yes	N/A	
26	India	No	N/A	Yes	N/A	A new tax treaty compliant with the Standards initialled
27	Indonesia	No	N/A	Yes	N/A	
28	Iran*	No	N/A	Yes	N/A	
29	Ireland	No	N/A	Yes	N/A	
30	Isle of Man	No	N/A	Yes	N/A	
31	Italy	No	N/A	Yes	N/A	
32	Japan	No	N/A	Yes	N/A	
33	Jersey	No	N/A	Yes	N/A	
34	Jordan*	No	N/A	Yes	N/A	
35	Kazakhstan	No	N/A	Yes	N/A	
36	Kenya	No	N/A	Yes	N/A	
37	Korea	No	N/A	Yes	N/A	
38	Kyrgyzstan*	No	N/A	Yes	N/A	
39	Latvia	No	N/A	Yes	N/A	
40	Lebanon*	No	N/A	Yes	N/A	
41	Luxembourg	No	N/A	Yes	N/A	
42	Malaysia	No	N/A	Yes	N/A	
43	Malta	No	N/A	Yes	N/A	
44	Mauritius	No	N/A	Yes	N/A	
45	Mexico	No	N/A	Yes	N/A	
46	Monaco	No	N/A	Yes	N/A	
47	Morocco	No	N/A	Yes	N/A	Expected to be in force on 30 June 2019
48	Nepal*	No	N/A	Yes	N/A	
49	Netherlands	No	N/A	Yes	N/A	
50	Nigeria	No	N/A	Yes	N/A	
51	North Macedonia	No	N/A	Yes	N/A	
52	Norway	No	N/A	Yes	N/A	
53	Pakistan	No	N/A	Yes	N/A	
54	Panama	No	N/A	Yes	N/A	
55	Philippines*	No	N/A	Yes	N/A	
56	Poland	No	N/A	Yes	N/A	
57	Portugal	No	N/A	Yes	N/A	
58	Romania	No	N/A	Yes	N/A	
59	Russia	No	N/A	Yes	N/A	
60	San Marino	No	N/A	Yes	N/A	
61	Senegal	No	N/A	Yes	N/A	

62	Serbia	No	N/A	Yes	N/A	
63	Seychelles	No	N/A	Yes	N/A	
64	Singapore	No	N/A	Yes	N/A	
65	Slovenia	No	N/A	Yes	N/A	
66	South Africa	No	N/A	Yes	N/A	
67	Spain	No	N/A	Yes	N/A	
68	Sri Lanka	No	N/A	Yes	N/A	
69	Sudan*	No	N/A	Yes	N/A	
70	Switzerland	No	N/A	Yes	N/A	
71	Syrian Arab Republic*	No	N/A	Yes	N/A	
72	Tunisia	No	N/A	Yes	N/A	
73	Turkey	No	N/A	Yes	N/A	
74	United Kingdom	No	N/A	Yes	N/A	
75	Venezuela*	No	N/A	Yes	N/A	Expected to be in force on 30 June 2019
76	Viet Nam	No	N/A	Yes	N/A	
77	Yemen*	No	N/A	Yes	N/A	

Romania

A. Progress in the implementation of the minimum standard

Romania has 88 tax agreements in force, as reported in its response to the Peer Review questionnaire.

Romania signed the MLI in 2017, listing 88 tax agreements.[125]

Romania is implementing the minimum standard through the inclusion of the preamble statement and the PPT.[126]

The agreements that will be modified by the MLI will come into compliance with the minimum standard once the provisions of the MLI take effect.

Romania signed a bilateral complying instrument with respect to its agreement with Spain.

B. Implementation issues

No jurisdiction has raised any concerns about their agreements with Romania.

Summary of the jurisdiction response – Romania

	Treaty partners	Compliance with the standard	If compliant, the alternative implemented	Signature of a complying instrument	The alternative implemented through the complying instrument (if not the MLI)	Comments
1	Albania*	No	N/A	Yes	N/A	
2	Algeria*	No	N/A	Yes	N/A	
3	Armenia	No	N/A	Yes	N/A	
4	Australia	No	N/A	Yes	N/A	
5	Austria	No	N/A	Yes	N/A	
6	Azerbaijan*	No	N/A	Yes	N/A	
7	Bangladesh*	No	N/A	Yes	N/A	
8	Belarus*	No	N/A	Yes	N/A	
9	Belgium	No	N/A	Yes	N/A	
10	Bosnia and Herzegovina*	No	N/A	Yes	N/A	
11	Bulgaria	No	N/A	Yes	N/A	
12	Canada	No	N/A	Yes	N/A	
13	China (People's Republic of)	No	N/A	Yes	N/A	
14	Croatia	No	N/A	Yes	N/A	
15	Cyprus*	No	N/A	Yes	N/A	
16	Czech Republic	No	N/A	Yes	N/A	
17	Democratic People's Republic of Korea*	No	N/A	Yes	N/A	
18	Denmark	No	N/A	Yes	N/A	
19	Ecuador*	No	N/A	Yes	N/A	
20	Egypt	No	N/A	Yes	N/A	
21	Estonia	No	N/A	Yes	N/A	

22	Ethiopia*	No	N/A	Yes	N/A	
23	Finland	No	N/A	Yes	N/A	
24	France	No	N/A	Yes	N/A	
25	Georgia	No	N/A	Yes	N/A	
26	Germany	No	N/A	Yes	N/A	
27	Greece	No	N/A	Yes	N/A	
28	Hong Kong (China)	No	N/A	Yes	N/A	
29	Hungary	No	N/A	Yes	N/A	
30	Iceland	No	N/A	Yes	N/A	
31	India	No	N/A	Yes	N/A	
32	Indonesia	No	N/A	Yes	N/A	
33	Iran*	No	N/A	Yes	N/A	
34	Ireland	No	N/A	Yes	N/A	
35	Israel	No	N/A	Yes	N/A	
36	Italy	No	N/A	Yes	N/A	
37	Japan	No	N/A	Yes	N/A	
38	Jordan*	No	N/A	Yes	N/A	
39	Kazakhstan	No	N/A	Yes	N/A	
40	Korea	No	N/A	Yes	N/A	
41	Kuwait*	No	N/A	Yes	N/A	
42	Latvia	No	N/A	Yes	N/A	
43	Lebanon*	No	N/A	Yes	N/A	
44	Lithuania	No	N/A	Yes	N/A	
45	Luxembourg	No	N/A	Yes	N/A	
46	North Macedonia	No	N/A	Yes	N/A	
47	Malaysia	No	N/A	Yes	N/A	
48	Malta	No	N/A	Yes	N/A	
49	Mexico	No	N/A	Yes	N/A	
50	Moldova*	No	N/A	Yes	N/A	
51	Montenegro*	No	N/A	Yes	N/A	
52	Morocco	No	N/A	Yes	N/A	
53	Namibia*	No	N/A	Yes	N/A	
54	Netherlands	No	N/A	Yes	N/A	
55	Nigeria	No	N/A	Yes	N/A	
56	Norway	No	N/A	Yes	N/A	
57	Pakistan	No	N/A	Yes	N/A	
58	Philippines*	No	N/A	Yes	N/A	
59	Poland	No	N/A	Yes	N/A	
60	Portugal	No	N/A	Yes	N/A	
61	Qatar	No	N/A	Yes	N/A	
62	Russia	No	N/A	Yes	N/A	
63	San Marino	No	N/A	Yes	N/A	
64	Saudi Arabia	No	N/A	Yes	N/A	
65	Serbia	No	N/A	Yes	N/A	
66	Singapore	No	N/A	Yes	N/A	
67	Slovak Republic	No	N/A	Yes	N/A	
68	Slovenia	No	N/A	Yes	N/A	
69	South Africa	No	N/A	Yes	N/A	
70	Spain	No	N/A	Yes	PPT alone	
71	Sri Lanka	No	N/A	Yes	N/A	
72	Sudan*	No	N/A	Yes	N/A	
73	Sweden	No	N/A	Yes	N/A	
74	Switzerland	No	N/A	Yes	N/A	

75	Syrian Arab Republic*	No	N/A	Yes	N/A	
76	Tajikistan*	No	N/A	Yes	N/A	
77	Thailand	No	N/A	Yes	N/A	
78	Tunisia	No	N/A	Yes	N/A	
79	Turkey	No	N/A	Yes	N/A	
80	Turkmenistan*		N/A	Yes	N/A	
81	Ukraine	No	N/A	Yes	N/A	
82	United Arab Emirates	No	N/A	Yes	N/A	
83	United Kingdom	No	N/A	Yes	N/A	
84	United States	No	N/A	Yes	N/A	
85	Uruguay	No	N/A	Yes	N/A	
86	Uzbekistan*	No	N/A	Yes	N/A	
87	Viet Nam	No	N/A	Yes	N/A	
88	Zambia	No	N/A	Yes	N/A	

Russian Federation

A. Progress in the implementation of the minimum standard

The Russian Federation has 85 tax agreements in force, as reported in its response to the Peer Review questionnaire. Two of those agreements, the agreements with Japan and Sweden, comply with the minimum standard.

The Russian Federation signed the MLI in 2017 and deposited its instrument of ratification on 18 June 2019, listing 70 tax agreements.[127] The MLI entered into force for Russia on 1 October 2019.

The Russian Federation is implementing the minimum standard through the inclusion of the preamble statement and the PPT combined with the LOB.[128]

The agreements that will be modified by the MLI will come into compliance with the minimum standard once the provisions of the MLI take effect.

The Russian Federation indicated in its response to the Peer Review questionnaire that bilateral negotiations would be used for its agreements with Brazil, Germany and Switzerland.

B. Implementation issues

No jurisdiction has raised any concerns about their agreements with the Russian Federation.

Summary of the jurisdiction response – Russian Federation

	Treaty partners	Compliance with the standard	If compliant, the alternative implemented	Signature of a complying instrument	The alternative implemented through the complying instrument (if not the MLI)	Comments
1	Albania*	No	N/A	Yes	N/A	
2	Algeria*	No	N/A	Yes	N/A	
3	Argentina	No	N/A	Yes	N/A	
4	Armenia	No	N/A	Yes	N/A	
5	Australia	No	N/A	Yes	N/A	
6	Austria	No	N/A	Yes	N/A	
7	Azerbaijan*	No	N/A	Yes	N/A	
8	Belarus*	No	N/A	Yes	N/A	
9	Belgium	No	N/A	Yes	N/A	
10	Botswana	No	N/A	Yes	N/A	
11	Brazil	No	N/A	No	N/A	
12	Bulgaria	No	N/A	Yes	N/A	
13	Canada	No	N/A	Yes	N/A	
14	Chile	No	N/A	Yes	N/A	
15	China (People's Republic of)	No	N/A	Yes	N/A	
16	Croatia	No	N/A	Yes	N/A	
17	Cuba*	No	N/A	Yes	N/A	
18	Cyprus*	No	N/A	Yes	N/A	
19	Czech Republic	No	N/A	Yes	N/A	

20	Democratic People's Republic of Korea*	No	N/A	No	N/A	
21	Denmark	No	N/A	Yes	N/A	
22	Ecuador*	No	N/A	Yes	N/A	
23	Egypt	No	N/A	Yes	N/A	
24	Finland	No	N/A	Yes	N/A	
25	France	No	N/A	Yes	N/A	
26	Germany	No	N/A	No	N/A	
27	Greece	No	N/A	Yes	N/A	
28	Hong Kong (China)	No	N/A	Yes	N/A	
29	Hungary	No	N/A	Yes	N/A	
30	Iceland	No	N/A	Yes	N/A	
31	India	No	N/A	Yes	N/A	
32	Indonesia	No	N/A	Yes	N/A	
33	Iran*	No	N/A	No	N/A	
34	Ireland	No	N/A	Yes	N/A	
35	Israel	No	N/A	Yes	N/A	
36	Italy	No	N/A	Yes	N/A	
37	Japan	Yes	PPT and LOB	N/A	N/A	
38	Kazakhstan	No	N/A	Yes	N/A	
39	Korea	No	N/A	Yes	N/A	
40	Kuwait*	No	N/A	Yes	N/A	
41	Kyrgyzstan*	No	N/A	No	N/A	
42	Latvia	No	N/A	Yes	N/A	
43	Lebanon*	No	N/A	Yes	N/A	
44	Lithuania	No	N/A	Yes	N/A	
45	Luxembourg	No	N/A	Yes	N/A	
46	North Macedonia	No	N/A	No	N/A	
47	Malaysia	No	N/A	Yes	N/A	
48	Mali*	No	N/A	No	N/A	
49	Malta	No	N/A	Yes	N/A	
50	Mexico	No	N/A	Yes	N/A	
51	Moldova*	No	N/A	Yes	N/A	
52	Mongolia	No	N/A	Yes	N/A	
53	Montenegro*	No	N/A	Yes	N/A	
54	Morocco	No	N/A	Yes	N/A	
55	Namibia*	No	N/A	No	N/A	
56	Netherlands	No	N/A	Yes	N/A	
57	New Zealand	No	N/A	Yes	N/A	
58	Norway	No	N/A	Yes	N/A	
59	Philippines*	No	N/A	Yes	N/A	
60	Poland	No	N/A	Yes	N/A	
61	Portugal	No	N/A	Yes	N/A	
62	Qatar	No	N/A	Yes	N/A	
63	Romania	No	N/A	Yes	N/A	
64	Saudi Arabia	No	N/A	Yes	N/A	
65	Serbia	No	N/A	Yes	N/A	
66	Singapore	No	N/A	Yes	N/A	
67	Slovak Republic	No	N/A	Yes	N/A	
68	Slovenia	No	N/A	Yes	N/A	
69	South Africa	No	N/A	Yes	N/A	
70	Spain	No	N/A	Yes	N/A	
71	Sri Lanka	No	N/A	Yes	N/A	
72	Sweden	Yes	PPT alone	N/A	N/A	

73	Switzerland	No	N/A	No	N/A	
74	Syrian Arab Republic*	No	N/A	No	N/A	
75	Tajikistan*	No	N/A	No	N/A	
76	Thailand	No	N/A	Yes	N/A	
77	Turkey	No	N/A	Yes	N/A	
78	Turkmenistan*	No	N/A	No	N/A	
79	Ukraine	No	N/A	Yes	N/A	
80	United Arab Emirates	No	N/A	Yes	N/A	
81	United Kingdom	No	N/A	Yes	N/A	
82	United States	No	N/A	Yes	N/A	
83	Uzbekistan*	No	N/A	No	N/A	
84	Venezuela*	No	N/A	Yes	N/A	
85	Viet Nam	No	N/A	Yes	N/A	

Saint Kitts and Nevis

A. Progress in the implementation of the minimum standard

Saint Kitts and Nevis has five tax agreements in force, as reported in its response to the Peer Review questionnaire, including the multilateral agreement among the members of the CARICOM concluded with ten treaty partners (the CARICOM Agreement).[129]

None of Saint Kitts and Nevis' agreements comply with the minimum standard or are subject to a complying instrument.

B. Implementation issues

Saint Kitts and Nevis is encouraged to implement the minimum standard in its agreements.

Saint Kitts and Nevis is encouraged to bring the CARICOM Agreement up to date by commencing talks among all the treaty partners.[130]

Summary of the jurisdiction response – Saint Kitts and Nevis

	Treaty partners	Compliance with the standard	If compliant, the alternative implemented	Signature of a complying instrument	The alternative implemented through the complying instrument (if not the MLI)	Comments
1	Antigua and Barbuda	No	N/A	No	N/A	CARICOM
2	Barbados	No	N/A	No	N/A	CARICOM
3	Belize	No	N/A	No	N/A	CARICOM
4	Dominica	No	N/A	No	N/A	CARICOM
5	Grenada	No	N/A	No	N/A	CARICOM
6	Guyana*	No	N/A	No	N/A	CARICOM
7	Jamaica	No	N/A	No	N/A	CARICOM
8	Monaco	No	N/A	No	N/A	
9	Saint Lucia	No	N/A	No	N/A	CARICOM
10	Saint Vincent and the Grenadines	No	N/A	No	N/A	CARICOM
11	San Marino	No	N/A	No	N/A	
12	Switzerland	No	N/A	No	N/A	
13	Trinidad and Tobago	No	N/A	No	N/A	CARICOM
14	United Kingdom	No	N/A	No	N/A	

Saint Lucia

A. Progress in the implementation of the minimum standard

Saint Lucia has two tax agreements, including the multilateral agreement among the members of the CARICOM concluded with ten treaty partners (the CARICOM Agreement).[131]

Neither of Saint Lucia's agreements comply with the minimum standard or are subject to a complying instrument.

B. Implementation issues

Saint Lucia is encouraged to implement the minimum standard in its agreements.

Saint Lucia is encouraged to bring the CARICOM Agreement up to date by commencing talks among all the treaty partners.[132]

Summary of the jurisdiction response – Saint Lucia

	Treaty partners	Compliance with the standard	If compliant, the alternative implemented	Signature of a complying instrument	The alternative implemented through the complying instrument (if not the MLI)	Comments
1	Antigua and Barbuda	No	N/A	No	N/A	CARICOM
2	Barbados	No	N/A	No	N/A	CARICOM
3	Belize	No	N/A	No	N/A	CARICOM
4	Dominica	No	N/A	No	N/A	CARICOM
5	Grenada	No	N/A	No	N/A	CARICOM
6	Guyana*	No	N/A	No	N/A	CARICOM
7	Jamaica	No	N/A	No	N/A	CARICOM
8	Saint Kitts and Nevis	No	N/A	No	N/A	CARICOM
9	Saint Vincent and the Grenadines	No	N/A	No	N/A	CARICOM
10	Switzerland	No	N/A	No	N/A	
11	Trinidad and Tobago	No	N/A	No	N/A	CARICOM

Saint Vincent and the Grenadines

A. Progress in the implementation of the minimum standard

Saint Vincent and the Grenadines has two tax agreements, as reported in its response to the Peer Review questionnaire, including the multilateral agreement among the members of the CARICOM concluded with ten treaty partners (the CARICOM Agreement).[133]

Neither of Saint Vincent and the Grenadines' agreements comply with the minimum standard or are subject to a complying instrument.

B. Implementation issues

Saint Vincent and the Grenadines is encouraged to implement the minimum standard in its agreements.

Saint Vincent and the Grenadines is encouraged to bring the CARICOM Agreement up to date by commencing talks among all the treaty partners.[134]

Summary of the jurisdiction response – Saint Vincent and the Grenadines

	Treaty partners	Compliance with the standard	If compliant, the alternative implemented	Signature of a complying instrument	The alternative implemented through the complying instrument (if not the MLI)	Comments
1	Antigua and Barbuda	No	N/A	No	N/A	CARICOM
2	Barbados	No	N/A	No	N/A	CARICOM
3	Belize	No	N/A	No	N/A	CARICOM
4	Dominica	No	N/A	No	N/A	CARICOM
5	Grenada	No	N/A	No	N/A	CARICOM
6	Guyana*	No	N/A	No	N/A	CARICOM
7	Jamaica	No	N/A	No	N/A	CARICOM
8	Saint Kitts and Nevis	No	N/A	No	N/A	CARICOM
9	Saint Lucia	No	N/A	No	N/A	CARICOM
10	Switzerland	No	N/A	No	N/A	
11	Trinidad and Tobago	No	N/A	No	N/A	CARICOM

San Marino

A. Progress in the implementation of the minimum standard

San Marino has 22 tax agreements in force, as reported in its response to the Peer Review questionnaire. Its agreement with Serbia complies with the minimum standard.

San Marino signed the MLI in 2017, listing 21 tax agreements.[135]

San Marino is implementing the minimum standard through the inclusion of the preamble statement and the PPT.[136]

The agreements that will be modified by the MLI will come into compliance with the minimum standard once the provisions of the MLI take effect.

B. Implementation issues

No jurisdiction has raised any concerns about their agreements with San Marino.

Summary of the jurisdiction response – San Marino

	Treaty partners	Compliance with the standard	If compliant, the alternative implemented	Signature of a complying instrument	The alternative implemented through the complying instrument (if not the MLI)	Comments
1	Austria	No	N/A	Yes	N/A	The treaty partner has not listed this agreement in its MLI position.
2	Azerbaijan*	No	N/A	Yes	N/A	Partial compliance (the treaty just lacks the new preamble).
3	Barbados	No	N/A	Yes	N/A	Partial compliance (the treaty just lacks the new preamble).
4	Belgium	No	N/A	Yes	N/A	
5	Croatia	No	N/A	Yes	N/A	
6	Cyprus*	No	N/A	Yes	N/A	
7	Georgia	No	N/A	Yes	N/A	
8	Greece	No	N/A	Yes	N/A	
9	Hungary	No	N/A	Yes	N/A	
10	Italy	No	N/A	Yes	N/A	A Partial compliance

						(the treaty just lacks the new preamble)
11	Liechtenstein	No	N/A	Yes	N/A	
12	Luxembourg	No	N/A	Yes	N/A	
13	Malaysia	No	N/A	Yes	N/A	
14	Malta	No	N/A	Yes	N/A	
15	Portugal	No	N/A	Yes	N/A	
16	Qatar	No	N/A	Yes	N/A	
17	Romania	No	N/A	Yes	N/A	
18	Saint Kitts and Nevis	No	N/A	Yes	N/A	
19	Serbia	Yes	PPT alone	N/A	N/A	
20	Seychelles	No	N/A	Yes	N/A	
21	Singapore	No	N/A	Yes	N/A	
22	Viet Nam	No	N/A	Yes	N/A	

Saudi Arabia

A. Progress in the implementation of the minimum standard

Saudi Arabia has 50 tax agreements in force, as reported in its response to the Peer Review questionnaire. Two of those agreements, the agreements with Bulgaria and the United Arab Emirates, comply with the minimum standard.

Saudi Arabia signed the MLI in 2018, listing 50 tax agreements.[137]

Saudi Arabia is implementing the minimum standard through the inclusion of the preamble statement and the PPT.[138]

The agreements that will be modified by the MLI will come into compliance with the minimum standard once the provisions of the MLI take effect.

B. Implementation issues

No jurisdiction has raised any concerns about their agreements with Saudi Arabia.

Summary of the jurisdiction response – Saudia Arabia

	Treaty partners	Compliance with the standard	If compliant, the alternative implemented	Signature of a complying instrument	The alternative implemented through the complying instrument (if not the MLI)	Comments
1	Algeria*	No	N/A	Yes	N/A	
2	Austria	No	N/A	Yes	N/A	
3	Azerbaijan*	No	N/A	Yes	N/A	
4	Bangladesh*	No	N/A	Yes	N/A	
5	Belarus*	No	N/A	Yes	N/A	
6	Bulgaria	Yes	PPT alone	N/A	N/A	
7	China (People's Republic of)	No	N/A	Yes	N/A	
8	Cyprus*	No	N/A	Yes	N/A	
9	Czech Republic	No	N/A	Yes	N/A	
10	Egypt	No	N/A	Yes	N/A	
11	Ethiopia*	No	N/A	Yes	N/A	
12	France	No	N/A	Yes	N/A	
13	Georgia	No	N/A	Yes	N/A	
14	Greece	No	N/A	Yes	N/A	
15	Hong Kong (China)	No	N/A	Yes	N/A	
16	Hungary	No	N/A	Yes	N/A	
17	India	No	N/A	Yes	N/A	
18	Ireland	No	N/A	Yes	N/A	
19	Italy	No	N/A	Yes	N/A	
20	Japan	No	N/A	Yes	N/A	
21	Jordan*	No	N/A	Yes	N/A	

22	Kazakhstan	No	N/A	Yes	N/A	
23	Korea	No	N/A	Yes	N/A	
24	Kyrgyzstan*	No	N/A	Yes	N/A	
25	Luxembourg	No	N/A	Yes	N/A	
26	North Macedonia	No	N/A	Yes	N/A	
27	Malaysia	No	N/A	Yes	N/A	
28	Malta	No	N/A	Yes	N/A	
29	Mexico	No	N/A	Yes	N/A	
30	Netherlands	No	N/A	Yes	N/A	
31	Pakistan	No	N/A	Yes	N/A	
32	Poland	No	N/A	Yes	N/A	
33	Portugal	No	N/A	Yes	N/A	
34	Romania	No	N/A	Yes	N/A	
35	Russia	No	N/A	Yes	N/A	
36	Singapore	No	N/A	Yes	N/A	
37	South Africa	No	N/A	Yes	N/A	
38	Spain	No	N/A	Yes	N/A	
39	Sweden	No	N/A	Yes	N/A	
40	Syrian Arab Republic*	No	N/A	Yes	N/A	
41	Tajikistan*	No	N/A	Yes	N/A	
42	Tunisia	No	N/A	Yes	N/A	
43	Turkey	No	N/A	Yes	N/A	
44	Turkmenistan*	No	N/A	Yes	N/A	
45	Ukraine	No	N/A	Yes	N/A	
46	United Arab Emirates	Yes	PPT alone	N/A	N/A	
47	United Kingdom	No	N/A	Yes	N/A	
48	Uzbekistan*	No	N/A	Yes	N/A	
49	Venezuela*	No	N/A	Yes	N/A	
50	Viet Nam	No	N/A	Yes	N/A	

Senegal

A. Progress in the implementation of the minimum standard

Senegal has 19 tax agreements in force, as reported in its response to the Peer Review questionnaire, including the multilateral Regulation 08/2008/COM adopting the rules for the avoidance of double taxation within the West African Economic and Monetary Union and the rule for assistance in tax matters (the UEMOA) concluded with seven partners. [139] Its agreement with Luxembourg complies with the minimum standard.

Senegal signed the MLI in 2017, listing 17 tax agreements.

Senegal is implementing the minimum standard through the inclusion of the preamble statement and the PPT combined with the LOB.[140]

The agreements that will be modified by the MLI will come into compliance with the minimum standard once the provisions of the MLI take effect.

Senegal indicated in its response to the Peer Review questionnaire that the UEMOA has not been listed under the MLI as it is a regulation of the West African Economic and Monetary Union.

B. Implementation issues

No jurisdiction has raised any concerns about their agreements with Senegal.

Senegal initiated the process to terminate its agreement with Mauritius.

Summary of the jurisdiction response – Senegal

	Treaty partners	Compliance with the standard	If compliant, the alternative implemented	Signature of a complying instrument	The alternative implemented through the complying instrument (if not the MLI)	Comments
1	Belgium	No	N/A	Yes	N/A	
2	Benin	No	N/A	No	N/A	
3	Burkina Faso	No	N/A	No	N/A	
4	Canada	No	N/A	Yes	N/A	
5	Chinese Taipei*	No	N/A	No	N/A	
6	Cote d'Ivoire	No	N/A	No	N/A	
7	France	No	N/A	Yes	N/A	
8	Guinea-Bissau*	No	N/A	No	N/A	
9	Italy	No	N/A	Yes	N/A	
10	Lebanon*	No	N/A	Yes	N/A	
11	Luxembourg	Yes	PPT alone	N/A	N/A	
12	Malaysia	No	N/A	Yes	N/A	
13	Mali*	No	N/A	No	N/A	
14	Mauritania*	No	N/A	Yes	N/A	
15	Mauritius	No	N/A	Yes	N/A	
16	Morocco	No	N/A	Yes	N/A	

17	Niger*	No	N/A	No	N/A	
18	Norway	No	N/A	Yes	N/A	
19	Portugal	No	N/A	Yes	N/A	
20	Qatar	No	N/A	Yes	N/A	
21	Spain	No	N/A	Yes	N/A	
22	Togo*	No	N/A	No	N/A	
23	Tunisia	No	N/A	Yes	N/A	
24	United Arab Emirates	No	N/A	Yes	N/A	
25	United Kingdom	No	N/A	Yes	N/A	

Serbia

A. Progress in the implementation of the minimum standard

Serbia has 59 tax agreements in force, as reported in its response to the Peer Review questionnaire. Eight of those agreements, the agreements with Austria, France, Lithuania, Poland, San Marino, Slovak Republic, Slovenia and the United Kingdom, comply with the minimum standard.

Serbia signed the MLI in 2017 and deposited its instrument of ratification on 5 June 2018, listing 58 tax agreements.[141] The MLI has entered into force for Serbia on 1 October 2018.

Serbia is implementing the minimum standard through the inclusion of the preamble statement and the PPT.[142]

The agreements modified by the MLI come into compliance with the minimum standard once the provisions of the MLI take effect. Other agreements listed under the MLI are expected to become compliant with the minimum standard by the end of 2019.

B. Implementation issues

No jurisdiction has raised any concerns about their agreements with Serbia.

Summary of the jurisdiction response – Serbia

	Treaty partners	Compliance with the standard	If compliant, the alternative implemented	Signature of a complying instrument	The alternative implemented through the complying instrument (if not the MLI)	Comments
1	Albania*	No	N/A	Yes	N/A	
2	Armenia	No	N/A	Yes	N/A	
3	Austria	Yes	PPT alone	N/A	N/A	
4	Azerbaijan*	No	N/A	Yes	N/A	
5	Belarus*	No	N/A	Yes	N/A	
6	Belgium	No	N/A	Yes	N/A	
7	Bosnia and Herzegovina*	No	N/A	Yes	N/A	
8	Bulgaria	No	N/A	Yes	N/A	
9	Canada	No	N/A	Yes	N/A	
10	China (People's Republic of)	No	N/A	Yes	N/A	
11	Croatia	No	N/A	Yes	N/A	
12	Cyprus*	No	N/A	Yes	N/A	
13	Czech Republic	No	N/A	Yes	N/A	
14	Democratic People's Republic of Korea*	No	N/A	Yes	N/A	
15	Denmark	No	N/A	Yes	N/A	
16	Egypt	No	N/A	Yes	N/A	
17	Estonia	No	N/A	Yes	N/A	
18	Finland	No	N/A	Yes	N/A	

19	France	Yes	PPT alone	N/A	N/A	
20	Georgia	No	N/A	Yes	N/A	
21	Germany	No	N/A	Yes	N/A	
22	Greece	No	N/A	Yes	N/A	
23	Hungary	No	N/A	Yes	N/A	
24	India	No	N/A	Yes	N/A	
25	Indonesia	No	N/A	Yes	N/A	
26	Iran*	No	N/A	Yes	N/A	
27	Ireland	No	N/A	Yes	N/A	
28	Italy	No	N/A	Yes	N/A	
29	Kazakhstan	No	N/A	Yes	N/A	
30	Korea	No	N/A	Yes	N/A	
31	Kuwait*	No	N/A	Yes	N/A	
32	Latvia	No	N/A	Yes	N/A	
33	Libya*	No	N/A	Yes	N/A	
34	Lithuania	Yes	PPT alone	N/A	N/A	
35	Luxembourg	No	N/A	Yes	N/A	
36	North Macedonia	No	N/A	Yes	N/A	
37	Malta	No	N/A	Yes	N/A	
38	Moldova*	No	N/A	Yes	N/A	
39	Montenegro*	No	N/A	Yes	N/A	
40	Netherlands	No	N/A	Yes	N/A	
41	Norway	No	N/A	Yes	N/A	
42	Pakistan	No	N/A	Yes	N/A	
43	Poland	Yes	PPT alone	N/A	N/A	
44	Qatar	No	N/A	Yes	N/A	
45	Romania	No	N/A	Yes	N/A	
46	Russia	No	N/A	Yes	N/A	
47	San Marino	Yes	PPT alone	N/A	N/A	
48	Slovak Republic	Yes	PPT alone	N/A	N/A	
49	Slovenia	Yes	PPT alone	N/A	N/A	
50	Spain	No	N/A	Yes	N/A	
51	Sri Lanka	No	N/A	Yes	N/A	
52	Sweden	No	N/A	Yes	N/A	
53	Switzerland	No	N/A	Yes	N/A	
54	Tunisia	No	N/A	Yes	N/A	
55	Turkey	No	N/A	Yes	N/A	
56	Ukraine	No	N/A	Yes	N/A	
57	United Arab Emirates	No	N/A	Yes	N/A	
58	United Kingdom	Yes	PPT alone	N/A	N/A	
59	Viet Nam	No	N/A	Yes	N/A	

Seychelles

A. Progress in the implementation of the minimum standard

The Seychelles has 28 tax agreements in force, as reported in its response to the Peer Review questionnaire.

The Seychelles signed the MLI in 2017, listing 28 tax agreements.

The Seychelles is implementing the minimum standard through the inclusion of the preamble statement and the PPT.[143]

The agreements that will be modified by the MLI will come into compliance with the minimum standard once the provisions of the MLI take effect.

B. Implementation issues

No jurisdiction has raised any concerns about their agreements with the Seychelles.

Summary of the jurisdiction response – Seychelles

	Treaty partners	Compliance with the standard	If compliant, the alternative implemented	Signature of a complying instrument	The alternative implemented through the complying instrument (if not the MLI)	Comments
1	Bahrain	No	N/A	Yes	N/A	
2	Barbados	No	N/A	Yes	N/A	
3	Belgium	No	N/A	Yes	N/A	
4	Bermuda	No	N/A	Yes	N/A	
5	Botswana	No	N/A	Yes	N/A	
6	China (People's Republic of)	No	N/A	Yes	N/A	
7	Cyprus*	No	N/A	Yes	N/A	
8	Ethiopia*	No	N/A	Yes	N/A	
9	Guernsey	No	N/A	Yes	N/A	
10	Indonesia	No	N/A	Yes	N/A	
11	Isle of Man	No	N/A	Yes	N/A	
12	Jersey	No	N/A	Yes	N/A	
13	Kenya	No	N/A	Yes	N/A	
14	Luxembourg	No	N/A	Yes	N/A	
15	Malaysia	No	N/A	Yes	N/A	
16	Mauritius	No	N/A	Yes	N/A	
17	Monaco	No	N/A	Yes	N/A	
18	Oman	No	N/A	Yes	N/A	
19	Qatar	No	N/A	Yes	N/A	
20	San Marino	No	N/A	Yes	N/A	
21	Singapore	No	N/A	Yes	N/A	
22	South Africa	No	N/A	Yes	N/A	
23	Sri Lanka	No	N/A	Yes	N/A	
24	Eswatini*	No	N/A	Yes	N/A	

25	Thailand	No	N/A	Yes	N/A	
26	United Arab Emirates	No	N/A	Yes	N/A	
27	Viet Nam	No	N/A	Yes	N/A	
28	Zambia	No	N/A	Yes	N/A	

Sierra Leone

A. Progress in the implementation of the minimum standard

Sierra Leone has three tax agreements in force, as reported in its response to the Peer Review questionnaire.

None of Sierra Leone's agreements comply with the minimum standard or are subject to a complying instrument.

B. Implementation issues

No jurisdiction has raised any concerns about their agreements with Sierra Leone.

Sierra Leone is encouraged to implement the minimum standard in its agreements.

Summary of the jurisdiction response – Sierra Leone

	Treaty partners	Compliance with the standard	If compliant, the alternative implemented	Signature of a complying instrument	The alternative implemented through the complying instrument (if not the MLI)	Comments
1	Norway	No	N/A	No	N/A	
2	South Africa	No	N/A	No	N/A	
3	United Kingdom	No	N/A	No	N/A	

Singapore

A. Progress in the implementation of the minimum standard

Singapore has 86 tax agreements in force, as reported in its response to the Peer Review questionnaire.

Singapore signed the MLI in 2017 and deposited its instrument of ratification on 21 December 2018, listing 84 tax agreements.[144] The MLI entered into force for Singapore on 1 April 2019.

Singapore is implementing the minimum standard in its tax agreements through the inclusion of the preamble statement and the PPT.[145]

The agreements that will be modified by the MLI will come into compliance with the minimum standard once the provisions of the MLI take effect. Some agreements listed under the MLI are expected to become compliant with the minimum standard by the end of 2019.

B. Implementation issues

No jurisdiction has raised any concerns about their agreements with Singapore.

Summary of the jurisdiction response – Singapore

	Treaty partners	Compliance with the standard	If compliant, the alternative implemented	Signature of a complying instrument	The alternative implemented through the complying instrument (if not the MLI)	Comments
1	Albania*	No	N/A	Yes	N/A	
2	Australia	No	N/A	Yes	N/A	
3	Austria	No	N/A	Yes	N/A	
4	Bahrain	No	N/A	Yes	N/A	
5	Bangladesh*	No	N/A	Yes	N/A	
6	Barbados	No	N/A	Yes	N/A	
7	Belarus*	No	N/A	Yes	N/A	
8	Belgium	No	N/A	Yes	N/A	
9	Brunei Darussalam	No	N/A	Yes	N/A	
10	Bulgaria	No	N/A	Yes	N/A	
11	Cambodia*	No	N/A	Yes	N/A	
12	Canada	No	N/A	Yes	N/A	
13	China (People's Republic of)	No	N/A	Yes	N/A	
14	Chinese Taipei*	No	N/A	No	N/A	Discussion with treaty partner is ongoing
15	Cyprus*	No	N/A	Yes	N/A	
16	Czech Republic	No	N/A	Yes	N/A	
17	Denmark	No	N/A	Yes	N/A	
18	Ecuador*	No	N/A	Yes	N/A	
19	Egypt	No	N/A	Yes	N/A	

20	Estonia	No	N/A	Yes	N/A	
21	Ethiopia*	No	N/A	Yes	N/A	
22	Fiji*	No	N/A	Yes	N/A	
23	Finland	No	N/A	Yes	N/A	
24	France	No	N/A	Yes	N/A	
25	Georgia	No	N/A	Yes	N/A	
26	Germany	No	N/A	Yes	N/A	Excluded from MLI by treaty partner
27	Ghana*	No	N/A	Yes	N/A	
28	Guernsey	No	N/A	Yes	N/A	
29	Hungary	No	N/A	Yes	N/A	
30	India	No	N/A	Yes	N/A	
31	Indonesia	No	N/A	Yes	N/A	
32	Ireland	No	N/A	Yes	N/A	
33	Isle of Man	No	N/A	Yes	N/A	
34	Israel	No	N/A	Yes	N/A	
35	Italy	No	N/A	Yes	N/A	
36	Japan	No	N/A	Yes	N/A	
37	Jersey	No	N/A	Yes	N/A	
38	Kazakhstan	No	N/A	Yes	N/A	
39	Korea	No	N/A	Yes	PPT alone	
40	Kuwait*	No	N/A	Yes	N/A	
41	Lao People's Democratic Republic*	No	N/A	Yes	N/A	
42	Latvia	No	N/A	Yes	N/A	
43	Libya*	No	N/A	Yes	N/A	
44	Liechtenstein	No	N/A	Yes	N/A	
45	Lithuania	No	N/A	Yes	N/A	
46	Luxembourg	No	N/A	Yes	N/A	
47	Malaysia	No	N/A	Yes	N/A	
48	Malta	No	N/A	Yes	N/A	
49	Mauritius	No	N/A	Yes	N/A	
50	Mexico	No	N/A	Yes	N/A	
51	Mongolia	No	N/A	Yes	N/A	
52	Morocco	No	N/A	Yes	N/A	
53	Myanmar*	No	N/A	Yes	N/A	
54	Netherlands	No	N/A	Yes	N/A	
55	New Zealand	No	N/A	Yes	N/A	
56	Nigeria	No	N/A	Yes	N/A	
57	Norway	No	N/A	Yes	N/A	Excluded from MLI by treaty partner
58	Oman	No	N/A	Yes	N/A	
59	Pakistan	No	N/A	Yes	N/A	
60	Panama	No	N/A	Yes	N/A	
61	Papua New Guinea	No	N/A	Yes	N/A	
62	Philippines*	No	N/A	Yes	N/A	
63	Poland	No	N/A	Yes	N/A	
64	Portugal	No	N/A	Yes	N/A	
65	Qatar	No	N/A	Yes	N/A	
66	Romania	No	N/A	Yes	N/A	

67	Russia	No	N/A	Yes	N/A	
68	Rwanda*	No	N/A	Yes	N/A	
69	San Marino	No	N/A	Yes	N/A	
70	Saudi Arabia	No	N/A	Yes	N/A	
71	Seychelles	No	N/A	Yes	N/A	
72	Slovak Republic	No	N/A	Yes	N/A	
73	Slovenia	No	N/A	Yes	N/A	
74	South Africa	No	N/A	Yes	N/A	
75	Spain	No	N/A	Yes	N/A	
76	Sri Lanka	No	N/A	Yes	N/A	
77	Sweden	No	N/A	Yes	N/A	Excluded from MLI by treaty partner
78	Switzerland	No	N/A	Yes	N/A	Excluded from MLI by treaty partner
79	Thailand	No	N/A	Yes	N/A	
80	Turkey	No	N/A	Yes	N/A	
81	Ukraine	No	N/A	Yes	N/A	
82	United Arab Emirates	No	N/A	Yes	N/A	
83	United Kingdom	No	N/A	Yes	N/A	
84	Uruguay	No	N/A	Yes	N/A	
85	Uzbekistan*	No	N/A	Yes	N/A	
86	Viet Nam	No	N/A	Yes	N/A	

Slovak Republic

A. Progress in the implementation of the minimum standard

The Slovak Republic has 70 tax agreements in force, as reported in its response to the Peer Review questionnaire. Ten of those agreements, the agreements with Australia, Austria, France, Israel, Japan, Lithuania, Poland, Serbia, Slovenia and the United Kingdom, comply with the minimum standard.

The Slovak Republic signed the MLI in 2017 and deposited its instrument of ratification on 20 September 2018, listing of 64 tax agreements. The MLI entered into force for the Slovak Republic on 1 January 2019.

The Slovak Republic is implementing the minimum standard through the inclusion of the preamble statement and the PPT, combined with the LOB.[146]

The agreements modified by the MLI come into compliance with the minimum standard once the provisions of the MLI take effect. Other agreements listed under the MLI are expected to become compliant with the minimum standard by the end of 2019. The Slovak Republic indicated in its response to the Peer Review questionnaire that the agreements not listed under the MLI were either not in force at the time of its signature or too old to be covered under the MLI. The Slovak Republic further indicated in that bilateral negotiations would be used with respect to its agreements with Armenia, Chinese Taipei, Ethiopia, Iran, Mongolia, and the United Arab Emirates.

B. Implementation issues

No jurisdiction has raised any concerns about their agreements with the Slovak Republic.

Summary of the jurisdiction response – Slovak Republic

	Treaty partners	Compliance with the standard	If compliant, the alternative implemented	Signature of a complying instrument	The alternative implemented through the complying instrument (if not the MLI)	Comments
1	Armenia	No	N/A	No	N/A	
2	Australia	Yes	PPT alone	N/A	N/A	
3	Austria	Yes	PPT alone	N/A	N/A	
4	Belarus*	No	N/A	Yes	N/A	
5	Belgium	No	N/A	Yes	N/A	
6	Bosnia and Herzegovina*	No	N/A	Yes	N/A	
7	Brazil	No	N/A	Yes	N/A	
8	Bulgaria	No	N/A	Yes	N/A	
9	Canada	No	N/A	Yes	N/A	
10	China (People's Republic of)	No	N/A	Yes	N/A	
11	Chinese Taipei*	No	N/A	No	N/A	
12	Croatia	No	N/A	Yes	N/A	
13	Cyprus*	No	N/A	Yes	N/A	
14	Czech Republic	No	N/A	Yes	N/A	
15	Denmark	No	N/A	Yes	N/A	

16	Estonia	No	N/A	Yes	N/A	
17	Ethiopia*	No	N/A	No	N/A	
18	Finland	No	N/A	Yes	N/A	
19	France	Yes	PPT alone	N/A	N/A	
20	Georgia	No	N/A	Yes	N/A	
21	Germany	No	N/A	Yes	N/A	
22	Greece	No	N/A	Yes	N/A	
23	Hungary	No	N/A	Yes	N/A	
24	Iceland	No	N/A	Yes	N/A	
25	India	No	N/A	Yes	N/A	
26	Indonesia	No	N/A	Yes	N/A	
27	Iran*	No	N/A	No	N/A	
28	Ireland	No	N/A	Yes	N/A	
29	Israel	Yes	PPT alone	N/A	N/A	
30	Italy	No	N/A	Yes	N/A	
31	Japan	Yes	PPT alone	N/A	N/A	
32	Kazakhstan	No	N/A	Yes	N/A	
33	Korea	No	N/A	Yes	N/A	
34	Kuwait*	No	N/A	Yes	N/A	
35	Latvia	No	N/A	Yes	N/A	
36	Libya*	No	N/A	Yes	N/A	
37	Lithuania	Yes	PPT alone	N/A	N/A	
38	Luxembourg	No	N/A	Yes	N/A	
39	North Macedonia	No	N/A	Yes	N/A	
40	Malaysia	No	N/A	Yes	N/A	
41	Malta	No	N/A	Yes	N/A	
42	Mexico	No	N/A	Yes	N/A	
43	Moldova*	No	N/A	Yes	N/A	
44	Mongolia	No	N/A	No	N/A	
45	Montenegro*	No	N/A	Yes	N/A	
46	Netherlands	No	N/A	Yes	N/A	
47	Nigeria	No	N/A	Yes	N/A	
48	Norway	No	N/A	Yes	N/A	
49	Poland	Yes	PPT alone	N/A	N/A	
50	Portugal	No	N/A	Yes	N/A	
51	Romania	No	N/A	Yes	N/A	
52	Russia	No	N/A	Yes	N/A	
53	Serbia	Yes	PPT alone	N/A	N/A	
54	Singapore	No	N/A	Yes	N/A	
55	Slovenia	Yes	PPT alone	N/A	N/A	
56	South Africa	No	N/A	Yes	N/A	
57	Spain	No	N/A	Yes	N/A	
58	Sri Lanka	No	N/A	Yes	N/A	
59	Sweden	No	N/A	Yes	N/A	
60	Switzerland	No	N/A	Yes	N/A	
61	Syrian Arab Republic*	No	N/A	Yes	N/A	
62	Tunisia	No	N/A	Yes	N/A	
63	Turkey	No	N/A	Yes	N/A	
64	Turkmenistan*	No	N/A	Yes	N/A	
65	Ukraine	No	N/A	Yes	N/A	
66	United Arab Emirates	No	N/A	No	N/A	
67	United Kingdom	Yes	PPT alone	N/A	N/A	

68	United States	No	N/A	Yes	N/A	
69	Uzbekistan*	No	N/A	Yes	N/A	
70	Viet Nam	No	N/A	Yes	N/A	

Slovenia

A. Progress in the implementation of the minimum standard

Slovenia has 59 tax agreements in force, as reported in its response to the Peer Review questionnaire. Nine of those agreements, the agreements with Austria, France, Japan, Israel, Lithuania, Poland, Serbia, Slovak Republic and the United Kingdom, comply with the minimum standard.

Slovenia signed the MLI in 2017 and deposited its instrument of ratification of the MLI on 22 March 2018, listing 55 tax agreements.[147] The MLI entered into force for Slovenia on 1 July 2018.

Slovenia is implementing the minimum standard through the inclusion of the preamble statement and the PPT.[148]

The agreements modified by the MLI come into compliance with the minimum standard once the provisions of the MLI take effect. Other agreements listed under the MLI are expected to become compliant with the minimum standard by the end of 2019.

Slovenia indicated in its response to the Peer Review questionnaire that bilateral negotiations would be used for its agreements with Germany, Montenegro* and Sweden.

B. Implementation issues

No jurisdiction has raised any concerns about their agreements with Slovenia.

Summary of the jurisdiction response – Slovenia

	Treaty partners	Compliance with the standard	If compliant, the alternative implemented	Signature of a complying instrument	The alternative implemented through the complying instrument (if not the MLI)	Comments
1	Albania*	No	N/A	Yes	N/A	
2	Armenia	No	N/A	Yes	N/A	
3	Austria	Yes	PPT alone	N/A	N/A	
4	Azerbaijan*	No	N/A	Yes	N/A	
5	Belarus*	No	N/A	Yes	N/A	
6	Belgium	No	N/A	Yes	N/A	
7	Bosnia and Herzegovina*	No	N/A	Yes	N/A	
8	Bulgaria	No	N/A	Yes	N/A	
9	Canada	No	N/A	Yes	N/A	
10	China (People's Republic of)	No	N/A	Yes	N/A	
11	Croatia	No	N/A	Yes	N/A	
12	Cyprus*	No	N/A	Yes	N/A	
13	Czech Republic	No	N/A	Yes	N/A	
14	Denmark	No	N/A	Yes	N/A	

15	Estonia	No	N/A	Yes	N/A	
16	Finland	No	N/A	Yes	N/A	
17	France	Yes	PPT alone	N/A	N/A	
18	Georgia	No	N/A	Yes	N/A	
19	Germany	No	N/A	No	N/A	
20	Greece	No	N/A	Yes	N/A	
21	Hungary	No	N/A	Yes	N/A	
22	Iceland	No	N/A	Yes	N/A	
23	India	No	N/A	Yes	N/A	
24	Iran*	No	N/A	Yes	N/A	
25	Ireland	No	N/A	Yes	N/A	
26	Israel	Yes	PPT alone	N/A	N/A	
27	Italy	No	N/A	Yes	N/A	
28	Japan	Yes	PPT alone	N/A	N/A	
29	Kazakhstan	No	N/A	Yes	N/A	
30	Korea	No	N/A	Yes	N/A	
31	Kosovo*	No	N/A	Yes	N/A	
32	Kuwait*	No	N/A	Yes	N/A	
33	Latvia	No	N/A	Yes	N/A	
34	Lithuania	Yes	PPT alone	N/A	N/A	
35	Luxembourg	No	N/A	Yes	N/A	
36	North Macedonia	No	N/A	Yes	N/A	
37	Malta	No	N/A	Yes	N/A	
38	Moldova*	No	N/A	Yes	N/A	
39	Montenegro*	No	N/A	No	N/A	
40	Netherlands	No	N/A	Yes	N/A	
41	Norway	No	N/A	Yes	N/A	
42	Poland	Yes	PPT alone	N/A	N/A	
43	Portugal	No	N/A	Yes	N/A	
44	Qatar	No	N/A	Yes	N/A	
45	Romania	No	N/A	Yes	N/A	
46	Russia	No	N/A	Yes	N/A	
47	Serbia	Yes	PPT alone	N/A	N/A	
48	Singapore	No	N/A	Yes	N/A	
49	Slovak Republic	Yes	PPT alone	N/A	N/A	
50	Spain	No	N/A	Yes	N/A	
51	Sweden	No	N/A	No	N/A	
52	Switzerland	No	N/A	Yes	N/A	
53	Thailand	No	N/A	Yes	N/A	
54	Turkey	No	N/A	Yes	N/A	
55	Ukraine	No	N/A	Yes	N/A	
56	United Arab Emirates	No	N/A	Yes	N/A	
57	United Kingdom	Yes	PPT alone	N/A	N/A	
58	United States	No	N/A	Yes	N/A	
59	Uzbekistan*	No	N/A	Yes	N/A	

South Africa

A. Progress in the implementation of the minimum standard

South Africa has 79 tax agreements in force, as reported in its response to the Peer Review questionnaire.

South Africa signed the MLI in 2017, listing 74 tax agreements.

South Africa is implementing the minimum standard through the inclusion of the preamble statement and the PPT.[149]

The agreements that will be modified by the MLI will come into compliance with the minimum standard once the provisions of the MLI take effect.

South Africa indicated in its response to the Peer Review questionnaire that bilateral negotiations would be used for its agreements with Brazil, Germany, Malawi* and Zambia.

B. Implementation issues

No jurisdiction has raised any concerns about their agreements with South Africa.

Summary of the jurisdiction response – South Africa

	Treaty partners	Compliance with the standard	If compliant, the alternative implemented	Signature of a complying instrument	The alternative implemented through the complying instrument (if not the MLI)	Comments
1	Algeria*	No	N/A	Yes	N/A	
2	Australia	No	N/A	Yes	N/A	
3	Austria	No	N/A	Yes	N/A	
4	Belarus*	No	N/A	Yes	N/A	
5	Belgium	No	N/A	Yes	N/A	
6	Botswana	No	N/A	Yes	N/A	
7	Brazil	No	N/A	Yes	N/A	
8	Bulgaria	No	N/A	Yes	N/A	
9	Cameroon	No	N/A	Yes	N/A	
10	Canada	No	N/A	Yes	N/A	
11	Chile	No	N/A	Yes	N/A	
12	China (People's Republic of)	No	N/A	Yes	N/A	
13	Chinese Taipei*	No	N/A	Yes	N/A	
14	Croatia	No	N/A	Yes	N/A	
15	Cyprus*	No	N/A	Yes	N/A	
16	Czech Republic	No	N/A	Yes	N/A	
17	Democratic Republic of the Congo	No	N/A	Yes	N/A	
18	Denmark	No	N/A	Yes	N/A	
19	Egypt	No	N/A	Yes	N/A	
20	Ethiopia*	No	N/A	Yes	N/A	

21	Finland	No	N/A	Yes	N/A	
22	France	No	N/A	Yes	N/A	
23	Germany	No	N/A	No	N/A	
24	Ghana*	No	N/A	Yes	N/A	
25	Greece	No	N/A	Yes	N/A	
26	Grenada*	No	N/A	No	N/A	
27	Hong Kong (China)	No	N/A	Yes	N/A	
28	Hungary	No	N/A	Yes	N/A	
29	India	No	N/A	Yes	N/A	
30	Indonesia	No	N/A	Yes	N/A	
31	Iran*	No	N/A	Yes	N/A	
32	Ireland	No	N/A	Yes	N/A	
33	Israel	No	N/A	Yes	N/A	
34	Italy	No	N/A	Yes	N/A	
35	Japan	No	N/A	Yes	N/A	
36	Kenya	No	N/A	Yes	N/A	
37	Korea	No	N/A	Yes	N/A	
38	Kuwait*	No	N/A	Yes	N/A	
39	Lesotho*	No	N/A	Yes	N/A	
40	Luxembourg	No	N/A	Yes	N/A	
41	Malawi*	No	N/A	No	N/A	
42	Malaysia	No	N/A	Yes	N/A	
43	Malta	No	N/A	Yes	N/A	
44	Mauritius	No	N/A	Yes	N/A	
45	Mexico	No	N/A	Yes	N/A	
46	Mozambique*	No	N/A	Yes	N/A	
47	Namibia*	No	N/A	Yes	N/A	
48	Netherlands	No	N/A	Yes	N/A	
49	New Zealand	No	N/A	Yes	N/A	
50	Nigeria	No	N/A	Yes	N/A	
51	Norway	No	N/A	Yes	N/A	
52	Oman	No	N/A	Yes	N/A	
53	Pakistan	No	N/A	Yes	N/A	
54	Poland	No	N/A	Yes	N/A	
55	Portugal	No	N/A	Yes	N/A	
56	Qatar	No	N/A	Yes	N/A	
57	Romania	No	N/A	Yes	N/A	
58	Russia Federation	No	N/A	Yes	N/A	
59	Rwanda*	No	N/A	Yes	N/A	
60	Saudi Arabia	No	N/A	Yes	N/A	
61	Seychelles	No	N/A	Yes	N/A	
62	Sierra Leone	No	N/A	No	N/A	
63	Singapore	No	N/A	Yes	N/A	
64	Slovak Republic	No	N/A	Yes	N/A	
65	Spain	No	N/A	Yes	N/A	
66	Eswatini*	No	N/A	Yes	N/A	
67	Sweden	No	N/A	Yes	N/A	
68	Switzerland	No	N/A	Yes	N/A	
69	Tanzania*	No	N/A	Yes	N/A	
70	Thailand	No	N/A	Yes	N/A	
71	Tunisia	No	N/A	Yes	N/A	
72	Turkey	No	N/A	Yes	N/A	
73	Uganda*	No	N/A	Yes	N/A	

74	Ukraine	No	N/A	Yes	N/A	
75	United Arab Emirates	No	N/A	Yes	N/A	
76	United Kingdom	No	N/A	Yes	N/A	
77	United States	No	N/A	Yes	N/A	
78	Zambia	No	N/A	No	N/A	
79	Zimbabwe*	No	N/A	Yes	N/A	

Spain

A. Progress in the implementation of the minimum standard

Spain has 92 tax agreements in force, as reported in its response to the Peer Review questionnaire. Its agreement with Mexico complies with the minimum standard.

Spain signed the MLI in 2017, listing 86 tax agreements.[150]

Spain is implementing the minimum standard in its tax agreements through the inclusion of the preamble statement and the PPT, combined with the LOB for its agreement with Japan.[151]

The agreements that will be modified by the MLI will come into compliance with the minimum standard once the provisions of the MLI take effect.

Spain signed a bilateral complying instrument with respect to its agreements with China, Japan and Romania.

Spain indicated in its response to the Peer Review questionnaire that bilateral negotiations would be used for its agreements with the Netherlands, Norway, Sweden and Ukraine.

B. Implementation issues

No jurisdiction has raised any concerns about their agreements with Spain.

Summary of the jurisdiction response – Spain

	Treaty partners	Compliance with the standard	If compliant, the alternative implemented	Signature of a complying instrument	The alternative implemented through the complying instrument (if not the MLI)	Comments
1	Albania*	No	N/A	Yes	N/A	
2	Algeria*	No	N/A	Yes	N/A	
3	Andorra	No	N/A	Yes	N/A	
4	Argentina	No	N/A	Yes	N/A	
5	Armenia	No	N/A	Yes	N/A	
6	Australia	No	N/A	Yes	N/A	
7	Austria	No	N/A	Yes	N/A	
8	Barbados	No	N/A	Yes	N/A	
9	Belgium	No	N/A	Yes	N/A	
10	Bolivia*	No	N/A	Yes	N/A	
11	Bosnia and Herzegovina*	No	N/A	Yes	N/A	
12	Brazil	No	N/A	Yes	N/A	
13	Bulgaria	No	N/A	Yes	N/A	
14	Canada	No	N/A	Yes	N/A	
15	Chile	No	N/A	Yes	N/A	
16	China (People's Republic of)	No	N/A	Yes	PPT alone	

17	Colombia	No	N/A	Yes	N/A	
18	Costa Rica	No	N/A	Yes	N/A	
19	Croatia	No	N/A	Yes	N/A	
20	Cuba*	No	N/A	Yes	N/A	
21	Cyprus*	No	N/A	Yes	N/A	
22	Czech Republic	No	N/A	Yes	N/A	
23	Dominican Republic	No	N/A	Yes	N/A	
24	Ecuador*	No	N/A	Yes	N/A	
25	Egypt	No	N/A	Yes	N/A	
26	El Salvador*	No	N/A	Yes	N/A	
27	Estonia	No	N/A	Yes	N/A	
28	Finland	No	N/A	Yes	N/A	
29	France	No	N/A	Yes	N/A	
30	Georgia	No	N/A	Yes	N/A	
31	Germany	No	N/A	Yes	N/A	
32	Greece	No	N/A	Yes	N/A	
33	Hong Kong (China)	No	N/A	Yes	N/A	
34	Hungary	No	N/A	Yes	N/A	
35	Iceland	No	N/A	Yes	N/A	
36	India	No	N/A	Yes	N/A	
37	Indonesia	No	N/A	Yes	N/A	
38	Iran*	No	N/A	Yes	N/A	
39	Ireland	No	N/A	Yes	N/A	
40	Israel	No	N/A	Yes	N/A	
41	Italy	No	N/A	Yes	N/A	
42	Jamaica	No	N/A	Yes	N/A	
43	Japan	No	N/A	Yes	PPT and LOB	
44	Kazakhstan	No	N/A	Yes	N/A	
45	Korea	No	N/A	Yes	N/A	
46	Kuwait*	No	N/A	Yes	N/A	
47	Kyrgyzstan*	No	N/A	Yes	N/A	
48	Latvia	No	N/A	Yes	N/A	
49	Lithuania	No	N/A	Yes	N/A	
50	Luxembourg	No	N/A	Yes	N/A	
51	North Macedonia	No	N/A	Yes	N/A	
52	Malaysia	No	N/A	Yes	N/A	
53	Malta	No	N/A	Yes	N/A	
54	Mexico	Yes	PPT alone	N/A	N/A	
55	Moldova*	No	N/A	Yes	N/A	
56	Morocco	No	N/A	Yes	N/A	
57	Netherlands	No	N/A	No	N/A	
58	New Zealand	No	N/A	Yes	N/A	
59	Nigeria	No	N/A	Yes	N/A	
60	Norway	No	N/A	No	N/A	
61	Oman	No	N/A	Yes	N/A	
62	Pakistan	No	N/A	Yes	N/A	
63	Panama	No	N/A	Yes	N/A	
64	Philippines*	No	N/A	Yes	N/A	
65	Poland	No	N/A	Yes	N/A	
66	Portugal	No	N/A	Yes	N/A	
67	Qatar	No	N/A	Yes	N/A	
68	Romania	No	N/A	Yes	PPT alone	
69	Russia	No	N/A	Yes	N/A	

70	Saudi Arabia	No	N/A	Yes	N/A	
71	Senegal	No	N/A	Yes	N/A	
72	Serbia	No	N/A	Yes	N/A	
73	Singapore	No	N/A	Yes	N/A	
74	Slovak Republic	No	N/A	Yes	N/A	
75	Slovenia	No	N/A	Yes	N/A	
76	South Africa	No	N/A	Yes	N/A	
77	Sweden	No	N/A	No	N/A	
78	Switzerland	No	N/A	Yes	N/A	
79	Tajikistan*	No	N/A	Yes	N/A	
80	Thailand	No	N/A	Yes	N/A	
81	Trinidad and Tobago	No	N/A	Yes	N/A	
82	Tunisia	No	N/A	Yes	N/A	
83	Turkey	No	N/A	Yes	N/A	
84	Turkmenistan*	No	N/A	Yes	N/A	
85	Ukraine	No	N/A	No	N/A	
86	United Arab Emirates	No	N/A	Yes	N/A	
87	United Kingdom	No	N/A	Yes	N/A	
88	United States	No	N/A	Yes	N/A	
89	Uruguay	No	N/A	Yes	N/A	
90	Uzbekistan*	No	N/A	Yes	N/A	
91	Venezuela*	No	N/A	Yes	N/A	
92	Viet Nam	No	N/A	Yes	N/A	

Sri Lanka

A. Progress in the implementation of the minimum standard

Sri Lanka has 47 tax agreements in force, as reported in its response to the Peer Review questionnaire.

None of Sri Lanka's agreements comply with the minimum standard or are subject to a complying instrument.

B. Implementation issues

No jurisdiction has raised any concerns about their agreements with Sri Lanka.

Sri Lanka is encouraged to implement the minimum standard in its agreements.

Summary of the jurisdiction response – Sri Lanka

	Treaty partners	Compliance with the standard	If compliant, the alternative implemented	Signature of a complying instrument	The alternative implemented through the complying instrument (if not the MLI)	Comments
1	Australia	No	N/A	No	N/A	
2	Bahrain	No	N/A	No	N/A	
3	Bangladesh*	No	N/A	No	N/A	
4	Belarus*	No	N/A	No	N/A	
5	Belgium	No	N/A	No	N/A	
6	Bosnia and Herzegovina*	No	N/A	No	N/A	
7	Canada	No	N/A	No	N/A	
8	China (People's Republic of)	No	N/A	No	N/A	
9	Croatia	No	N/A	No	N/A	
10	Czech Republic	No	N/A	No	N/A	
11	Denmark	No	N/A	No	N/A	
12	Finland	No	N/A	No	N/A	
13	France	No	N/A	No	N/A	
14	Germany	No	N/A	No	N/A	
15	India	No	N/A	No	N/A	
16	Indonesia	No	N/A	No	N/A	
17	Iran*	No	N/A	No	N/A	
18	Italy	No	N/A	No	N/A	
19	Japan	No	N/A	No	N/A	
20	Korea	No	N/A	No	N/A	
21	Kuwait*	No	N/A	No	N/A	
22	Luxembourg	No	N/A	No	N/A	
23	North Macedonia	No	N/A	No	N/A	
24	Malaysia	No	N/A	No	N/A	
25	Mauritius	No	N/A	No	N/A	

26	Montenegro*	No	N/A	No	N/A	
27	Nepal*	No	N/A	No	N/A	
28	Netherlands	No	N/A	No	N/A	
29	Norway	No	N/A	No	N/A	
30	Oman	No	N/A	No	N/A	
31	Pakistan	No	N/A	No	N/A	
32	Philippines*	No	N/A	No	N/A	
33	Poland	No	N/A	No	N/A	
34	Qatar	No	N/A	No	N/A	
35	Romania	No	N/A	No	N/A	
36	Russia	No	N/A	No	N/A	
37	Serbia	No	N/A	No	N/A	
38	Seychelles	No	N/A	No	N/A	
39	Singapore	No	N/A	No	N/A	
40	Slovak Republic	No	N/A	No	N/A	
41	Sweden	No	N/A	No	N/A	
42	Switzerland	No	N/A	No	N/A	
43	Thailand	No	N/A	No	N/A	
44	United Arab Emirates	No	N/A	No	N/A	
45	United Kingdom	No	N/A	No	N/A	
46	United States	No	N/A	No	N/A	
47	Viet Nam	No	N/A	No	N/A	

Sweden

A. Progress in the implementation of the minimum standard

Sweden has 81 tax agreements, as reported in its response to the Peer Review questionnaire, including the multilateral Nordic Convention concluded with Denmark, the Faroe Islands, Finland, Iceland and Norway (the "Nordic Convention").[152] Its agreement with the Russian Federation complies with the minimum standard.

Sweden signed the MLI in 2017 and deposited its instrument of ratification on 22 June 2018, listing 64 tax agreements. The MLI entered into force for Sweden on 1 October 2018.

Sweden is implementing the minimum standard through the inclusion of the preamble statement and the PPT.[153]

The agreements that will be modified by the MLI will come into compliance with the minimum standard once the provisions of the MLI take effect.

Sweden signed a bilateral complying instrument with respect to its agreements with Brazil and Portugal. Further, the Parties to the Nordic Convention signed a complying instrument in 2018.

Sweden indicated in its response to the Peer Review questionnaire that bilateral negotiations would be used with respect to its agreements with Germany, Singapore, Slovenia and Spain.

B. Implementation issues

No jurisdiction has raised any concerns about their agreements with Sweden.

Summary of the jurisdiction response – Sweden

	Treaty partners	Compliance with the standard	If compliant, the alternative implemented	Signature of a complying instrument	The alternative implemented through the complying instrument (if not the MLI)	Comments
1	Albania*	No	N/A	Yes	N/A	
2	Argentina	No	N/A	Yes	N/A	
3	Armenia	No	N/A	Yes	N/A	
4	Australia	No	N/A	No	N/A	
5	Austria	No	N/A	No	N/A	
6	Azerbaijan*	No	N/A	Yes	N/A	
7	Bangladesh*	No	N/A	Yes	N/A	
8	Barbados	No	N/A	Yes	N/A	
9	Belarus*	No	N/A	Yes	N/A	
10	Belgium	No	N/A	Yes	N/A	
11	Bolivia*	No	N/A	Yes	N/A	
12	Bosnia and Herzegovina*	No	N/A	No	N/A	
13	Botswana	No	N/A	Yes	N/A	
14	Brazil	No	N/A	Yes	PPT and LOB	

15	Bulgaria	No	N/A	Yes	N/A	
16	Canada	No	N/A	Yes	N/A	
17	Chile	No	N/A	Yes	N/A	
18	China (People's Republic of)	No	N/A	Yes	N/A	
19	Croatia	No	N/A	No	N/A	
20	Cyprus*	No	N/A	Yes	N/A	
21	Czech Republic	No	N/A	Yes	N/A	
22	Denmark	No	N/A	Yes	PPT alone	
23	Egypt	No	N/A	Yes	N/A	
24	Estonia	No	N/A	Yes	N/A	
25	Faroe Islands	No	N/A	Yes	PPT alone	
26	Finland	No	N/A	Yes	PPT alone	
27	France	No	N/A	No	N/A	
28	Gambia*	No	N/A	Yes	N/A	
29	Georgia	No	N/A	Yes	N/A	
30	Germany	No	N/A	No	N/A	
31	Greece	No	N/A	Yes	N/A	
32	Hungary	No	N/A	Yes	N/A	
33	Iceland	No	N/A	Yes	PPT alone	
34	India	No	N/A	Yes	N/A	
35	Indonesia	No	N/A	Yes	N/A	
36	Ireland	No	N/A	Yes	N/A	
37	Israel	No	N/A	Yes	N/A	
38	Italy	No	N/A	Yes	N/A	
39	Jamaica	No	N/A	Yes	N/A	
40	Japan	No	N/A	Yes	N/A	
41	Kazakhstan	No	N/A	Yes	N/A	
42	Kenya	No	N/A	Yes	N/A	
43	Korea	No	N/A	Yes	N/A	
44	Kosovo*	No	N/A	No	N/A	
45	Latvia	No	N/A	Yes	N/A	
46	Lithuania	No	N/A	Yes	N/A	
47	Luxembourg	No	N/A	Yes	N/A	
48	North Macedonia	No	N/A	Yes	N/A	
49	Malaysia	No	N/A	Yes	N/A	
50	Malta	No	N/A	Yes	N/A	
51	Mauritius	No	N/A	Yes	N/A	
52	Mexico	No	N/A	Yes	N/A	
53	Montenegro*	No	N/A	No	N/A	
54	Namibia*	No	N/A	Yes	N/A	
55	Netherlands	No	N/A	Yes	N/A	
56	New Zealand	No	N/A	Yes	N/A	
57	Nigeria	No	N/A	Yes	N/A	
58	Norway	No	N/A	Yes	PPT alone	
59	Pakistan	No	N/A	Yes	N/A	
60	Philippines*	No	N/A	Yes	N/A	
61	Poland	No	N/A	Yes	N/A	
62	Portugal	No	N/A	Yes	PPT alone	
63	Romania	No	N/A	Yes	N/A	
64	Russian Federation	Yes	PPT alone	N/A	N/A	
65	Saudi Arabia	No	N/A	Yes	N/A	
66	Serbia	No	N/A	No	N/A	
67	Singapore	No	N/A	No	N/A	

68	Slovak Republic	No	N/A	Yes	N/A	
69	Slovenia	No	N/A	No	N/A	
70	South Africa	No	N/A	Yes	N/A	
71	Spain	No	N/A	No	N/A	
72	Sri Lanka	No	N/A	Yes	N/A	
73	Switzerland	No	N/A	Yes	PPT alone	
74	Tanzania*	No	N/A	Yes	N/A	
75	Thailand	No	N/A	Yes	N/A	
76	Trinidad and Tobago	No	N/A	Yes	N/A	
77	Tunisia	No	N/A	Yes	N/A	
78	Turkey	No	N/A	Yes	N/A	
79	Ukraine	No	N/A	Yes	N/A	
80	United Kingdom	No	N/A	Yes	N/A	
81	United States	No	N/A	Yes	N/A	
82	Venezuela*	No	N/A	Yes	N/A	
83	Viet Nam	No	N/A	Yes	N/A	
84	Zambia	No	N/A	Yes	N/A	
85	Zimbabwe*	No	N/A	Yes	N/A	

Switzerland

A. Progress in the implementation of the minimum standard

Switzerland has 106 tax agreements in force, as reported in its response to the Peer Review questionnaire. Three of those agreements, the agreements with Kosovo*, Latvia and Zambia, comply with the minimum standard.

Switzerland signed the MLI in 2017, listing 14 tax agreements.

Switzerland is implementing the minimum standard through the inclusion of the preamble statement and the PPT.[154]

The agreements that will be modified by the MLI will come into compliance with the minimum standard once the provisions of the MLI take effect.

Switzerland signed a bilateral complying instrument with respect to its agreements with Iran*, Ireland, Korea, the Netherlands, Norway, Sweden, Ukraine and the United Kingdom

Switzerland indicated in its response to the Peer Review questionnaire that it would only list an agreement under the MLI if it agrees with its treaty partner on how the MLI modifies their agreement. The agreement with Mexico will be added to Switzerland's list of covered tax agreements under the MLI.

Switzerland further indicated in its response to the Peer Review questionnaire that it has entered or intends to enter into bilateral negotiations with more than 45 of its treaty partners.[155] Bilateral negotiations would be used for agreements with Algeria*, Armenia, Australia, Belgium, Bulgaria, Canada, China, Colombia, Côte d'Ivoire, Croatia, Cyprus*, Denmark, Egypt, Estonia, Finland, France, Georgia, Germany, Greece, Hong Kong (China), Hungary, Indonesia, Israel, Jamaica, Japan, Kazakhstan, Kuwait*, Kyrgyzstan*, Malaysia, Malta, New Zealand, Peru, Romania, Russia, Serbia, Singapore, the Slovak Republic, Slovenia, Spain, Sri Lanka, Tunisia, the United States, Uruguay and Viet Nam.

Switzerland mentioned that there is no concern for treaty shopping with respect to some of its treaty partners (Anguilla, Antigua and Barbuda*, Barbados, Belize, British Virgin Islands, Dominica, Gambia*, Grenada, Malawi*, Montserrat, Saint Kitts and Nevis, Saint Lucia, and Saint Vincent and the Grenadines).

B. Implementation issues

No jurisdiction has raised any concerns about their agreements with Switzerland.

Summary of the jurisdiction response – Switzerland

	Treaty partners	Compliance with the standard	If compliant, the alternative implemented	Signature of a complying instrument	The alternative implemented through the complying instrument (if not the MLI)	Comments
1	Albania*	No	N/A	No	N/A	
2	Algeria*	No	N/A	No	N/A	
3	Anguilla	No	N/A	No	N/A	
4	Antigua and Barbuda	No	N/A	No	N/A	
5	Argentina	No	N/A	Yes	N/A	
6	Armenia	No	N/A	No	N/A	
7	Australia	No	N/A	No	N/A	

8	Austria	No	N/A	Yes	N/A	
9	Azerbaijan*	No	N/A	No	N/A	
10	Bangladesh*	No	N/A	No	N/A	
11	Barbados	No	N/A	No	N/A	
12	Belarus*	No	N/A	No	N/A	
13	Belgium	No	N/A	No	N/A	
14	Belize	No	N/A	No	N/A	
15	British Virgin Islands	No	N/A	No	N/A	
16	Bulgaria	No	N/A	No	N/A	
17	Canada	No	N/A	No	N/A	
18	Chile	No	N/A	Yes	N/A	
19	China (People's Republic of)	No	N/A	No	N/A	
20	Chinese Taipei*	No	N/A	No	N/A	
21	Colombia	No	N/A	No	N/A	
22	Cote d'Ivoire	No	N/A	No	N/A	
23	Croatia	No	N/A	No	N/A	
24	Cyprus*	No	N/A	No	N/A	
25	Czech Republic	No	N/A	Yes	N/A	
26	Denmark	No	N/A	No	N/A	
27	Dominica	No	N/A	No	N/A	
28	Ecuador*	No	N/A	No	N/A	
29	Egypt	No	N/A	No	N/A	
30	Estonia	No	N/A	No	N/A	
31	Finland	No	N/A	No	N/A	
32	France	No	N/A	No	N/A	
33	Gambia*	No	N/A	No	N/A	
34	Georgia	No	N/A	No	N/A	
35	Germany	No	N/A	No	N/A	
36	Ghana*	No	N/A	No	N/A	
37	Greece	No	N/A	No	N/A	
38	Grenada	No	N/A	No	N/A	
39	Hong Kong (China)	No	N/A	No	N/A	
40	Hungary	No	N/A	No	N/A	
41	Iceland	No	N/A	Yes	N/A	
42	India	No	N/A	Yes	N/A	
43	Indonesia	No	N/A	No	N/A	
44	Iran*	No	N/A	Yes	PPT alone	
45	Ireland	No	N/A	Yes	PPT alone	
46	Israel	No	N/A	No	N/A	
47	Italy	No	N/A	Yes	N/A	
48	Jamaica	No	N/A	No	N/A	
49	Japan	No	N/A	No	N/A	
50	Kazakhstan	No	N/A	No	N/A	
51	Korea	No	N/A	Yes	PPT alone	
52	Kosovo*	Yes	PPT alone	N/A	N/A	
53	Kuwait*	No	N/A	No	N/A	
54	Kyrgyzstan*	No	N/A	No	N/A	
55	Latvia	Yes	PPT alone	N/A	N/A	
56	Liechtenstein	No	N/A	Yes	N/A	
57	Lithuania	No	N/A	Yes	N/A	
58	Luxembourg	No	N/A	Yes	N/A	

59	North Macedonia	No	N/A	No	N/A	
60	Malawi*	No	N/A	No	N/A	
61	Malaysia	No	N/A	No	N/A	
62	Malta	No	N/A	No	N/A	
63	Mexico	No	N/A	No	N/A	
64	Moldova*	No	N/A	No	N/A	
65	Mongolia	No	N/A	No	N/A	
66	Montenegro*	No	N/A	No	N/A	
67	Montserrat	No	N/A	No	N/A	
68	Morocco	No	N/A	No	N/A	
69	Netherlands	No	N/A	Yes	PPT alone	
70	New Zealand	No	N/A	No	N/A	
71	Norway	No	N/A	Yes	PPT alone	
72	Oman	No	N/A	No	N/A	
73	Pakistan	No	N/A	No	N/A	PPT, but missing preamble
74	Peru	No	N/A	No	N/A	
75	Philippines*	No	N/A	No	N/A	
76	Poland	No	N/A	Yes	N/A	
77	Portugal	No	N/A	Yes	N/A	
78	Qatar	No	N/A	No	N/A	
79	Romania	No	N/A	No	N/A	
80	Russia	No	N/A	No	N/A	
81	Saint Kitts and Nevis	No	N/A	No	N/A	
82	Saint Lucia	No	N/A	No	N/A	
83	Saint Vincent and the Grenadines	No	N/A	No	N/A	
84	Serbia	No	N/A	No	N/A	
85	Singapore	No	N/A	No	N/A	
86	Slovak Republic	No	N/A	No	N/A	
87	Slovenia	No	N/A	No	N/A	
88	South Africa	No	N/A	Yes	N/A	
89	Spain	No	N/A	No	N/A	
90	Sri Lanka	No	N/A	No	N/A	
91	Sweden	No	N/A	Yes	PPT alone	
92	Tajikistan*	No	N/A	No	N/A	
93	Thailand	No	N/A	No	N/A	
94	Trinidad and Tobago	No	N/A	No	N/A	
95	Tunisia	No	N/A	No	N/A	
96	Turkey	No	N/A	Yes	N/A	
97	Turkmenistan*	No	N/A	No	N/A	
98	Ukraine	No	N/A	Yes	PPT alone	
99	United Arab Emirates	No	N/A	No	N/A	
100	United Kingdom	No	N/A	Yes	PPT alone	
101	United States	No	N/A	No	N/A	
102	Uruguay	No	N/A	No	N/A	
103	Uzbekistan*	No	N/A	No	N/A	
104	Venezuela*	No	N/A	No	N/A	
105	Viet Nam	No	N/A	No	N/A	
106	Zambia	Yes	PPT alone	N/A	N/A	

Thailand

A. Progress in the implementation of the minimum standard

Thailand has 61 tax agreements in force, as reported in its response to the Peer Review questionnaire.

None of Thailand's agreements comply with the minimum standard or are subject to a complying instrument.

B. Implementation issues

No jurisdiction has raised any concerns about their agreements with Thailand.

Thailand is encouraged to implement the minimum standard in its agreements.

Summary of the jurisdiction response - Thailand

	Treaty partners	Compliance with the standard	If compliant, the alternative implemented	Signature of a complying instrument	The alternative implemented through the complying instrument (if not the MLI)	Comments
1	Armenia	No	N/A	No	N/A	
2	Australia	No	N/A	No	N/A	
3	Austria	No	N/A	No	N/A	
4	Bahrain	No	N/A	No	N/A	
5	Bangladesh*	No	N/A	No	N/A	
6	Belarus*	No	N/A	No	N/A	
7	Belgium	No	N/A	No	N/A	
8	Bulgaria	No	N/A	No	N/A	
9	Cambodia*	No	N/A	No	N/A	
10	Canada	No	N/A	No	N/A	
11	Chile	No	N/A	No	N/A	
12	China (People's Republic of)	No	N/A	No	N/A	
13	Chinese Taipei*	No	N/A	No	N/A	
14	Cyprus*	No	N/A	No	N/A	
15	Czech Republic	No	N/A	No	N/A	
16	Denmark	No	N/A	No	N/A	
17	Estonia	No	N/A	No	N/A	
18	Finland	No	N/A	No	N/A	
19	France	No	N/A	No	N/A	
20	Germany	No	N/A	No	N/A	
21	Hong Kong (China)	No	N/A	No	N/A	
22	Hungary	No	N/A	No	N/A	
23	India	No	N/A	No	N/A	
24	Indonesia	No	N/A	No	N/A	
25	Ireland	No	N/A	No	N/A	
26	Israel	No	N/A	No	N/A	

27	Italy	No	N/A	No	N/A		
28	Japan	No	N/A	No	N/A		
29	Korea	No	N/A	No	N/A		
30	Kuwait*	No	N/A	No	N/A		
31	Lao People's Democratic Republic*	No	N/A	No	N/A		
32	Luxembourg	No	N/A	No	N/A		
33	Malaysia	No	N/A	No	N/A		
34	Mauritius	No	N/A	No	N/A		
35	Myanmar*	No	N/A	No	N/A		
36	Nepal*	No	N/A	No	N/A		
37	Netherlands	No	N/A	No	N/A		
38	New Zealand	No	N/A	No	N/A		
39	Norway	No	N/A	No	N/A		
40	Oman	No	N/A	No	N/A		
41	Pakistan	No	N/A	No	N/A		
42	Philippines*	No	N/A	No	N/A		
43	Poland	No	N/A	No	N/A		
44	Romania	No	N/A	No	N/A		
45	Russia	No	N/A	No	N/A		
46	Seychelles	No	N/A	No	N/A		
47	Singapore	No	N/A	No	N/A		
48	Slovenia	No	N/A	No	N/A		
49	South Africa	No	N/A	No	N/A		
50	Spain	No	N/A	No	N/A		
51	Sri Lanka	No	N/A	No	N/A		
52	Sweden	No	N/A	No	N/A		
53	Switzerland	No	N/A	No	N/A		
54	Tajikistan*	No	N/A	No	N/A		
55	Turkey	No	N/A	No	N/A		
56	Ukraine	No	N/A	No	N/A		
57	United Arab Emirates	No	N/A	No	N/A		
58	United Kingdom	No	N/A	No	N/A		
59	United States	No	N/A	No	N/A		
60	Uzbekistan*	No	N/A	No	N/A		
61	Viet Nam	No	N/A	No	N/A		

Trinidad and Tobago

A. Progress in the implementation of the minimum standard

Trinidad and Tobago has 17 tax agreements in force, as reported in its response to the Peer Review questionnaire, including the multilateral agreement among the members of the CARICOM concluded with ten treaty partners (the CARICOM Agreement).[156]

None of Trinidad and Tobago's agreements comply with the minimum standard or are subject to a complying instrument.

B. Implementation issues

Trinidad and Tobago is encouraged to implement the minimum standard in its agreements.

Trinidad and Tobago is encouraged to bring the CARICOM Agreement up to date by commencing talks among all the treaty partners.[157]

Summary of the jurisdiction response – Trinidad and Tobago

	Treaty partners	Compliance with the standard	If compliant, the alternative implemented	Signature of a complying instrument	The alternative implemented through the complying instrument (if not the MLI)	Comments
1	Antigua and Barbuda	No	N/A	No	N/A	CARICOM
2	Barbados	No	N/A	No	N/A	CARICOM
3	Belize	No	N/A	No	N/A	CARICOM
4	Brazil	No	N/A	No	N/A	
5	Canada	No	N/A	No	N/A	
6	China (People's Republic of)	No	N/A	No	N/A	
7	Denmark	No	N/A	No	N/A	
8	Dominica	No	N/A	No	N/A	CARICOM
9	France	No	N/A	No	N/A	
10	Germany	No	N/A	No	N/A	
11	Grenada*	No	N/A	No	N/A	CARICOM
12	Guyana*	No	N/A	No	N/A	CARICOM
13	India	No	N/A	No	N/A	
14	Italy	No	N/A	No	N/A	
15	Jamaica	No	N/A	No	N/A	CARICOM
16	Luxembourg	No	N/A	No	N/A	
17	Norway	No	N/A	No	N/A	
18	Saint Kitts and Nevis	No	N/A	No	N/A	CARICOM
19	Saint Lucia	No	N/A	No	N/A	CARICOM

20	Saint Vincent and the Grenadines	No	N/A	No	N/A	CARICOM
21	Spain	No	N/A	No	N/A	
22	Sweden	No	N/A	No	N/A	
23	Switzerland	No	N/A	No	N/A	
24	United Kingdom	No	N/A	No	N/A	
25	United States	No	N/A	No	N/A	
26	Venezuela*	No	N/A	No	N/A	

Tunisia

A. Progress in the implementation of the minimum standard

Tunisia has 55 tax agreements in force, as reported in its response to the Peer Review questionnaire, including the Arab Maghreb Union Income Agreement concluded with four treaty partners. [158]

Tunisia signed the MLI in 2018, listing 55 tax agreements.

Tunisia implementing the minimum standard through the inclusion of the preamble statement and the PPT.[159]

The agreements that will be modified by the MLI will come into compliance with the minimum standard once the provisions of the MLI take effect.

B. Implementation issues

No jurisdiction has raised any concerns about their agreements with Tunisia.

Summary of the jurisdiction response – Tunisia

	Treaty partners	Compliance with the standard	If compliant, the alternative implemented	Signature of a complying instrument	The alternative implemented through the complying instrument (if not the MLI)	Comments
1	Algeria*	No	N/A	Yes	N/A	
2	Austria	No	N/A	Yes	N/A	
3	Belgium	No	N/A	Yes	N/A	
4	Burkina Faso	No	N/A	Yes	N/A	
5	Cameroon	No	N/A	Yes	N/A	
6	Canada	No	N/A	Yes	N/A	
7	China (People's Republic of)	No	N/A	Yes	N/A	
8	Cote d'Ivoire	No	N/A	Yes	N/A	
9	Czech Republic	No	N/A	Yes	N/A	
10	Denmark	No	N/A	Yes	N/A	
11	Egypt	No	N/A	Yes	N/A	
12	Ethiopia*	No	N/A	Yes	N/A	
13	France	No	N/A	Yes	N/A	
14	Germany	No	N/A	Yes	N/A	
15	Greece	No	N/A	Yes	N/A	
16	Hungary	No	N/A	Yes	N/A	
17	Indonesia	No	N/A	Yes	N/A	
18	Iran*	No	N/A	Yes	N/A	
19	Italy	No	N/A	Yes	N/A	
20	Jordan*	No	N/A	Yes	N/A	
21	Korea	No	N/A	Yes	N/A	
22	Kuwait*	No	N/A	Yes	N/A	

23	Lebanon*	No	N/A	Yes	N/A	
24	Libya*	No	N/A	Yes	N/A	
25	Luxembourg	No	N/A	Yes	N/A	
26	Mali*	No	N/A	Yes	N/A	
27	Malta	No	N/A	Yes	N/A	
28	Mauritania*	No	N/A	Yes	N/A	
29	Mauritius	No	N/A	Yes	N/A	
30	Morocco	No	N/A	Yes	N/A	
31	Netherlands	No	N/A	Yes	N/A	
32	Norway	No	N/A	Yes	N/A	
33	Oman	No	N/A	Yes	N/A	
34	Pakistan	No	N/A	Yes	N/A	
35	Poland	No	N/A	Yes	N/A	
36	Portugal	No	N/A	Yes	N/A	
37	Qatar	No	N/A	Yes	N/A	
38	Romania	No	N/A	Yes	N/A	
39	Saudi Arabia	No	N/A	Yes	N/A	
40	Senegal	No	N/A	Yes	N/A	
41	Serbia	No	N/A	Yes	N/A	
42	Slovak Republic	No	N/A	Yes	N/A	
43	South Africa	No	N/A	Yes	N/A	
44	Spain	No	N/A	Yes	N/A	
45	Sudan*	No	N/A	Yes	N/A	
46	Sweden	No	N/A	Yes	N/A	
47	Switzerland	No	N/A	Yes	N/A	
48	Syrian Arab Republic*	No	N/A	Yes	N/A	
49	Turkey	No	N/A	Yes	N/A	
50	United Arab Emirates	No	N/A	Yes	N/A	
51	United Kingdom	No	N/A	Yes	N/A	
52	United States	No	N/A	Yes	N/A	
53	Viet Nam	No	N/A	Yes	N/A	
54	Yemen*	No	N/A	Yes	N/A	
55	Algeria* (UMA)	No	N/A	Yes	N/A	
56	Libya* (UMA)	No	N/A	Yes	N/A	
57	Mauritania* (UMA)	No	N/A	Yes	N/A	
58	Morocco (UMA)	No	N/A	Yes	N/A	

Turks and Caicos Islands

A. Progress in the implementation of the minimum standard

The Turks and Caicos Islands has no tax agreements in force, as reported in its response to the Peer Review questionnaire.

B. Implementation issues

No jurisdiction has raised any concerns about the Turks and Caicos Islands.

Turkey

A. Progress in the implementation of the minimum standard

Turkey has 86 tax agreements in force, as reported in its response to the Peer Review questionnaire.

Turkey signed the MLI in 2017, listing 86 tax agreements.[160]

Turkey is implementing the minimum standard through the inclusion of the preamble statement and the PPT.[161]

The agreements that will be modified by the MLI will come into compliance with the minimum standard once the provisions of the MLI take effect.

B. Implementation issues

No jurisdiction has raised any concerns about their agreements with Turkey.

Summary of the jurisdiction response – Turkey

	Treaty partners	Compliance with the standard	If compliant, the alternative implemented	Signature of a complying instrument	The alternative implemented through the complying instrument (if not the MLI)	Comments
1	Albania*	No	N/A	Yes	N/A	
2	Algeria*	No	N/A	Yes	N/A	
3	Australia	No	N/A	Yes	N/A	
4	Austria	No	N/A	Yes	N/A	
5	Azerbaijan*	No	N/A	Yes	N/A	
6	Bahrain	No	N/A	Yes	N/A	
7	Bangladesh*	No	N/A	Yes	N/A	
8	Belarus*	No	N/A	Yes	N/A	
9	Belgium	No	N/A	Yes	N/A	
10	Bosnia and Herzegovina*	No	N/A	Yes	N/A	
11	Brazil	No	N/A	Yes	N/A	
12	Bulgaria	No	N/A	Yes	N/A	
13	Canada	No	N/A	Yes	N/A	
14	China (People's Republic of)	No	N/A	Yes	N/A	
15	Croatia	No	N/A	Yes	N/A	
16	Czech Republic	No	N/A	Yes	N/A	
17	Denmark	No	N/A	Yes	N/A	
18	Egypt	No	N/A	Yes	N/A	
19	Estonia	No	N/A	Yes	N/A	
20	Ethiopia*	No	N/A	Yes	N/A	
21	Finland	No	N/A	Yes	N/A	
22	France	No	N/A	Yes	N/A	
23	Gambia*	No	N/A	Yes	N/A	

24	Georgia	No	N/A	Yes	N/A	
25	Germany	No	N/A	Yes	N/A	
26	Greece	No	N/A	Yes	N/A	
27	Hungary	No	N/A	Yes	N/A	
28	India	No	N/A	Yes	N/A	
29	Indonesia	No	N/A	Yes	N/A	
30	Iran*	No	N/A	Yes	N/A	
31	Ireland	No	N/A	Yes	N/A	
32	Israel	No	N/A	Yes	N/A	
33	Italy	No	N/A	Yes	N/A	
34	Japan	No	N/A	Yes	N/A	
35	Jordan*	No	N/A	Yes	N/A	
36	Kazakhstan	No	N/A	Yes	N/A	
37	Korea	No	N/A	Yes	N/A	
38	Kosovo*	No	N/A	Yes	N/A	
39	Kuwait*	No	N/A	Yes	N/A	
40	Kyrgyzstan*	No	N/A	Yes	N/A	
41	Latvia	No	N/A	Yes	N/A	
42	Lebanon*	No	N/A	Yes	N/A	
43	Lithuania	No	N/A	Yes	N/A	
44	Luxembourg	No	N/A	Yes	N/A	
45	North Macedonia	No	N/A	Yes	N/A	
46	Malaysia	No	N/A	Yes	N/A	
47	Malta	No	N/A	Yes	N/A	
48	Mexico	No	N/A	Yes	N/A	
49	Moldova*	No	N/A	Yes	N/A	
50	Mongolia	No	N/A	Yes	N/A	
51	Montenegro*	No	N/A	Yes	N/A	
52	Morocco	No	N/A	Yes	N/A	
53	Netherlands	No	N/A	Yes	N/A	
54	New Zealand	No	N/A	Yes	N/A	
55	Norway	No	N/A	Yes	N/A	
56	Oman	No	N/A	Yes	N/A	
57	Pakistan	No	N/A	Yes	N/A	
58	Philippines*	No	N/A	Yes	N/A	
59	Poland	No	N/A	Yes	N/A	
60	Portugal	No	N/A	Yes	N/A	
61	Qatar	No	N/A	Yes	N/A	
62	Romania	No	N/A	Yes	N/A	
63	Russia	No	N/A	Yes	N/A	
64	Saudi Arabia	No	N/A	Yes	N/A	
65	Serbia	No	N/A	Yes	N/A	
66	Singapore	No	N/A	Yes	N/A	
67	Slovak Republic	No	N/A	Yes	N/A	
68	Slovenia	No	N/A	Yes	N/A	
69	South Africa	No	N/A	Yes	N/A	
70	Spain	No	N/A	Yes	N/A	
71	Sudan*	No	N/A	Yes	N/A	
72	Sweden	No	N/A	Yes	N/A	
73	Switzerland	No	N/A	Yes	N/A	
74	Syrian Arab Republic*	No	N/A	Yes	N/A	
75	Tajikistan*	No	N/A	Yes	N/A	
76	Thailand	No	N/A	Yes	N/A	

77	Tunisia	No	N/A	Yes	N/A	
78	Turkish Republic of Northern Cyprus*	No	N/A	Yes	N/A	
79	Turkmenistan*	No	N/A	Yes	N/A	
80	Ukraine	No	N/A	Yes	N/A	
81	United Arab Emirates	No	N/A	Yes	N/A	
82	United Kingdom	No	N/A	Yes	N/A	
83	United States	No	N/A	Yes	N/A	
84	Uzbekistan*	No	N/A	Yes	N/A	
85	Viet Nam	No	N/A	Yes	N/A	
86	Yemen*	No	N/A	Yes	N/A	

Ukraine

A. Progress in the implementation of the minimum standard

Ukraine has 75 tax agreements in force, as reported in its response to the Peer Review questionnaire.

Ukraine signed the MLI on 23 July 2018, listing 75 tax agreements.[162]

Ukraine is implementing the minimum standard through the inclusion of the preamble statement and the PPT.[163]

The agreements that will be modified by the MLI will come into compliance with the minimum standard once the provisions of the MLI take effect.

Ukraine signed a bilateral complying instrument with respect to its agreements with the Netherlands, Switzerland and the United Kingdom.

B. Implementation issues

No jurisdiction has raised any concerns about their agreements with Ukraine.

Summary of the jurisdiction response – Ukraine

	Treaty partners	Compliance with the standard	If compliant, the alternative implemented	Signature of a complying instrument	The alternative implemented through the complying instrument (if not the MLI)	Comments
1	Algeria*	No	N/A	Yes	N/A	
2	Armenia	No	N/A	Yes	N/A	
3	Austria	No	N/A	Yes	N/A	
4	Azerbaijan*	No	N/A	Yes	N/A	
5	Belarus*	No	N/A	Yes	N/A	
6	Belgium	No	N/A	Yes	N/A	
7	Brazil	No	N/A	Yes	N/A	
8	Bulgaria	No	N/A	Yes	N/A	
9	Canada	No	N/A	Yes	N/A	
10	China (People's Republic of)	No	N/A	Yes	N/A	
11	Croatia	No	N/A	Yes	N/A	
12	Cuba*	No	N/A	Yes	N/A	
13	Cyprus*	No	N/A	Yes	N/A	
14	Czech Republic	No	N/A	Yes	N/A	
15	Denmark	No	N/A	Yes	N/A	
16	Egypt	No	N/A	Yes	N/A	
17	Estonia	No	N/A	Yes	N/A	
18	Finland	No	N/A	Yes	N/A	
19	France	No	N/A	Yes	N/A	
20	Georgia	No	N/A	Yes	N/A	
21	Germany	No	N/A	Yes	N/A	
22	Greece	No	N/A	Yes	N/A	
23	Hungary	No	N/A	Yes	N/A	

24	Iceland	No	N/A	Yes	N/A	
25	India	No	N/A	Yes	N/A	
26	Indonesia	No	N/A	Yes	N/A	
27	Iran*	No	N/A	Yes	N/A	
28	Ireland	No	N/A	Yes	N/A	
29	Israel	No	N/A	Yes	N/A	
30	Italy	No	N/A	Yes	N/A	
31	Japan	No	N/A	Yes	N/A	
32	Jordan*	No	N/A	Yes	N/A	
33	Kazakhstan	No	N/A	Yes	N/A	
34	Korea	No	N/A	Yes	N/A	
35	Kuwait*	No	N/A	Yes	N/A	
36	Kyrgyzstan*	No	N/A	Yes	N/A	
37	Latvia	No	N/A	Yes	N/A	
38	Lebanon*	No	N/A	Yes	N/A	
39	Libya*	No	N/A	Yes	N/A	
40	Lithuania	No	N/A	Yes	N/A	
41	Luxembourg	No	N/A	Yes	N/A	
42	North Macedonia	No	N/A	Yes	N/A	
43	Malaysia	No	N/A	Yes	N/A	
44	Malta	No	N/A	Yes	N/A	
45	Mexico	No	N/A	Yes	N/A	
46	Moldova*	No	N/A	Yes	N/A	
47	Mongolia	No	N/A	Yes	N/A	
48	Montenegro*	No	N/A	Yes	N/A	
49	Morocco	No	N/A	Yes	N/A	
50	Netherlands	No	N/A	Yes	PPT alone	
51	Norway	No	N/A	Yes	N/A	
52	Pakistan	No	N/A	Yes	N/A	
53	Poland	No	N/A	Yes	N/A	
54	Portugal	No	N/A	Yes	N/A	
55	Romania	No	N/A	Yes	N/A	
56	Russia	No	N/A	Yes	N/A	
57	Saudi Arabia	No	N/A	Yes	N/A	
58	Serbia	No	N/A	Yes	N/A	
59	Singapore	No	N/A	Yes	N/A	
60	Slovak Republic	No	N/A	Yes	N/A	
61	Slovenia	No	N/A	Yes	N/A	
62	South Africa	No	N/A	Yes	N/A	
63	Spain	No	N/A	Yes	N/A	
64	Sweden	No	N/A	Yes	N/A	
65	Switzerland	No	N/A	Yes	PPT alone	
66	Syrian Arab Republic*	No	N/A	Yes	N/A	
67	Tajikistan*	No	N/A	Yes	N/A	
68	Thailand	No	N/A	Yes	N/A	
69	Turkey	No	N/A	Yes	N/A	
70	Turkmenistan*	No	N/A	Yes	N/A	
71	United Arab Emirates	No	N/A	Yes	N/A	
72	United Kingdom	No	N/A	Yes	PPT alone	
73	United States	No	N/A	Yes	N/A	
74	Uzbekistan*	No	N/A	Yes	N/A	
75	Viet Nam	No	N/A	Yes	N/A	

United Arab Emirates

A. Progress in the implementation of the minimum standard

The United Arab Emirates has 92 tax agreements in force, as reported in its response to the Peer Review questionnaire. Its agreement with Saudi Arabia complies with the minimum standard.

The United Arab Emirates signed the MLI in 2018 and deposited its instrument of ratification on 29 May 2019, listing 91 tax agreements.[164]

The United Arab Emirates is implementing the minimum standard through the inclusion of the preamble statement and the PPT.[165]

The agreements that will be modified by the MLI will come into compliance with the minimum standard once the provisions of the MLI take effect.

B. Implementation issues

No jurisdiction has raised any concerns about their agreements with the United Arab Emirates.

Summary of the jurisdiction response – United Arab Emirates

	Treaty partners	Compliance with the standard	If compliant, the alternative implemented	Signature of a complying instrument	The alternative implemented through the complying instrument (if not the MLI)	Comments
1	Albania*	No	N/A	Yes	N/A	
2	Algeria*	No	N/A	Yes	N/A	
3	Andorra	No	N/A	Yes	N/A	
4	Argentina	No	N/A	Yes	N/A	
5	Armenia	No	N/A	Yes	N/A	
6	Austria	No	N/A	Yes	N/A	
7	Azerbaijan*	No	N/A	Yes	N/A	
8	Bangladesh*	No	N/A	Yes	N/A	
9	Barbados	No	N/A	Yes	N/A	
10	Belarus*	No	N/A	Yes	N/A	
11	Belgium	No	N/A	Yes	N/A	
12	Bosnia and Herzegovina*	No	N/A	Yes	N/A	
13	Brunei Darussalam	No	N/A	Yes	N/A	
14	Bulgaria	No	N/A	Yes	N/A	
15	Canada	No	N/A	Yes	N/A	
16	China (People's Republic of)	No	N/A	Yes	N/A	
17	Comoros*	No	N/A	Yes	N/A	
18	Croatia	No	N/A	Yes	N/A	
19	Cyprus*	No	N/A	Yes	N/A	
20	Czech Republic	No	N/A	Yes	N/A	

21	Egypt	No	N/A	Yes	N/A	
22	Estonia	No	N/A	Yes	N/A	
23	Fiji*	No	N/A	Yes	N/A	
24	Finland	No	N/A	Yes	N/A	
25	France	No	N/A	Yes	N/A	
26	Georgia	No	N/A	Yes	N/A	
27	Germany	No	N/A	Yes	N/A	
28	Greece	No	N/A	Yes	N/A	
29	Guinea*	No	N/A	Yes	N/A	
30	Hong Kong (China)	No	N/A	Yes	N/A	
31	Hungary	No	N/A	Yes	N/A	
32	India	No	N/A	Yes	N/A	
33	Indonesia	No	N/A	Yes	N/A	
34	Ireland	No	N/A	Yes	N/A	
35	Italy	No	N/A	Yes	N/A	
36	Japan	No	N/A	Yes	N/A	
37	Jersey	No	N/A	Yes	N/A	
38	Jordan*	No	N/A	Yes	N/A	
39	Kazakhstan	No	N/A	Yes	N/A	
40	Kenya	No	N/A	Yes	N/A	
41	Korea	No	N/A	Yes	N/A	
42	Kosovo*	No	N/A	Yes	N/A	
43	Kyrgyzstan*	No	N/A	Yes	N/A	
44	Latvia	No	N/A	Yes	N/A	
45	Lebanon*	No	N/A	Yes	N/A	
46	Liechtenstein	No	N/A	Yes	N/A	
47	Lithuania	No	N/A	Yes	N/A	
48	Luxembourg	No	N/A	Yes	N/A	
49	North Macedonia	No	N/A	Yes	N/A	
50	Malaysia	No	N/A	Yes	N/A	
51	Maldives	No	N/A	Yes	N/A	
52	Malta	No	N/A	Yes	N/A	
53	Mauritius	No	N/A	Yes	N/A	
54	Mexico	No	N/A	Yes	N/A	
55	Moldova*	No	N/A	Yes	N/A	
56	Montenegro*	No	N/A	Yes	N/A	
57	Morocco	No	N/A	Yes	N/A	
58	Mozambique*	No	N/A	Yes	N/A	
59	Netherlands	No	N/A	Yes	N/A	
60	New Zealand	No	N/A	Yes	N/A	
61	Pakistan	No	N/A	Yes	N/A	
62	Panama	No	N/A	Yes	N/A	
63	Philippines*	No	N/A	Yes	N/A	
64	Poland	No	N/A	Yes	N/A	
65	Portugal	No	N/A	Yes	N/A	
66	Romania	No	N/A	Yes	N/A	
67	Russia	No	N/A	Yes	N/A	
68	Saudi Arabia	Yes	PPT alone	N/A	N/A	
69	Senegal	No	N/A	Yes	N/A	
70	Serbia	No	N/A	Yes	N/A	
71	Seychelles	No	N/A	Yes	N/A	
72	Singapore	No	N/A	Yes	N/A	
73	Slovak Republic	No	N/A	Yes	N/A	

74	Slovenia	No	N/A	Yes	N/A	
75	South Africa	No	N/A	Yes	N/A	
76	Spain	No	N/A	Yes	N/A	
77	Sri Lanka	No	N/A	Yes	N/A	
78	Sudan*	No	N/A	Yes	N/A	
79	Switzerland	No	N/A	Yes	N/A	
80	Syrian Arab Republic*	No	N/A	Yes	N/A	
81	Tajikistan*	No	N/A	Yes	N/A	
82	Thailand	No	N/A	Yes	N/A	
83	Tunisia	No	N/A	Yes	N/A	
84	Turkey	No	N/A	Yes	N/A	
85	Turkmenistan*	No	N/A	Yes	N/A	
86	Ukraine	No	N/A	Yes	N/A	
87	United Kingdom	No	N/A	Yes	N/A	
88	Uruguay	No	N/A	Yes	N/A	
89	Uzbekistan*	No	N/A	Yes	N/A	
90	Venezuela*	No	N/A	Yes	N/A	
91	Viet Nam	No	N/A	Yes	N/A	
92	Yemen*	No	N/A	Yes	N/A	

United Kingdom

A. Progress in the implementation of the minimum standard

The United Kingdom has 129 tax agreements in force, as reported in its response to the Peer Review questionnaire. Sixteen of those agreements, the agreements with Australia, Austria, Belarus*, Cyprus*, France, Guernsey, Isle of Man, Japan, Jersey, Lithuania, New Zealand, Poland, Serbia, Slovak Republic, Slovenia, and Uzbekistan*, comply with the minimum standard.

The United Kingdom signed the MLI in 2017 and deposited its instrument of ratification on 29 June 2018, listing 120 tax agreements. The MLI entered into force for the United Kingdom on 1 October 2018.[166]

The United Kingdom is implementing the minimum standard through the inclusion of the preamble statement and the PPT.[167]

The agreements modified by the MLI come into compliance with the minimum standard once the provisions of the MLI take effect. Other agreements listed under the MLI are expected to become compliant with the minimum standard by the end of 2019. The United Kingdom's agreements with the Falkland Islands*, Guernsey, Isle of Man, Jersey and Montserrat are not listed under the MLI as they are arrangements with Crown Dependencies and overseas territories. Bilateral negotiations are being used to update these agreements.

The United Kingdom signed a bilateral complying instrument with respect to its agreements with Israel, Switzerland and Ukraine.[168]

The United Kingdom indicated in its response to the Peer Review questionnaire that bilateral negotiations would be used with respect to its agreement with Germany.

B. Implementation issues

No jurisdiction has raised any concerns about their agreements with the United Kingdom.

Summary of the jurisdiction response – United Kingdom

	Treaty partners	Compliance with the standard	If compliant, the alternative implemented	Signature of a complying instrument	The alternative implemented through the complying instrument (if not the MLI)	Comments
1	Albania*	No	N/A	Yes	N/A	
2	Algeria*	No	N/A	Yes	N/A	
3	Antigua and Barbuda	No	N/A	Yes	N/A	
4	Argentina	No	N/A	Yes	N/A	
5	Armenia	No	N/A	Yes	N/A	
6	Australia	Yes	PPT alone	N/A	N/A	
7	Austria	Yes	PPT alone	N/A	N/A	
8	Azerbaijan*	No	N/A	Yes	N/A	
9	Bahrain	No	N/A	Yes	N/A	
10	Bangladesh*	No	N/A	Yes	N/A	
11	Barbados	No	N/A	Yes	N/A	

12	Belarus*	Yes	PPT alone	N/A	N/A	
13	Belgium	No	N/A	Yes	N/A	
14	Belize	No	N/A	Yes	N/A	
15	Bolivia*	No	N/A	Yes	N/A	
16	Bosnia and Herzegovina*	No	N/A	Yes	N/A	
17	Botswana	No	N/A	Yes	N/A	
18	Brunei Darussalam	No	N/A	Yes	N/A	
19	Bulgaria	No	N/A	Yes	N/A	
20	Canada	No	N/A	Yes	N/A	
21	Chile	No	N/A	Yes	N/A	
22	China (People's Republic of)	No	N/A	Yes	N/A	
23	Chinese Taipei*	No	N/A	No	N/A	
24	Cote d'Ivoire	No	N/A	Yes	N/A	
25	Croatia	No	N/A	Yes	N/A	
26	Cyprus*	Yes	PPT alone	N/A	N/A	
27	Czech Republic	No	N/A	Yes	N/A	
28	Denmark	No	N/A	Yes	N/A	
29	Egypt	No	N/A	Yes	N/A	
30	Estonia	No	N/A	Yes	N/A	
31	Ethiopia*	No	N/A	Yes	N/A	
32	Falkland Islands*	No	N/A	No	N/A	
33	Faroe Islands	No	N/A	Yes	N/A	
34	Fiji*	No	N/A	Yes	N/A	
35	Finland	No	N/A	Yes	N/A	MLI has effect from 1/1/2020
36	France	Yes	PPT alone	N/A	N/A	
37	Gambia*	No	N/A	Yes	N/A	
38	Georgia	No	N/A	Yes	N/A	MLI has effect from 1/1/2020
39	Germany	No	N/A	No	N/A	
40	Ghana*	No	N/A	Yes	N/A	
41	Greece	No	N/A	Yes	N/A	
42	Grenada*	No	N/A	Yes	N/A	
43	Guernsey	Yes	PPT alone	N/A	N/A	
44	Guyana*	No	N/A	Yes	N/A	
45	Hong Kong (China)	No	N/A	Yes	N/A	
46	Hungary	No	N/A	Yes	N/A	
47	Iceland	No	N/A	Yes	N/A	
48	India	No	N/A	Yes	N/A	
49	Indonesia	No	N/A	Yes	N/A	
50	Ireland	No	N/A	Yes	N/A	MLI has effect from 1/1/2020
51	Isle of Man	Yes	PPT alone	N/A	N/A	
52	Israel	No	N/A	Yes	PPT alone	Amending protocol signed
53	Italy	No	N/A	Yes	N/A	
54	Jamaica	No	N/A	Yes	N/A	
55	Japan	Yes	PPT and LOB	N/A	N/A	
56	Jersey	Yes	PPT alone	N/A	N/A	
57	Jordan*	No	N/A	Yes	N/A	

58	Kazakhstan	No	N/A	Yes	N/A	
59	Kenya	No	N/A	Yes	N/A	
60	Kiribati*	No	N/A	Yes	N/A	
61	Korea	No	N/A	Yes	N/A	
62	Kosovo*	No	N/A	Yes	N/A	
63	Kuwait*	No	N/A	Yes	N/A	
64	Latvia	No	N/A	Yes	N/A	
65	Lesotho*[169]	No	N/A	Yes	N/A	
66	Libya*	No	N/A	Yes	N/A	
67	Liechtenstein	No	N/A	Yes	N/A	
68	Lithuania	Yes	PPT alone	N/A	N/A	
69	Luxembourg	No	N/A	Yes	N/A	MLI has effect from 1/1/2020
70	North Macedonia	No	N/A	Yes	N/A	
71	Malawi*	No	N/A	Yes	N/A	
72	Malaysia	No	N/A	Yes	N/A	
73	Malta	No	N/A	Yes	N/A	MLI has effect from 1/1/2020
74	Mauritius	No	N/A	Yes	N/A	
75	Mexico	No	N/A	Yes	N/A	
76	Moldova*	No	N/A	Yes	N/A	
77	Mongolia	No	N/A	Yes	N/A	
78	Montenegro*	No	N/A	Yes	N/A	
79	Montserrat	No	N/A	No	N/A	
80	Morocco	No	N/A	Yes	N/A	
81	Myanmar*	No	N/A	Yes	N/A	
82	Namibia*	No	N/A	Yes	N/A	
83	Netherlands	No	N/A	Yes	N/A	MLI has effect from 1/1/2020
84	New Zealand	Yes	PPT alone	N/A	N/A	
85	Nigeria	No	N/A	Yes	N/A	
86	Norway	No	N/A	Yes	N/A	
87	Oman	No	N/A	Yes	N/A	
88	Pakistan	No	N/A	Yes	N/A	
89	Panama	No	N/A	Yes	N/A	
90	Papua New Guinea	No	N/A	Yes	N/A	
91	Philippines*	No	N/A	Yes	N/A	
92	Poland	Yes	PPT alone	N/A	N/A	
93	Portugal	No	N/A	Yes	N/A	
94	Qatar	No	N/A	Yes	N/A	
95	Romania	No	N/A	Yes	N/A	
96	Russia	No	N/A	Yes	N/A	
97	Saint Kitts and Nevis	No	N/A	Yes	N/A	
98	Saudi Arabia	No	N/A	Yes	N/A	
99	Senegal	No	N/A	Yes	N/A	
100	Serbia	Yes	PPT alone	N/A	N/A	
101	Sierra Leone	No	N/A	Yes	N/A	
102	Singapore	No	N/A	Yes	N/A	MLI has effect from 1/1/2020
103	Slovak Republic	Yes	PPT alone	N/A	N/A	
104	Slovenia	Yes	PPT alone	N/A	N/A	
105	Solomon	No	N/A	Yes	N/A	

	Islands*					
106	South Africa	No	N/A	Yes	N/A	
107	Spain	No	N/A	Yes	N/A	
108	Sri Lanka	No	N/A	Yes	N/A	
109	Sudan*	No	N/A	Yes	N/A	
110	Eswatini*	No	N/A	Yes	N/A	
111	Sweden	No	N/A	Yes	N/A	MLI to enter into effect when Sweden have completed their internal procedures
112	Switzerland	No	N/A	Yes	PPT alone	Amending protocol awaiting ratification in Switzerland
113	Tajikistan*	No	N/A	Yes	N/A	
114	Thailand	No	N/A	Yes	N/A	
115	Trinidad and Tobago	No	N/A	Yes	N/A	
116	Tunisia	No	N/A	Yes	N/A	
117	Turkey	No	N/A	Yes	N/A	
118	Turkmenistan*	No	N/A	Yes	N/A	
119	Tuvalu*	No	N/A	Yes	N/A	
120	Uganda*	No	N/A	Yes	N/A	
121	Ukraine	No	N/A	Yes	PPT alone	Amending protocol awaiting ratification in Ukraine
122	United Arab Emirates	No	N/A	Yes	N/A	
123	United States	No	N/A	Yes	N/A	
124	Uruguay	No	N/A	Yes	N/A	
125	Uzbekistan*	Yes	PPT alone	N/A	N/A	
126	Venezuela*	No	N/A	Yes	N/A	
127	Viet Nam	No	N/A	Yes	N/A	
128	Zambia	No	N/A	Yes	N/A	
129	Zimbabwe*	No	N/A	Yes	N/A	

United States

A. Progress in the implementation of the minimum standard

The United States has 66 tax agreements in force, as reported in its response to the Peer Review questionnaire.

The United States has implemented LOB clauses in most of its agreements. It started to include anti-treaty-shopping measures in 1962,[170] and since the seventies, LOB clauses (which initially targeted investment or holding companies) have appeared in agreements concluded by the United States. All of the United States' agreements are supplemented by its anti-conduit regulations.[171]

The 2016 US Model Convention contains an express statement that the tax treaty should not create opportunities for non-taxation or reduced taxation through tax evasion or avoidance (including through treaty-shopping arrangements aimed at obtaining reliefs provided in this Convention for the indirect benefit of residents of third states).

The United States expects to comply with the minimum standard through a detailed LOB which is not available through the MLI. Therefore, the United States did not sign the MLI and will implement the minimum standard bilaterally.

The United States' agreements with the following 45 jurisdictions contain an LOB and are supplemented by domestic anti-conduit rules: Australia, Austria, Bangladesh*, Barbados, Belgium, Bulgaria, Canada, China (People's Republic of), Cyprus*, Czech Republic, Denmark, Estonia, Finland, France, Germany, Iceland, India, Indonesia, Ireland, Israel, Italy, Jamaica, Japan, Kazakhstan, Latvia, Lithuania, Luxembourg, Malta, Mexico, the Netherlands, New Zealand, Portugal, Russia, Slovak Republic, Slovenia, South Africa, Spain, Sri Lanka, Sweden, Switzerland, Thailand, Tunisia, Turkey, Ukraine, Venezuela*. Signed conventions with Hungary and Poland contain an LOB and are supplemented by domestic anti-conduit rules. The agreements with Egypt, Korea, Morocco, Norway, and Trinidad and Tobago have a limited anti-treaty shopping rule and are supplemented by domestic anti-conduit rules. The agreement with the United Kingdom contains an LOB and anti-conduit rules and is supplemented by domestic anti-conduit rules.

B. Implementation issues

No jurisdiction has raised any concerns about their agreements with the United States.

Summary of the jurisdiction response – United States

	Treaty partners	Compliance with the standard	If compliant, the alternative implemented	Signature of a complying instrument	The alternative implemented through the complying instrument (if not the MLI)	Comments
1	Armenia	No	N/A	No	N/A	
2	Australia	No	N/A	No	N/A	LOB supplemented by domestic anti-conduit rules

3	Austria	No	N/A	No	N/A	LOB supplemented by domestic anti-conduit rules
4	Azerbaijan*	No	N/A	No	N/A	
5	Bangladesh*	No	N/A	No	N/A	LOB supplemented by domestic anti-conduit rules
6	Barbados	No	N/A	No	N/A	LOB supplemented by domestic anti-conduit rules
7	Belarus*	No	N/A	No	N/A	
8	Belgium	No	N/A	No	N/A	LOB supplemented by domestic anti-conduit rules
9	Bulgaria	No	N/A	No	N/A	LOB supplemented by domestic anti-conduit rules
10	Canada	No	N/A	No	N/A	LOB supplemented by domestic anti-conduit rules
11	China (People's Republic of)	No	N/A	No	N/A	LOB supplemented by domestic anti-conduit rules
12	Cyprus*	No	N/A	No	N/A	LOB supplemented by domestic anti-conduit rules
13	Czech Republic	No	N/A	No	N/A	LOB supplemented by domestic anti-conduit rules
14	Denmark	No	N/A	No	N/A	LOB supplemented by domestic anti-conduit rules
15	Egypt	No	N/A	No	N/A	Limited anti-treaty shopping rule supplemented by domestic anti-conduit rules
16	Estonia	No	N/A	No	N/A	LOB supplemented by domestic anti-conduit rules
17	Finland	No	N/A	No	N/A	LOB supplemented by domestic anti-conduit rules
18	France	No	N/A	No	N/A	LOB supplemented by domestic anti-conduit rules
19	Georgia	No	N/A	No	N/A	Has not listed the treaty under the MLI.
20	Germany	No	N/A	No	N/A	LOB supplemented by domestic anti-conduit rules
21	Greece	No	N/A	No	N/A	
22	Hungary	No	N/A	No	N/A	LOB in a signed convention, supplemented by domestic anti-conduit rules
23	Iceland	No	N/A	No	N/A	LOB supplemented by domestic anti-conduit rules
24	India	No	N/A	No	N/A	LOB supplemented by domestic anti-conduit rules
25	Indonesia	No	N/A	No	N/A	LOB supplemented by domestic anti-conduit rules
26	Ireland	No	N/A	No	N/A	LOB supplemented by domestic anti-conduit rules
27	Israel	No	N/A	No	N/A	LOB supplemented by domestic anti-conduit rules
28	Italy	No	N/A	No	N/A	LOB supplemented by domestic anti-conduit rules
29	Jamaica	No	N/A	No	N/A	LOB supplemented by domestic anti-conduit rules
30	Japan	No	N/A	No	N/A	LOB supplemented by domestic anti-conduit rules
31	Kazakhstan	No	N/A	No	N/A	LOB supplemented by domestic anti-conduit rules
32	Korea	No	N/A	No	N/A	Limited anti-treaty shopping rule supplemented by

						domestic anti-conduit rules
33	Kyrgyzstan*	No	N/A	No	N/A	
34	Latvia	No	N/A	No	N/A	LOB supplemented by domestic anti-conduit rules
35	Lithuania	No	N/A	No	N/A	LOB supplemented by domestic anti-conduit rules
36	Luxembourg	No	N/A	No	N/A	LOB supplemented by domestic anti-conduit rules
37	Malta	No	N/A	No	N/A	LOB supplemented by domestic anti-conduit rules
38	Mexico	No	N/A	No	N/A	LOB supplemented by domestic anti-conduit rules
39	Moldova*	No	N/A	No	N/A	
40	Morocco	No	N/A	No	N/A	Limited anti-treaty shopping rule supplemented by domestic anti-conduit rules
41	Netherlands	No	N/A	No	N/A	LOB supplemented by domestic anti-conduit rules
42	New Zealand	No	N/A	No	N/A	LOB supplemented by domestic anti-conduit rules
43	Norway	No	N/A	No	N/A	Limited anti-treaty shopping rule supplemented by domestic anti-conduit rules
44	Pakistan	No	N/A	No	N/A	
45	Philippines*	No	N/A	No	N/A	
46	Poland	No	N/A	No	N/A	LOB in a signed convention, supplemented by domestic anti-conduit rules
47	Portugal	No	N/A	No	N/A	LOB supplemented by domestic anti-conduit rules
48	Romania	No	N/A	No	N/A	
49	Russia	No	N/A	No	N/A	LOB supplemented by domestic anti-conduit rules
50	Slovak Republic	No	N/A	No	N/A	LOB supplemented by domestic anti-conduit rules
51	Slovenia	No	N/A	No	N/A	LOB supplemented by domestic anti-conduit rules
52	South Africa	No	N/A	No	N/A	LOB supplemented by domestic anti-conduit rules
53	Spain	No	N/A	No	N/A	LOB supplemented by domestic anti-conduit rules
54	Sri Lanka	No	N/A	No	N/A	LOB supplemented by domestic anti-conduit rules
55	Sweden	No	N/A	No	N/A	LOB supplemented by domestic anti-conduit rules
56	Switzerland	No	N/A	No	N/A	LOB supplemented by domestic anti-conduit rules
57	Tajikistan*	No	N/A	No	N/A	
58	Thailand	No	N/A	No	N/A	LOB supplemented by domestic anti-conduit rules
59	Trinidad and Tobago	No	N/A	No	N/A	Limited anti-treaty shopping rule supplemented by domestic anti-conduit rules
60	Tunisia	No	N/A	No	N/A	LOB supplemented by domestic anti-conduit rules
61	Turkey	No	N/A	No	N/A	LOB supplemented by domestic anti-conduit rules
62	Turkmenistan*	No	N/A	No	N/A	.

63	Ukraine	No	N/A	No	N/A	LOB supplemented by domestic anti-conduit rules
64	United Kingdom	No	N/A	No	N/A	LOB and anti-conduit rules in the treaty supplemented by domestic anti-conduit rules
65	Uzbekistan*	No	N/A	No	N/A	
66	Venezuela*	No	N/A	No	N/A	LOB supplemented by domestic anti-conduit rules

Uruguay

A. Progress in the implementation of the minimum standard

Uruguay has 21 tax agreements in force, as reported in its response to the Peer Review questionnaire. Two of those agreements, the agreements with Chile and Paraguay, comply with the minimum standard.

Uruguay signed the MLI in 2017, listing 20 tax agreements.

Uruguay is implementing the minimum standard through the inclusion of the preamble statement and the PPT combined with the LOB.[172]

The agreements that will be modified by the MLI will come into compliance with the minimum standard once the provisions of the MLI take effect.

B. Implementation issues

No jurisdiction has raised any concerns about their agreements with Uruguay.

Summary of the jurisdiction response – Uruguay

	Treaty partners	Compliance with the standard	If compliant, the alternative implemented	Signature of a complying instrument	The alternative implemented through the complying instrument (if not the MLI)	Comments
1	Belgium	No	N/A	Yes	N/A	
2	Chile	Yes	PPT and LOB	N/A	N/A	
3	Ecuador*	No	N/A	Yes	N/A	
4	Finland	No	N/A	Yes	N/A	
5	Germany	No	N/A	Yes	N/A	
6	Hungary	No	N/A	Yes	N/A	
7	India	No	N/A	Yes	N/A	
8	Korea	No	N/A	Yes	N/A	
9	Liechtenstein	No	N/A	Yes	N/A	
10	Luxembourg	No	N/A	Yes	N/A	
11	Malta	No	N/A	Yes	N/A	
12	Mexico	No	N/A	Yes	N/A	
13	Paraguay	Yes	PPT and LOB	N/A	N/A	
14	Portugal	No	N/A	Yes	N/A	
15	Romania	No	N/A	Yes	N/A	
16	Singapore	No	N/A	Yes	N/A	
17	Spain	No	N/A	Yes	N/A	
18	Switzerland	No	N/A	Yes	N/A	
19	United Arab Emirates	No	N/A	Yes	N/A	
20	United Kingdom	No	N/A	Yes	N/A	
21	Viet Nam	No	N/A	Yes	N/A	

Viet Nam

A. Progress in the implementation of the minimum standard

Viet Nam has 76 tax agreements in force, as reported in its response to the Peer Review questionnaire.

None of Viet Nam's agreements comply with the minimum standard or are subject to a complying instrument.

B. Implementation issues

No jurisdiction has raised any concerns about their agreements with Viet Nam.

Viet Nam is encouraged to implement the minimum standard in its agreements.

Summary of the jurisdiction response – Viet Nam

	Treaty partners	Compliance with the standard	If compliant, the alternative implemented	Signature of a complying instrument	The alternative implemented through the complying instrument (if not the MLI)	Comments
1	Australia	No	N/A	No	N/A	
2	Austria	No	N/A	No	N/A	
3	Azerbaijan*	No	N/A	No	N/A	
4	Bangladesh*	No	N/A	No	N/A	
5	Belarus*	No	N/A	No	N/A	
6	Belgium	No	N/A	No	N/A	
7	Brunei Darussalam	No	N/A	No	N/A	
8	Bulgaria	No	N/A	No	N/A	
9	Cambodia	No	N/A	No	N/A	
10	Canada	No	N/A	No	N/A	
11	China (People's Republic of)	No	N/A	No	N/A	
12	Chinese Taipei*	No	N/A	No	N/A	
13	Croatia	No	N/A	No	N/A	
14	Cuba*	No	N/A	No	N/A	
15	Czech Republic	No	N/A	No	N/A	
16	Democratic People's Republic of Korea*	No	N/A	No	N/A	
17	Denmark	No	N/A	No	N/A	
18	Estonia	No	N/A	No	N/A	
19	Finland	No	N/A	No	N/A	
20	France	No	N/A	No	N/A	
21	Germany	No	N/A	No	N/A	
22	Hong Kong (China)	No	N/A	No	N/A	
23	Hungary	No	N/A	No	N/A	
24	Iceland	No	N/A	No	N/A	
25	India	No	N/A	No	N/A	
26	Indonesia	No	N/A	No	N/A	

27	Iran*	No	N/A	No	N/A	
28	Ireland	No	N/A	No	N/A	
29	Israel	No	N/A	No	N/A	"Mini" PPTs in Article 28
30	Italy	No	N/A	No	N/A	
31	Japan	No	N/A	No	N/A	
32	Kazakhstan	No	N/A	No	N/A	
33	Korea	No	N/A	No	N/A	
34	Kuwait*	No	N/A	No	N/A	
35	Lao People's Democratic Republic*	No	N/A	No	N/A	
36	Latvia	No	N/A	No	N/A	
37	Luxembourg	No	N/A	No	N/A	
38	Macau (China)	No	N/A	No	N/A	
39	Malaysia	No	N/A	No	N/A	
40	Malta	No	N/A	No	N/A	
41	Mongolia	No	N/A	No	N/A	
42	Morocco	No	N/A	No	N/A	
43	Mozambique*	No	N/A	No	N/A	
44	Myanmar*	No	N/A	No	N/A	
45	Netherlands	No	N/A	No	N/A	
46	New Zealand	No	N/A	No	N/A	"Mini" PPTs in dividend, interest, royalty Articles
47	Norway	No	N/A	No	N/A	
48	Oman	No	N/A	No	N/A	"Mini" PPTs in dividend, interest, royalty, technical fees Articles
49	Pakistan	No	N/A	No	N/A	
50	Palestinian Authority*	No	N/A	No	N/A	
51	Panama	No	N/A	No	N/A	
52	Philippines*	No	N/A	No	N/A	
53	Poland	No	N/A	No	N/A	
54	Portugal	No	N/A	No	N/A	"Mini" PPT in 1(c) of the Protocol
55	Qatar	No	N/A	No	N/A	
56	Romania	No	N/A	No	N/A	
57	Russia	No	N/A	No	N/A	
58	San Marino	No	N/A	No	N/A	
59	Saudi Arabia	No	N/A	No	N/A	
60	Serbia	No	N/A	No	N/A	
61	Seychelles	No	N/A	No	N/A	
62	Singapore	No	N/A	No	N/A	
63	Slovak Republic	No	N/A	No	N/A	
64	Spain	No	N/A	No	N/A	
65	Sri Lanka	No	N/A	No	N/A	
66	Sweden	No	N/A	No	N/A	
67	Switzerland	No	N/A	No	N/A	

68	Thailand	No	N/A	No	N/A	
69	Tunisia	No	N/A	No	N/A	
70	Turkey	No	N/A	No	N/A	
71	Ukraine	No	N/A	No	N/A	"Mini" PPTs in interest, royalty Articles
72	United Arab Emirates	No	N/A	No	N/A	
73	United Kingdom	No	N/A	No	N/A	"Mini" PPTs in interest and royalty Articles
74	Uruguay	No	N/A	No	N/A	
75	Uzbekistan*	No	N/A	No	N/A	Mini" PPTs in royalty Articles
76	Venezuela*	No	N/A	No	N/A	

Zambia

A. Progress in the implementation of the minimum standard

Zambia has 23 tax agreements in force, as reported in its response to the Peer Review questionnaire. Its agreement with Switzerland complies with the minimum standard. Zambia has not signed the MLI.

B. Implementation issues

No jurisdiction has raised any concerns about their agreements with Zambia.

Summary of the jurisdiction response – Zambia

	Treaty partners	Compliance with the standard	If compliant, the alternative implemented	Signature of a complying instrument	The alternative implemented through the complying instrument (if not the MLI)	Comments
1	Botswana	No	N/A	No	N/A	
2	Canada	No	N/A	No	N/A	
3	China (People's Republic of)	No	N/A	No	N/A	
4	Denmark	No	N/A	No	N/A	
5	Finland	No	N/A	No	N/A	
6	France	No	N/A	No	N/A	
7	Germany	No	N/A	No	N/A	
8	India	No	N/A	No	N/A	
9	Ireland	No	N/A	No	N/A	
10	Italy	No	N/A	No	N/A	
11	Japan	No	N/A	No	N/A	
12	Kenya	No	N/A	No	N/A	
13	Mauritius	No	N/A	No	N/A	
14	Netherlands	No	N/A	No	N/A	
15	Norway	No	N/A	No	N/A	
16	Romania	No	N/A	No	N/A	
17	Seychelles	No	N/A	No	N/A	
18	South Africa	No	N/A	No	N/A	
19	Sweden	No	N/A	No	N/A	
20	Switzerland	Yes	PPT alone	No	N/A	
21	Tanzania	No	N/A	No	N/A	
22	Uganda*	No	N/A	No	N/A	
23	United Kingdom	No	N/A	No	N/A	

Notes

[1] For all of its agreements listed under the MLI, Andorra is implementing the preamble statement (Article 6 of the MLI). For five of its agreements listed under the MLI, Andorra is implementing the PPT (Article 7 of the MLI). Andorra made a reservation pursuant to Article 7(15)(b) of the MLI not to apply Article 7(1) with respect to agreements which already contain a PPT. Two of Andorra's agreements are within the scope of this reservation

[2] In total, Antigua and Barbuda identified 12 "agreements" in its List of Tax agreements: two bilateral agreements and the CARICOM agreement concluded with ten of its treaty partners.

[3] Revisions to the CARICOM Agreement requires an agreement from its eleven treaty partners.

[4] For 15 of its agreements listed under the MLI, Argentina is implementing the preamble statement (Article 6 of the MLI) and the PPT (Article 7 of the MLI). Two of Argentina's agreements, the agreements with Chile and Mexico, are within the scope of reservations made by Argentina pursuant to Article 6(4) and Article 7(15)(b) of the MLI. Argentina also opted for the simplified LOB under Article 7(6) of the MLI.

[5] For its agreements listed under the MLI, Armenia is implementing the preamble statement (Article 6 of the MLI) and the PPT (Article 7 of the MLI). Armenia also opted for the simplified LOB under Article 7(6) of the MLI.

[6] A new agreement with Israel entered into force in December 2019 and also complies with the minimum standard.

[7] The agreement with Germany, already compliant with the minimum standard, has not been listed under the MLI.

[8] For its agreements listed under the MLI, Australia is implementing the preamble statement (Article 6 of the MLI) and the PPT (Article 7 of the MLI).

[9] For its agreements listed under the MLI, Austria is implementing the preamble statement (Article 6 of the MLI) and the PPT (Article 7 of the MLI).

[10] Austria made a reservation under Article 35(3) of the MLI (Entry into Effect).

[11] In total, Barbados identified 40 "agreements" in its List of Tax agreements: 30 bilateral agreements and the CARICOM agreement concluded with ten of its treaty partners.

[12] In total, Barbados listed 33 agreements under the MLI, three of which (the agreements with Ghana*, Rwanda* and the Slovak Republic) are not yet in force. Barbados also listed the CARICOM Agreement.

[13] For its agreements listed under the MLI, Barbados is implementing the preamble statement (Article 6 of the MLI) and the PPT (Article 7 of the MLI).

[14] Revisions to the CARICOM Agreement requires an agreement from its eleven treaty partners.

[15] In total, Belgium listed 99 agreements under the MLI, nine of which (the agreements with Botswana, the Isle of Man, Macau (China), Oman, Qatar, and Uganda* and the new agreements with Moldova*, Russia and Tajikistan*) are not yet in force.

[16] For its agreements listed under the MLI, Belgium is implementing the preamble statement (Article 6 of the MLI) and the PPT (Article 7 of the MLI).

[17] In total, Belize identified 13 "agreements" in its List of Tax agreements: 10 bilateral agreements and the CARICOM agreement concluded with ten of its treaty partners.

[18] Revisions to the CARICOM Agreement requires an agreement from its eleven treaty partners.

[19] Règlement n°08/2008/CM des pays de l'Union économique et monétaire Ouest Africaine (UEMOA) du 26 septembre 2008 portant adoption des règles visant à éviter la double imposition au sein de l'UEMOA et des règles d'assistance en matière fiscale. In total, Benin identified nine "agreements" in its List of Tax agreements: two bilateral agreements and the UEMOA.

[20] For 65 of its agreements listed under the MLI, Bulgaria is implementing the preamble statement (Article 6 of the MLI). For its 66 agreements listed under the MLI, Bulgaria is implementing the PPT (Article 7 of the MLI). Bulgaria also opted for the simplified LOB under Article 7(6) of the MLI. Bulgaria made a reservation pursuant to Article 6(4) not to apply Article 6(1) with respect to agreements, which already contain the relevant preamble language. One of Bulgaria's agreements, the agreement with Romania, is within the scope of this reservation.

[21] Règlement n°08/2008/CM des pays de l'Union économique et monétaire Ouest Africaine (UEMOA) du 26 septembre 2008 portant adoption des règles visant à éviter la double imposition au sein de l'UEMOA et des règles d'assistance en matière fiscale. In total, Burkina Faso identified nine "agreements" in its List of Tax agreements: two bilateral agreements and the UEMOA concluded with seven of its treaty partners.

[22] In total, Burkina Faso listed three agreements under the MLI, one of which (the agreement with the Morocco) is not yet in force.

[23] For its agreements listed under the MLI, Burkina Faso is implementing the preamble statement (Article 6 of the MLI) and the PPT (Article 7 of the MLI).

[24] In total, Cameroon listed five agreements under the MLI, one of which (the agreement with Morocco) is not yet in force

[25] For its agreements listed under the MLI, Cameroon is implementing the preamble statement (Article 6 of the MLI) and the PPT (Article 7 of the MLI).

[26] For its agreements listed under the MLI, Canada is implementing the preamble statement (Article 6 of the MLI) and the PPT (Article 7 of the MLI). Canada also expressed a statement, in accordance with Article 7(17)(a) of the MLI, that while it accepts the application of the PPT under the MLI, it intends where possible to adopt an LOB provision in addition to or in replacement of the PPT through bilateral negotiation.

[27] This is an Arrangement for the Avoidance of Double Taxation and the Prevention of Fiscal Evasion with Respect to Taxes on Income between the Canadian Trade Office in Taipei and the Taipei Economic and Cultural Office in Canada.

[28] In total, Chile listed 34 agreements under the MLI, one of which (the agreement with the United States) is not yet in force. The agreements with Argentina, China, Italy, Japan and Uruguay are already compliant and were listed under the MLI.

[29] For 28 of its agreements listed under the MLI, Chile is implementing the preamble statement (Article 6 of the MLI) and the PPT (Article 7 of the MLI). Chile also opted for the simplified LOB under Article 7(6) of the MLI and expressed a statement that while Chile accepts the application of the PPT under the MLI, it intends where possible to adopt an LOB provision through bilateral negotiation. Chile made a reservation pursuant to Article 6(4) not to apply Article 6(1) with respect to agreements, which already contain the relevant preamble language. Chile also made a reservation pursuant to Article 7(15)(b) not to apply Article 7(1) with respect to agreements which already contain a PPT. Five of Chile's agreements are within the scope of these reservations.

[30] In total, China listed 101 agreements under the MLI, one of which (the agreement with Uganda*) is not yet in force.

[31] For its agreements listed under the MLI, China is implementing the preamble statement (Article 6 of the MLI) and the PPT (Article 7 of the MLI).

[32] The Decision of the Commission of the Andean Community 578 on the regime for the avoidance of double taxation and the prevention of fiscal evasion, adopted on 4 May 2004. The current members of the Andean Community are Bolivia*, Colombia, Ecuador* and Peru. In total, Colombia identified 12 "agreements" in its List of Tax agreements: nine bilateral agreements and the Andean Community Agreement.

[33] In total, Colombia listed 10 agreements under the MLI, one of which (the agreement with France) is not yet in force.

[34] For its agreements listed under the MLI, Colombia is implementing the preamble statement (Article 6 of the MLI) and the PPT (Article 7 of the MLI). Colombia also opted for the simplified LOB under Article 7(6) of the MLI.

[35] Bolivia* and Ecuador* are not members of the BEPS Inclusive Framework.

[36] Colombia and Switzerland are finalising an Amending Protocol expected for signature during the summer of 2019. The Protocol adopts the preamble statement and the PPT.

[37] For its agreements listed under the MLI, Costa Rica is implementing the preamble statement (Article 6 of the MLI) and the PPT (Article 7 of the MLI).

[38] Règlement n°08/2008/CM des pays de l'Union économique et monétaire Ouest Africaine (UEMOA) du 26 septembre 2008 portant adoption des règles visant à éviter la double imposition au sein de l'UEMOA et des règles d'assistance en matière fiscale. In total, Côte d'Ivoire identified 18 "agreements" in its List of Tax agreements: 11 bilateral agreements and the UEMOA.

[39] In total, Cote d'Ivoire listed 11 agreements under the MLI, one of which (the agreement with Turkey) is not yet in force. The UEMOA has not been listed under the MLI, as it is a regulation of the West African Economic and Monetary Union.

[40] For its agreements listed under the MLI, Côte d'Ivoire is implementing the preamble statement (Article 6 of the MLI) and the PPT (Article 7 of the MLI). Côte d'Ivoire also opted for the asymmetrical application of the simplified LOB under Article 7(7)(b) of the MLI.

[41] For its agreements listed under the MLI, Croatia is implementing the preamble statement (Article 6 of the MLI) and the PPT (Article 7 of the MLI). This number appears in the Croatian MLI position to be filed after 30 June 2019.

[42] For its agreements listed under the MLI, Curacao is implementing the preamble statement (Article 6 of the MLI) and the PPT (Article 7 of the MLI).

[43] The Czech Republic continues to apply the treaty with former Serbia & Montenegro to both Serbia and Montenegro*.

[44] For its agreements provisionally listed under the MLI, the Czech Republic is implementing the preamble statement (Article 6 of the MLI) and the PPT (Article 7 of the MLI).

[45] See the Multilateral convention concluded by Denmark, Finland, the Faroe Islands, Iceland, Norway and Sweden: for the avoidance of double taxation with respect to taxes on income and on capital (1996, 1997, and 2008). In total, Denmark identified 73 "agreements" in its List of Tax agreements: 69 bilateral agreements and the Nordic Convention concluded with four of its treaty partners.

[46] For its agreements listed under the MLI, Denmark is implementing the preamble statement (Article 6 of the MLI) and the PPT (Article 7 of the MLI). Denmark has also accepted to implement a simplified LOB in agreements concluded with partners that opted in for the simplified LOB (Article 7(7)(a) of the MLI).

[47] In total, Dominica identified 12 "agreements" in its List of Tax agreements: two bilateral agreements and the CARICOM Agreement.

[48] Revisions to the CARICOM Agreement requires an agreement from its eleven treaty partners.

[49] For its agreements listed under the MLI, Egypt is implementing the preamble statement (Article 6 of the MLI) and the PPT (Article 7 of the MLI).

[50] In total, Estonia listed 58 agreements under the MLI, two of which (the agreements with Morocco and Russia) are not yet in force.

[51] For its agreements listed under the MLI, Estonia is implementing the preamble statement (Article 6 of the MLI) and the PPT (Article 7 of the MLI).

52 See the Multilateral convention concluded by Denmark, Finland, the Faroe Islands, Iceland, Norway and Sweden: for the avoidance of double taxation with respect to taxes on income and on capital (1996, 1997, and 2008). In total, the Faroe Islands identified eight "agreements" in its List of Tax agreements: three bilateral agreements and the Nordic Convention.

[53] See the Multilateral convention concluded by Denmark, Finland, the Faroe Islands, Iceland, Norway and Sweden: for the avoidance of double taxation with respect to taxes on income and on capital (1996, 1997, and 2008). In total, Finland identified 77 "agreements" in its List of Tax agreements: 72 bilateral agreements and the Nordic Convention concluded with five of its treaty partners.

[54] In total, Finland listed 70 agreements under the MLI, one of which (the agreement with Portugal) is not yet in force.

[55] For its agreements listed under the MLI, Finland is implementing the preamble statement (Article 6 of the MLI) and the PPT (Article 7 of the MLI).

[56] In total, France listed 91 agreements under the MLI, one of which (the agreement with Colombia) is not yet in force.

[57] For its agreements listed under the MLI, France is implementing the preamble statement (Article 6 of the MLI) and the PPT (Article 7 of the MLI).

[58] For its agreements listed under the MLI, Gabon is implementing the preamble statement (Article 6 of the MLI) and the PPT (Article 7 of the MLI).

[59] For its agreements listed under the MLI, Georgia is implementing the preamble statement (Article 6 of the MLI) and the PPT (Article 7 of the MLI).

[60] One of the agreements listed by Germany under the MLI, the agreement with Japan, is already compliant with the minimum standard (inclusion of the preamble statement and the PPT combined with the LOB).

[61] For its 35 agreements listed under the MLI, Germany is implementing the preamble statement (Article 6 of the MLI). For 31 of its agreements listed under the MLI, Germany is implementing the PPT (Paragraph 1 of Article 7 of the MLI). Germany made a reservation pursuant to Article 7(15)(b) of the MLI not to apply Article 7(1) with respect to agreements which already contain a PPT. Four of Germany's agreements are within the scope of this reservation.

[62] For its agreements listed under the MLI, Greece is implementing the preamble statement (Article 6 of the MLI) and the PPT (Article 7 of the MLI). Greece also opted for the simplified LOB under Article 7(7)(b) of the MLI.

[63] In total, Grenada identified 13 "agreements" in its List of Tax agreements: three bilateral agreements and the CARICOM Agreement.

[64] Revisions to the CARICOM Agreement requires an agreement from its eleven treaty partners.

[65] For its agreements listed under the MLI, Guernsey is implementing the preamble statement (Article 6 of the MLI) and the PPT (Article 7 of the MLI).

[66] The agreement with Belarus*, which is already compliant, is also listed under the MLI.

[67] For 35 of its agreements listed under the MLI, Hong Kong is implementing the preamble statement (Article 6 of the MLI). For 34 of its agreements listed under the MLI, Hong Kong is implementing the PPT (Article 7 of the MLI). Hong Kong made a reservation pursuant to Article 6(4) not to apply Article 6(1) with respect to agreements, which already contain the relevant preamble language. One of Hong Kong's agreements is within the scope of this reservation. Hong Kong made a reservation pursuant to Article 7(15)(b) not to apply Article 7(1) with respect to agreements, which already contain a PPT. Two of Hong Kong's agreements are within the scope of this reservation.

[68] For its agreements listed under the MLI, Hungary is implementing the preamble statement (Article 6 of the MLI) and the PPT (Article 7 of the MLI).

[69] See the Multilateral convention concluded by Denmark, Finland, the Faroe Islands, Iceland, Norway and Sweden: for the avoidance of double taxation with respect to taxes on income and on capital (1996, 1997, and 2008). In total, Iceland identified 45 "agreements" in its List of Tax agreements: 40 bilateral agreements and the Nordic Convention concluded with five of its treaty partners.

[70] For its agreements listed under the MLI, Iceland is implementing the preamble statement (Article 6 of the MLI) and the PPT (Article 7 of the MLI). Iceland has also accepted to implement a simplified LOB in agreements concluded with partners that opted in for the simplified LOB under Article 7(7)(a) of the MLI.

[71] For its agreements listed under the MLI, India is implementing the preamble statement (Article 6 of the MLI), the PPT (Article 7 of the MLI) and the simplified LOB (Article 7(6) of the MLI).

[72] Indonesia listed 47 tax agreements in a revised provisional MLI Position submitted to the Secretariat on 15 February 2019.

[73] For its agreements listed under the MLI, Indonesia is implementing the preamble statement (Article 6 of the MLI) and the PPT (Article 7 of the MLI).

[74] In total, Ireland listed 71 agreements under the MLI, one of which (the agreement with Ghana*) is not yet in force.

[75] For its agreements listed under the MLI, Ireland is implementing the preamble statement (Article 6 of the MLI) and the PPT (Article 7 of the MLI).

[76] For its agreements listed under the MLI, the Isle of Man is implementing the preamble statement (Article 6 of the MLI) and the PPT (Article 7 of the MLI).

[77] In total, Israel listed 53 agreements under the MLI, one of which (the agreement with North Macedonia) is not yet in force.

[78] For its agreements listed under the MLI, Israel is implementing the preamble statement (Article 6 of the MLI) and the PPT (Article 7 of the MLI).

[79] In total, Italy listed 84 agreements under the MLI, three of which (the agreements with Gabon, Kenya and Mongolia) are not yet in force and one of which is terminated (the former agreement with Romania). The figures presented here are still provisional. The final figures will be available following the approval of the MLI by the Parliament.

[80] For its 80 agreements listed under the MLI, Italy is implementing the preamble statement (Article 6 of the MLI). For 67 of its agreements listed under the MLI, Italy is implementing the PPT (Article 7 of the MLI). Thirteen of Italy's agreements, the agreements with Azerbaijan*, Estonia, Hong Kong, Iceland, Kazakhstan, Kuwait*, Latvia, Lebanon*, Lithuania, Mongolia, Qatar, San Marino and Saudi Arabia, are within the scope of a reservation made by Italy under Article 7(15)(b) of the MLI. Italy made a reservation pursuant to Article 7(15)(b) not to apply Article 7(1) with respect to agreements, which already contain a PPT.

[81] In total, Jamaica identified 23 "agreements" in its List of Tax agreements: 13 bilateral agreements and the CARICOM Agreement.

[82] For its agreements listed under the MLI, Jamaica is implementing the preamble statement (Article 6 of the MLI) and the PPT (Article 7 of the MLI). Jamaica has opted for the simplified LOB under Article 7(7)(a) of the MLI.

[83] Revisions to the CARICOM Agreement requires an agreement from its eleven treaty partners.

[84] The agreement with Germany which is already compliant was also listed under the MLI.

[85] For 38 of its agreements listed under the MLI, Japan is implementing the preamble statement (Article 6 of the MLI). For 38 of its agreements listed under the MLI, Japan is implementing the PPT (Article 7 of the MLI). Japan made a reservation pursuant to Article 6(4) not to apply Article 6(1) with respect to agreements, which already contain the relevant preamble language. One of Japan's agreements is within the scope of this reservation.

[86] For its agreements listed under the MLI, Jersey is implementing the preamble statement (Article 6 of the MLI) and the PPT (Article 7 of the MLI).

[87] For its agreements listed under the MLI, Kazakhstan is implementing the preamble statement (Article 6 of the MLI) and the PPT (Article 7 of the MLI). Kazakhstan also opted for the simplified LOB pursuant to Article 7(6) of the MLI.

[88] For its agreements listed under the MLI, Korea is implementing the preamble statement (Article 6 of the MLI) and the PPT (Article 7 of the MLI).

[89] For its agreements listed under the MLI, Latvia is implementing the preamble statement (Article 6 of the MLI) and the PPT (Article 7 of the MLI).

[90] For its agreements listed under the MLI, Liechtenstein is implementing the preamble statement (Article 6 of the MLI) and the PPT (Article 7 of the MLI).

[91] For its agreements listed under the MLI, Lithuania is implementing the preamble statement (Article 6 of the MLI) and the PPT (Article 7 of the MLI).

[92] For its agreements listed under the MLI, Luxembourg is implementing the preamble statement (Article 6 of the MLI) and the PPT (Article 7 of the MLI).

[93] In total, Malaysia listed 73 agreements under the MLI, one of which (the agreement with Senegal) is not yet in force.

[94] For its agreements listed under the MLI, Malaysia is implementing the preamble statement (Article 6 of the MLI) and the PPT (Article 7 of the MLI).

[95] In total, Malta listed 73 agreements under the MLI, one of which (the agreement with Curacao) is not yet in force.

[96] For its agreements listed under the MLI, Malta is implementing the preamble statement (Article 6 of the MLI) and the PPT (Article 7 of the MLI).

[97] Malta chose to replace, under Article 35(3) of the MLI, the reference to "taxable periods beginning on or after the expiration of a period" with a reference to "taxable periods beginning on or after 1 January of the next calendar year beginning on or after the expiration of a period" for the purposes of its own application of Article 35(1)(b) and (5)(b).

[98] Mauritius listed 41 tax agreements in a revised provisional MLI position.

[99] For its agreements listed under the MLI, Mauritius is implementing the preamble statement (Article 6 of the MLI) and the PPT (Article 7 of the MLI). Mauritius stated that while it accepts the application of the PPT under the MLI, it intends where possible to adopt an LOB provision through bilateral negotiation.

[100] In total, Mexico listed 61 agreements under the MLI, one of which (the agreement with Guatemala*) is not yet in force. The agreements with Argentina, Philippines* and Spain which are already compliant were listed under the MLI.

[101] For 57 of its agreements listed under the MLI, Mexico is implementing the preamble statement (Article 6 of the MLI) and the PPT (Article 7 of the MLI). Mexico also opted for the simplified LOB under Article 7(6) of the MLI. Mexico made a reservation pursuant to Article 6(4) not to apply Article 6(1) with respect to agreements which already contain the relevant preamble language and a reservation pursuant to Article 7(15)(b) not to apply Article 7(1) with respect to agreements which already contain a PPT Three of Mexico's agreements are within the scope of the reservations.

[102] The agreement with Liechtenstein, already compliant with the minimum standard, was not listed under the MLI.

[103] For its agreements listed under the MLI, Monaco is implementing the preamble statement (Article 6 of the MLI) and the PPT (Article 7 of the MLI).

[104] In total, Morocco identified 56 "agreements" in its List of Tax agreements: 52 bilateral agreements and the Arab Maghreb Union Income Tax Agreement concluded with four of its treaty partners.

[105] In total, Morocco listed 76 agreements under the MLI, 23 of which (the agreements with Albania*, Azerbaijan*, Bangladesh*, Burkina Faso, Cameroon, Democratic Republic of the Congo, Estonia, Ethiopia*, Ghana*, Guinea-Bissau*, Iran*, Lithuania, Madagascar*, Mauritius, Rwanda*, Sao Tome and Principe*, Saudi Arabia, Serbia, Slovenia, South Sudan*, Yemen* and Zambia, and the new agreements with Qatar) are not yet in force.

[106] For its agreements listed under the MLI, Morocco is implementing the preamble statement (Article 6 of the MLI) and the PPT (Article 7 of the MLI).

[107] For its agreements listed under the MLI, the Netherlands is implementing the preamble statement (Article 6 of the MLI) and the PPT (Article 7 of the MLI). The Netherlands' agreements with Aruba, Curacao and Sint Maarten* are not listed under the MLI as they are arrangements governed by the domestic law of the Kingdom of the Netherlands.

[108] The agreements with Ghana* and Uzbekistan* are subject to a bilateral complying instrument and listed under the MLI.

[109] For its agreements listed under the MLI, New Zealand is implementing the preamble statement (Article 6 of the MLI) and the PPT (Article 7 of the MLI).

[110] For its agreements listed under the MLI, Nigeria is implementing the preamble statement (Article 6 of the MLI) and the PPT (Article 7 of the MLI).

[111] North Macedonia signed the agreement with the former Federal Republic of Yugoslavia.

[112] North Macedonia signed the agreement with the former Federal Republic of Yugoslavia.

[113] See the Multilateral convention concluded by Denmark, Finland, the Faroe Islands, Iceland, Norway and Sweden: for the avoidance of double taxation with respect to taxes on income and on capital (1996, 1997, and 2008). In total, Norway identified 88 "agreements" in its List of Tax agreements: 83 bilateral agreements and the Nordic Convention concluded with five of its treaty partners.

[114] For its agreements listed under the MLI, Norway is implementing the preamble statement (Article 6 of the MLI) and the PPT (Article 7 of the MLI). Norway stated that while it accepts the application of the PPT under the MLI, it intends where possible to adopt an LOB provision through bilateral negotiation. Norway has also accepted to implement a simplified LOB in agreements concluded with partners that opted in for the simplified LOB under Article 7(7)(a) of the MLI.

[115] For its agreements listed under the MLI, Pakistan is implementing the preamble statement (Article 6 of the MLI) and the PPT (Article 7 of the MLI).

[116] For its agreements listed under the MLI, Panama is implementing the preamble statement (Article 6 of the MLI) and the PPT (Article 7 of the MLI).

[117] The Decision of the Commission of the Andean Community 578 on the regime for the avoidance of double taxation and the prevention of fiscal evasion, adopted on 4 May 2004. The current members of the Andean Community are Bolivia*, Colombia, Ecuador* and Peru. In total, Peru identified 10 “agreements” in its List of Tax agreements: seven bilateral agreements and the Andean Community (Decision 578).

[118] For its agreements listed under the MLI, Peru is implementing the preamble statement (Article 6 of the MLI) and the PPT (Article 7 of the MLI). Peru also expressed a statement that while it accepts the application of the PPT under the MLI, it intends where possible to adopt an LOB provision through bilateral negotiation.

[119] In total, Poland listed 78 agreements under the MLI, one of which (the new agreement with Malaysia) is not yet in force. Another listed agreement (the new agreement with Sri Lanka) entered into force on 14 June 2019.

[120] For its agreements listed under the MLI, Poland is implementing the preamble statement (Article 6 of the MLI) and the PPT (Article 7 of the MLI). Poland expressed a statement that while it accepts the application of the PPT under the MLI, it intends where possible to adopt an LOB provision through bilateral negotiation.

[121] In total, Portugal listed 79 agreements under the MLI, two of which (the agreements with Timor Leste* and with Finland) are not yet in force.

[122] For its agreements listed under the MLI, Portugal is implementing the preamble statement (Article 6 of the MLI) and the PPT (Article 7 of the MLI).

[123] In total, Qatar listed 84 agreements under the MLI in its provisional MLI Position, seven of which (the agreements with Belgium, Eritrea*, Ethiopia*, Gambia*, Mauritania* and Paraguay, and the new agreement with Morocco) are not yet in force and one which has been terminated (the previous agreement with Turkey).

[124] For its agreements listed under the MLI, Qatar is implementing the preamble statement (Article 6 of the MLI) and the PPT (Article 7 of the MLI).

[125] In total, Romania listed 91 agreements under the MLI, two of which (the former agreements with China and Italy) are terminated and one of which has been replaced (the agreement concluded by the Socialist Federal Republic of Yugoslavia*). New DTCs with China and Italy entered into force in 2018 and the DTC with Bosnia and Herzegovina entered into force in 2019. The old DTCs with those states will be removed from the notification list regarding the agreements covered by the MLI.

[126] For its agreements listed under the MLI, Romania is implementing the preamble statement (Article 6 of the MLI) and the PPT (Article 7 of the MLI).

[127] In total, the Russian Federation listed 71 agreements under the MLI, one of which (the new agreement with Belgium) is not yet in force.

[128] For its agreements listed under the MLI, the Russian Federation is implementing the preamble statement (Article 6 of the MLI) and the PPT (Article 7 of the MLI). The Russian Federation also opted for the simplified LOB under Article 7(6) of the MLI.

[129] In total, Saint Kitts and Nevis identified 14 "agreements" in its List of Tax agreements: four bilateral agreements and the CARICOM agreement concluded with ten of its treaty partners.

[130] Revisions to the CARICOM Agreement requires an agreement from its eleven treaty partners.

[131] In total, Saint Lucia identified 11 "agreements" in its List of Tax agreements: one bilateral agreement and the CARICOM agreement concluded with ten of its treaty partners.

[132] Revisions to the CARICOM Agreement requires an agreement from its eleven treaty partners.

[133] In total, Saint Vincent and the Grenadines identified 11 "agreements" in its List of Tax agreements: one bilateral agreement and the CARICOM agreement concluded with ten of its treaty partners.

[134] Revisions to the CARICOM Agreement requires an agreement from its eleven treaty partners.

[135] In total, San Marino listed 22 agreements under the MLI, one of which (the agreement with the United Arab Emirates) is not yet in force.

[136] For its agreements listed under the MLI, San Marino is implementing the preamble statement (Article 6 of the MLI). For 18 of its agreements listed under the MLI, San Marino is implementing the PPT (Article 7 of the MLI). San Marino made a reservation pursuant to Article 7(15)(b) not to apply Article 7(1) with respect to agreements which already contain a PPT. Three of San Marino's agreements are within the scope of this reservation.

[137] In total, Saudi Arabia listed 53 agreements under the MLI, three of which (the agreements with Gabon, Morocco and Switzerland) are not yet in force.

[138] For its agreements listed under the MLI, Saudi Arabia is implementing the preamble statement (Article 6 of the MLI) and the PPT (Article 7 of the MLI).

[139] Règlement n°08/2008/CM des pays de l'Union économique et monétaire Ouest Africaine (UEMOA) du 26 septembre 2008 portant adoption des règles visant à éviter la double imposition au sein de l'UEMOA et des règles d'assistance en matière fiscale. In total, Senegal identified 25 "agreements" in its List of Tax agreements: 18 bilateral agreements and the UEMOA with seven partners.

[140] For its agreements listed under the MLI, Senegal is implementing the preamble statement (Article 6 of the MLI) and the PPT (Article 7 of the MLI). Senegal also opted for the simplified LOB under Article 7(6) of the MLI and stated that, while it accepts the application of the PPT under the MLI, it intends where possible to adopt an LOB provision through bilateral negotiation.

[141] In total, Serbia listed 64 agreements under the MLI, five of which (the agreements with Ghana*, Guinea*, Morocco*, Palestine* and Zimbabwe*) are not yet in force. The agreement with Malaysia, also listed under the MLI, has been terminated.

[142] For its agreements listed under the MLI, Serbia is implementing the preamble statement (Article 6 of the MLI) and the PPT (Article 7 of the MLI).

[143] For its agreements listed under the MLI, the Seychelles is implementing the preamble statement (Article 6 of the MLI) and the PPT (Article 7 of the MLI). The Seychelles expressed a statement that while it accepts the application of the PPT under the MLI, it intends where possible to adopt an LOB provision through bilateral negotiation.

[144] In total, Singapore listed 86 agreements under the MLI, two of which (the agreement with Kenya and Tunisia) are not yet in force.

[145] For its agreements listed under the MLI, Singapore is implementing the preamble statement (Article 6 of the MLI) and the PPT (Article 7 of the MLI).

[146] For its agreements listed under the MLI, the Slovak Republic is implementing the preamble statement (Article 6 of the MLI) and the PPT (Article 7 of the MLI). The Slovak Republic also opted for the simplified LOB under Article 7(6) of the MLI.

[147] In total, Slovenia listed 57 agreements under the MLI, two of which (the agreements with Egypt and Morocco) are not yet in force.

[148] For its agreements listed under the MLI, Slovenia is implementing the preamble statement (Article 6 of the MLI) and the PPT (Article 7 of the MLI).

[149] For its agreements listed under the MLI, South Africa is implementing the preamble statement (Article 6 of the MLI) and the PPT (Article 7 of the MLI).

[150]In total, Spain listed 89 agreements under the MLI, three of which (the agreements with Azerbaijan*, Belarus* and Cabo Verde) are not yet in force. The agreement with Mexico, which is already compliant, was also listed under the MLI. The agreement with Romania is subject to a bilateral complying instrument and listed under the MLI.

[151] For 87 of its agreements listed under the MLI, Spain is implementing the preamble statement (Article 6 of the MLI). For 86 of its agreements listed under the MLI, Spain is implementing the PPT (Article 7 of the MLI). Spain made a reservation pursuant to Article 6(4) and Article 7(15)(b) of the MLI and three of Spain's agreements are within the scope of this reservation (the agreements with Andorra, Mexico and Romania).

[152] See the Multilateral convention concluded by Denmark, Finland, the Faroe Islands, Iceland, Norway and Sweden: for the avoidance of double taxation with respect to taxes on income and on capital (1996, 1997, 2008 and 2018). In total, Sweden identified 85 "agreements" in its List of Tax agreements: 80 bilateral agreements and the Nordic Convention concluded with five of its treaty partners.

[153] For its agreements listed under the MLI, Sweden is implementing the preamble statement (Article 6 of the MLI) and the PPT (Article 7 of the MLI).

[154] For its agreements listed under the MLI, Switzerland is implementing the preamble statement (Article 6 of the MLI) and the PPT (Article 7 of the MLI).

[155] Each of them has been contacted with a proposal for a protocol amending the tax agreement and corresponding negotiations have been suggested.

[156] In total, Trinidad and Tobago identified 26 "agreements" in its List of Tax agreements: 16 bilateral agreements and the CARICOM agreement concluded with ten of its treaty partners.

[157] Revisions to the CARICOM Agreement requires an agreement from its eleven treaty partners.

[158] In total, Tunisia identified 58 "agreements" in its List of Tax agreements: 54 bilateral agreements and the Arab Maghreb Union Income Tax Agreement concluded with four of its treaty partners.

[159] For its agreements listed under the MLI, Tunisia is implementing the preamble statement (Article 6 of the MLI) and the PPT (Article 7 of the MLI).

[160] In total, Turkey listed 95 agreements under the MLI, eight of which (the agreements with Argentina, Chad*, Cote d'Ivoire, Palestine*, Rwanda*, Senegal, Somalia* and Venezuela*) are not yet in force and one which has been terminated (the previous agreement with Qatar).

[161] For its agreements listed under the MLI, Turkey is implementing the preamble statement (Article 6 of the MLI) and the PPT (Article 7 of the MLI).

[162] In total, Ukraine listed 76 agreements under the MLI, one of which (the agreement with Malaysia) is not yet in force.

[163] For its agreements listed under the MLI, Ukraine is implementing the preamble statement (Article 6 of the MLI) and the PPT (Article 7 of the MLI).

[164] In total, the United Arab Emirates listed 114 agreements under the MLI, 23 of which (the agreements with Angola*, Antigua and Barbuda, Belize, Benin, Bermuda, Burundi*, Cameroon, Colombia, Costa Rica, Ecuador*, Equatorial Guinea*, Ethiopia*, Gambia*, Iraq*, Libya*, Mali*, Mauritania*, Nigeria, Palestine*, Paraguay, Rwanda*, St Kitts and Nevis and Uganda*) are not yet in force.

[165] For its agreements listed under the MLI, the United Arab Emirates is implementing the preamble statement (Article 6 of the MLI) and the PPT (Article 7 of the MLI).

[166] In total, the United Kingdom listed 121 agreements under the MLI, one of which (the agreement with Kyrgyzstan*) is not yet in force.

[167] For 117 of its agreements listed under the MLI, the United Kingdom is implementing the preamble statement (Article 6 of the MLI). For its 120 agreements listed under the MLI, the United Kingdom is implementing the PPT (Article 7 of the MLI). The United Kingdom made a reservation pursuant to Article 6(4) not to apply Article 6(1) with respect to agreements, which already contain the relevant preamble language. Three of the United Kingdom's agreements are within the scope of this reservation.

[168] The agreements with Israel and Ukraine are subject to a bilateral complying instrument and are listed under the MLI.

[169] The agreement is subject to a complying instrument as the new agreement with Lesotho was listed under the MLI.

[170] With respect to the United States' agreement with Luxembourg.

[171] See I.R.C. §7701(l), Treas. Reg. § 1.881-3, added to the Internal Revenue Code by section 13238 of the Omnibus Budget Reconciliation Act of 1993, P.L. 103-66. It allows the Internal Revenue Service to re-characterise any multiple-party financing transaction as being a transaction directly among any two or more of its parties whenever appropriate to prevent the avoidance of the United States' tax.

[172] For its agreements listed under the MLI, Uruguay is implementing the preamble statement (Article 6 of the MLI) and the PPT (Article 7 of the MLI). Uruguay also opted for the simplified LOB under Article 7(6) of the MLI.

www.ingramcontent.com/pod-product-compliance
Ingram Content Group UK Ltd.
Pitfield, Milton Keynes, MK11 3LW, UK
UKHW051458290926
15471UKWH00008B/1283

9 789264 408999